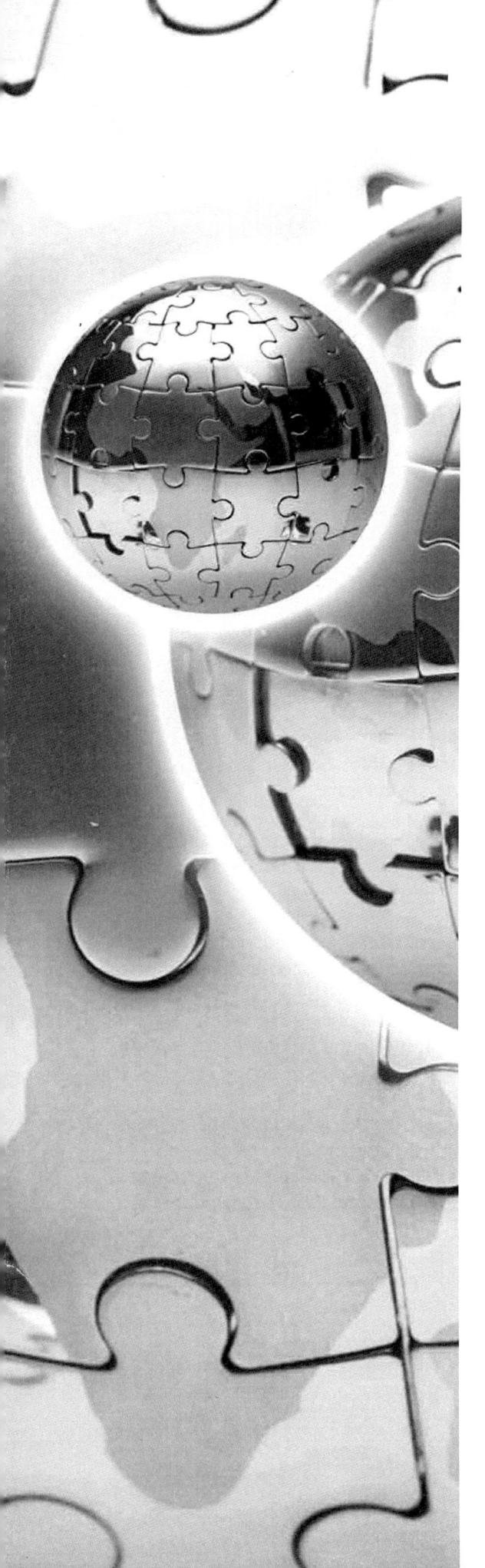

Investment Operations Certificate

Asset Servicing

Edition 14, April 2017

This workbook relates to syllabus version 12.0 and will cover exams from **11 July 2017 to 30 August 2018**

APPROVED WORKBOOK

Welcome to the Investment Operations Certificate (IOC) Programme study material for the Asset Servicing unit.

This workbook has been written to prepare you for the Chartered Institute for Securities & Investment's Asset Servicing examination.

Published by:
Chartered Institute for Securities & Investment
© Chartered Institute for Securities & Investment 2017
20 Fenchurch Street
London
EC3M 3BY
Tel: +44 20 7645 0600
Fax: +44 20 7645 0601

Email: customersupport@cisi.org
www.cisi.org/qualifications

Author:
Mark Tarran

Reviewers:
Paul Taylor
Ian Ashworth

This is an educational workbook only and the Chartered Institute for Securities & Investment accepts no responsibility for persons undertaking trading or investments in whatever form.

While every effort has been made to ensure its accuracy, no responsibility for loss occasioned to any person acting or refraining from action as a result of any material in this publication can be accepted by the publisher or authors.

All rights reserved. No part of this publication may be reproduced, stored in a retrieval system, or transmitted, in any form or by any means, electronic, mechanical, photocopying, recording or otherwise without the prior permission of the copyright owner.

Warning: any unauthorised act in relation to all or any part of the material in this publication may result in both a civil claim for damages and criminal prosecution.

A learning map, which contains the full syllabus, appears at the end of this workbook. The syllabus can also be viewed on cisi.org and is also available by contacting the Customer Support Centre on +44 20 7645 0777. Please note that the examination is based upon the syllabus. Candidates are reminded to check the Candidate Update area details (cisi.org/candidateupdate) on a regular basis for updates as a result of industry change(s) that could affect their examination.

The questions contained in this workbook are designed as an aid to revision of different areas of the syllabus and to help you consolidate your learning chapter by chapter.

Workbook version: 14.2 (September 2017)

Learning and Professional Development with the CISI

The Chartered Institute for Securities & Investment is the leading professional body for those who work in, or aspire to work in, the investment sector, and we are passionately committed to enhancing knowledge, skills and integrity – the three pillars of professionalism at the heart of our Chartered body.

CISI examinations are used extensively by firms to meet the requirements of government regulators. Besides the regulators in the UK, where the CISI head office is based, CISI examinations are recognised by a wide range of governments and their regulators, from Singapore to Dubai and the US. Around 50,000 examinations are taken each year, and it is compulsory for candidates to use CISI workbooks to prepare for CISI examinations so that they have the best chance of success. Our workbooks are normally revised every year by experts who themselves work in the industry and also by our Accredited Training Partners, who offer training and elearning to help prepare candidates for the examinations. Information for candidates is also posted on a special area of our website: cisi.org/candidateupdate.

This workbook not only provides a thorough preparation for the examination it refers to, it is also a valuable desktop reference for practitioners, and studying from it counts towards your Continuing Professional Development (CPD). Mock examination papers, for most of our titles, will be made available on our website, as an additional revision tool.

CISI examination candidates are automatically registered, without additional charge, as student members for one year (should they not be members of the CISI already), and this enables you to use a vast range of online resources, including CISI TV, free of any additional charge. The CISI has more than 40,000 members, and nearly half of them have already completed relevant qualifications and transferred to a core membership grade. You will find more information about the next steps for this at the end of this workbook.

Capital Instruments and Transactions	1
The Life Cycle of an Event	29
Mandatory Events	55
Voluntary Events	87
Corporate Governance	115
Tax	129
Participants	147
Legal and Compliance	163
Risk and Controls	183
Glossary and Abbreviations	195
Multiple Choice Questions	213
Syllabus Learning Map	229

It is estimated that this workbook will require approximately 80 hours of study time.

What next?
See the back of this book for details of CISI membership.

Need more support to pass your exam?
See our section on Accredited Training Partners.

Want to leave feedback?
Please email your comments to learningresources@cisi.org

Chapter One
Capital Instruments and Transactions

1.	Introduction	3
2.	Equities	3
3.	Debt Instruments	11
4.	Transaction Types	17
5.	Depositary Receipts (DRs) and CREST Depositary Interests (CDIs)	20
6.	Warrants	23

This syllabus area will provide approximately 5 of the 50 examination questions

1. Introduction

Companies, municipalities and governments require finance to fund growth, capital projects and restructuring. To achieve this, companies have a choice of either issuing equity or borrowing, whereas municipalities and governments can only raise finance by borrowing.

The commercial marketplace where this is achieved is known as the capital markets.

Different financial instruments and specialised transaction types, such as **stock lending** and **repo**, are created to meet the specific needs of both sellers and buyers. This chapter describes the following main categories:

- equities
- debt instruments
- stock lending and repo transactions
- **depositary receipts**, and
- warrants.

2. Equities

In return for providing cash to a company, an investor (or shareholder) receives a number of shares, which confer part-ownership of the company.

The shareholder will receive a return on their cash in the following ways:

1. **Capital growth** – the value of the shares may increase if the company is making good profits or the market believes that the company will be profitable in the future. The share price may also increase if there is speculation about a **takeover** offer being made, when a premium to the existing share price would be expected. (A fall in the share price may occur if the company makes losses, or the market believes that future profits will not be as good as expected, ie, when a company issues a profits warning.)
2. **Dividends** – when a company makes a profit it will usually pay an element of this to shareholders on a regular basis; this is known as a **dividend**.
3. **Other ways** – the company may also decide to distribute profits in other ways, for example, by giving shares to existing investors on a pro rata basis at no cost to the investor. This is usually referred to as a **stock dividend** or **bonus issue**. Although a bonus issue is sometimes referred to as a stock dividend, it should be noted that it is not a dividend payment in the true sense.

2.1 Classes of Share Capital

All companies will issue **ordinary shares** but they may also issue preference and deferred shares.

Learning Objective

1.1.1 Know the characteristics of ordinary shares in respect of: dividend payment; voting rights; repayment rights in the event of liquidation; conversion rights

1.1.2 Know the characteristics of preference shares in respect of: dividend payment; voting rights; repayment rights in the event of liquidation; conversion rights

1.1.3 Know the characteristics of deferred shares in respect of: dividend payment; voting rights; repayment rights in the event of liquidation; conversion rights

---

2.1.1 Ordinary Shares

Ordinary shareholders own the company and, as such, have the right to:

- attend and vote at shareholder meetings, including the **annual general meeting (AGM)** or any **extraordinary general meetings (EGMs)**
- automatically receive the annual report and accounts
- share in the company's profits, according to the number of shares held, by receiving any declared dividend
- maintain, appoint or remove the directors of the company at an AGM
- approve the appointment of the accountants at an AGM
- share in the remaining assets of the company if it is liquidated
- receive any scrip issue in proportion to their existing holdings
- be offered any **new issue** in proportion to their existing holdings (known as subscription rights), and
- be consulted in special circumstances, eg, when a merger is proposed.

2.1.2 Preference Shares

Preference shares are so named because the shareholder takes preference over the ordinary shareholder for dividend payments and liquidation payments. The features of preference shares are:

- the dividend is a fixed amount per share
- following **liquidation**, shares are repaid at their nominal value, if there are sufficient funds after the creditors have been paid, and
- they carry no, or limited, voting rights.

A dividend is not guaranteed, as the company can decide not to pay one. If a dividend *is* paid, however, the preference shareholders receive the payment first, even if the ordinary shareholder receives nothing.

Preference shares can be cumulative or non-cumulative:

- **Cumulative preference shares** – if no dividend is paid in a given period, the foregone dividend is carried forward to the next payment period and accumulates, so that it must be paid prior to paying any other dividend on ordinary shares.
- **Non-cumulative preference shares** – if a dividend is not paid in a given period, it is not carried forward, therefore in this respect it is similar to an ordinary share.

2.1.3 Deferred Shares

Deferred shares are less common than ordinary or preference shares. A holder of deferred shares will only receive a dividend if the ordinary shareholders have received a specified minimum payment.

Deferred shares do not always carry voting rights; this depends upon why they were issued and the description of the shares, in the first instance.

2.1.4 Conversion Rights

Preference shares and deferred shares may be issued with conversion rights (see Section 2.2). A conversion right is the right to convert preference or deferred shares into ordinary shares. There are two types of conversion rights: optional and mandatory.

- **Optional conversion rights** – these permit the holder to elect to convert their preference or deferred shares into ordinary shares at some time in the future.
- **Mandatory conversion rights** – these require the holder to convert their preference or deferred shares into ordinary shares at some time in the future.

2.1.5 Priority for Payment

Once a company has decided to make available an amount for distribution, this is the order in which the funds are allocated:

1. cumulative preference shares
2. non-cumulative preference shares
3. ordinary shares
4. deferred shares.

If the company goes into liquidation, the assets are generally sold and the proceeds will be paid out in the following order:

1. any form of loan secured by a fixed charge (eg, a line of company assets; a mortgage on buildings owned by the company)
2. preferential creditors (eg, unpaid wages, pensions, tax and National Insurance payments)
3. floating charge loans and bonds secured on company assets (assets owned by the shareholders as part-owners of the company, rather than a loan made to the company by a financial institution on a fixed asset of the company)
4. unsecured loans and bonds and other unsecured creditors
5. subordinated loan stocks

6. preference shares
7. ordinary shares
8. deferred shares.

2.2 Convertible Preference Shares

Learning Objective

1.1.4 Know the characteristics of convertible preference shares in respect of: dividend payment; voting rights; repayment rights in the event of liquidation; conversion rights

1.1.5 Know the reasons why a company may issue convertible preference shares rather than ordinary shares: when newly established; to benefit investors and issuers

Convertible preference shares can be converted (exchanged) into ordinary shares. They rank in the same place as preference shares in item 6 in Section 2.1.5, and the income they pay is the same as other preference shares. The issue documentation will state the conversion terms and whether this can occur at any time or over specific periods.

The advantage of this for the investor is that they can vary the characteristics of their instrument depending on the fortunes of the company. If the company is new and has not yet established a secure profit stream, preference shares may be more attractive than ordinary shares. Preferential shareholders will receive a fixed dividend that has to be paid before any of the other shareholders. On the other hand, as the company grows and profits increase, an ordinary shareholding may be more attractive because it could receive an ongoing dividend above the fixed dividend of the preference share.

By purchasing a convertible preference share, the investor gets the best of both worlds. The **issuer** benefits, too, as the instrument is more attractive to investors than either ordinary shares or preference shares alone. As a preference share, convertibles do not usually carry voting rights, but they do rank above ordinary shares in the event of the issuer going into liquidation. Convertible preference shares usually pay a fixed dividend, but some individual issues may have other dividend terms.

2.3 Issuing Additional Share Capital

Learning Objective

1.1.6 Know the difference between authorised and issued share capital

Under the Companies Act 2006, shares can be issued by the company to shareholders for a value equal to or greater than their nominal value.

If a company requires capital for expansion, there are several options available. It can:

- issue a bond
- take out a loan, or
- issue additional shares.

Capital Instruments and Transactions

Each company will look to keep the cost of raising capital as low as possible and the resulting overall mix of finance (bonds, loans and shares) will depend on the type of industry and the reputation and financial health of the firm.

If a company decides to issue new shares, and the existing shareholders were not offered the shares prior to other investors, the result would be that they would end up owning a smaller part of the company than they did before the new shares were issued. To prevent this, existing shareholders have **pre-emption rights**. This means that they are given the option of buying the additional shares in a fixed proportion to their existing holdings. To do this, they have to increase their cash investment.

To prevent a company's board from using this dilution of shareholding as a lever to gain additional investment, any issue of additional shares, therefore, has to be authorised by the shareholders at an AGM or EGM of the company. Once the new issue is authorised, it is the responsibility of the board to decide when and how many shares are actually issued, up to, but not exceeding, the limit authorised at the AGM/EGM. A company will often maintain unissued, **authorised share capital** in order to raise funds at short notice, without further referral to its shareholders.

Example

A company requires £1 million to fund an expansion plan. This equates to issuing an additional 10% of shares. This resolution is passed at the AGM. The board then decides to wait until the mid-year results are released, as it anticipates an increase in the share price based on the results. When results are declared, the share price does indeed increase and it is only necessary to issue an additional 8% of shares to raise £1 million. The board then retains the right to issue the remaining 2% of shares during the remainder of the year, or at any other time, as authorised.

The example above shows the difference between authorised and **issued share capital**. At each AGM, the board may raise a resolution to authorise the issue of additional share capital, as this will give it more flexibility in the financing of the company during the year without having to wait until the next AGM or needing to call an EGM. The board, although authorised, is not bound to issue the additional share capital.

To summarise: issued share capital refers to shares which have been allotted and issued and are held by shareholders. Shares in the authorised share capital are available to be issued. Not all of the authorised share capital needs to be issued.

2.3.1 Additional Share Capital with Restrictions

Learning Objective

1.1.7 Know the meaning of ranking *pari passu*

In some circumstances, a company may decide to issue new shares with a restriction in force for a period of time, specifically if they are issued within a particular accounting period, eg, that they will not attract a dividend for a given period, or that they are not allotted voting rights for the first year. This would prevent a negative impact on dividend distributions for existing shareholders.

Once these shares start trading on the **secondary market**, they are registered under a separate securities identification number and will trade at a lower price than the existing shares until the end of the restricted period. The lower price **margin** would essentially reflect the element of the declared dividend.

If the shares do not rank for the dividend, they will be restricted, and prefaced as RFD plus a date ('ranking for dividend' from this date). Once the restricted period is over, the share price of both instruments will move to the same level and they will share a single identification number. They are then treated as equal in all respects, a term known as ranking pari passu.

2.4 Corporate Actions

Learning Objective

1.1.8 Know the meaning of the following benefit distribution events: dividends; scrip dividends; bonus issues

1.1.9 Know the meaning of the following events: subdivisions (splits); consolidations (reverse splits); demergers (spin-offs); rights issues; tender offers; takeovers; mergers; scheme of arrangement

Corporate actions are covered in more detail in Chapters 2, 3 and 4 but are introduced briefly here. They can be defined as any issue which affects a company's share capital or materially affects its shareholders. Most types of corporate actions (eg, dividends and **rights issues** to name but a few) are instigated by the issuer of the securities concerned. A few (such as the exercise of warrants) are instigated by investors, and events such as takeovers are instigated by third parties.

A corporate action is usually:

- a benefit distribution, or
- a stock event.

These events apply to both bond markets and equity markets.

They can be divided into three generic categories:

- **mandatory corporate actions**, which do not require an investment decision on the part of the shareholder
- **voluntary corporate actions**, which typically require the shareholder to make an investment decision as to whether to take up an offer made by the company or to exercise a right, and
- events which contain both a mandatory element and an optional element, known as mandatory corporate actions with options.

For more on these categories, see Chapter 2, Section 1.

A benefit distribution is a corporate action in which an issuer (a company or government) distributes a benefit in the form of cash or stock to those investors holding the underlying security. As a result of the distribution, the nature of the underlying securities is unchanged.

Examples are:

- cash dividends
- scrip dividends – these are when, if the investor chooses, the dividend is paid out in the form of additional shares, and
- bonus (or capitalisation) issues, when shareholders are given additional shares for no additional cost.

The benefit distribution associated with bonds is the interest (coupon) payment.

A stock event is a category of corporate action that involves an investor's holding of a security being replaced by cash, another security or a combination of the two. In the case of equities, examples of stock events include the following:

- A **subdivision** or **stock split** – when a single share is replaced with two or more shares. This reduces the price of each share to a range that is considered to be more attractive to investors. Small private investors are thought to prefer lower share prices, ie, less than £10 per share. Additionally, a subdivision will increase the number of shares in existence and, therefore, their liquidity.
- A **consolidation** or **reverse split** – the reverse of a subdivision. Two or more shares are replaced with a single share. This increases the price of a share and is often used following a price collapse. If a share is only worth 2p, almost any buyer will be able to buy hundreds or thousands of them, but there is often a psychological fear of buying because it looks 'too cheap'. In this situation, the company may consolidate to make the shares look more 'normally priced'.
- A **demerger** or **spin-off** – when a company is split into two or more companies. An example is when a parent company demerges a division, so it can realise the value in that division to further its other operations. This happened when BT demerged its mobile phone arm, BT Cellnet, which became a separately quoted company, O2.
- A **capital repayment** – when a company pays back part of the issued capital to its shareholders. The capital reduction is paid to the holder, and the original security is exchanged for new securities appropriate to the new capital value.
- A **rights issue** – a type of stock event that involves a shareholder exercising their right to buy new shares that are being issued by the company. In a rights issue, the investor is given, free of charge, a 'rights security' by the company. To take up the new shares, the investor returns their holding of the rights security to the issuer together with the subscription payment for the new shares, and, in return, they are credited with the new shares. Thus, the old rights security is replaced with the new shares.

Tender offers are offers made by the issuing company, or by another company, to the issuer's shareholders to buy a set amount of its issued share capital over a given period of time.

Mergers (or takeovers) are events when two or more companies combine their capital and then operate their business as one company. A hostile takeover refers to a bid in which the management of the target company opposes the takeover and may obstruct the takeover process. The bidding company is often referred to as a 'predator'. A merger, or recommended takeover, may also be achieved by means of a scheme of arrangement.

The definition of a scheme of arrangement is 'a systematic plan or arrangement for achieving a particular object or effect'. So, in terms that are relevant to corporate actions, it is an arrangement by a company to restructure the company in some way, shape or form, which may range from a rebranding of the company by way of changing the name of the company to a complex subdivision with various subsidiaries of the parent company being spun off and receiving separate stock exchange listings in various countries with a cash component.

2.4.1 The Effect of Corporate Actions on Share Prices

A corporate action is designed to have some effect on the share price. Part of this effect may be purely mathematical, ie, if the number of shares is doubled in a subdivision, the price is halved. However, many corporate actions convey information to the market about the state of the company. A subdivision is seen as an expression of confidence by management that the share price will continue to rise. As a result, the price after the subdivision may be more than the maths alone would indicate.

The table below shows the possible impact on share price following certain events. Although corporate actions are generally thought of as applying to equities, there are events that affect debt securities also.

Event	Event type	Possible impact on share price on ex-date	Other factors to consider
Dividend	Distribution of profits	Reduction of share price by distribution amount	When the dividend is announced, there may be an adjustment of share price reflecting how closely the dividend is in line with market predictions
Bonus issue	Free distribution of shares	Reduction of share price proportionate to increase in shares now available with same net worth	Reasons for issuing of bonus shares will also impact the price on the announcement date (usually reducing it)
Rights issue	Option to buy new shares at a discounted price		Larger impact will be the market perception of an event, taking into account the discount amount and take-up volumes
Subdivision	Existing shares are split to increase available shares		Largest impact will be the mathematical difference in more shares with the same net asset value (NAV), ie, double the shares = half the price
Consolidation	Existing shares are consolidated, leading to a reduction in the number of shares available	Increase in share price due to fewer being available with same net worth	Occasionally, there may be a negative impact on share price due to the market's taking a negative view of this event

Takeover	The gaining of control of a company by another, or by any private body	Increase of the existing company share price by a premium based upon the capital value, under the terms of the offer	Takeovers eliminate the stock of the target company – its stock is no longer traded. The impact of the takeover on the price of the bidding company's shares is dependent on market reaction and is unpredictable
Capital repayment	Repayment of part of issued share capital	Reduction proportionate to the capital return	Dependent on market conditions and opportunities

3. Debt Instruments

3.1 Types of Fixed-Interest Security (UK)

Learning Objective

1.2.1 Know the interest payment (fixed, floating or zero rate), frequency of payment (annual, semi-annual, quarterly, other), term (fixed, dual-dated, perpetual, other) and redemption (early, partial) for: government bonds; Treasury bills; commercial paper; certificates of deposit; corporate bonds; asset-backed securities; floating-rate notes; amortising bonds; zero coupon bonds; bearer bonds

This section introduces the main types of fixed-interest securities traded in the UK capital and money markets. These are:

- **bonds** (government and corporate)
- **Treasury bills**
- **commercial paper**
- **certificates of deposit**
- **asset-backed securities**, and
- **floating-rate notes**.

Each of these securities is briefly described below.

3.1.1 Bonds

Bonds are long-term securities (ie, generally three- to 30-year terms, but can be longer, eg, War Loan) on which interest payments are usually made at fixed periods. The bonds represent a loan issued by governments, municipalities, corporations or financial institutions.

Bonds differ from equities in a number of ways. The main difference is that bondholders are creditors of a company rather than its part-owners. This means the bondholder has certain rights in the event of the company's liquidation, but has limited potential to gain from the company's success. Bonds provide investors with a regular source of income in the form of interest payments, without many of the risks associated with holding equity.

To some degree, bonds and equities compete with each other for investors' money. Depending on the availability of customised instruments, and the prevailing economic environment, investors will have a preference for either debt instruments or equities. Because of the principles of portfolio theory, and the need to offset risk, it is unlikely that an investor will hold only debt or equity, but the ratio of each will certainly change over time. Until the credit crunch of 2007/08 it was generally accepted that in times of economic growth investors would prefer to hold equity, and in times of economic stagnation they would prefer to hold bonds, as these would pay interest regardless of the issuer's economic strength. However, in the current economic climate investors have had concerns about both equity and debt investments, and many professional investors have decided to include such instruments as gold and other physical commodities, as well as equities and bonds, in their portfolios.

Bonds have an interest or **coupon** rate that is determined at the time of issue. This usually forms part of the description of the asset, along with the maturity date, eg, 5% Treasury 2025. The interest is paid at regular intervals, commonly either semi-annually or annually.

The maturity date is the date on which the issuer will repay the value of the bond to the investors; in other words, after this date the bond will cease to exist and there will be no further coupon payments.

Dual-dated bonds are bonds with a band of maturity dates. The issuer can choose to redeem them between the first and the final maturity date after making an announcement to the market.

Perpetual bonds are bonds that will never mature, ie, the issuer will carry on paying the interest for the perpetual future.

Bonds may be issued either in **registered** form, when evidence of ownership is proven by an entry in a **register** of bondholders, or in **bearer** form, where possession of the bond is proof of ownership. In practice, virtually all bearer bonds are deposited into a **central securities depository (CSD)** or international central securities depository (ICSD), and it is the CSD's records that provide such proof of ownership. The roles of CSDs and ICSDs are described in more detail in Chapter 7, Section 2.10.

Amortising bonds pay back both interest and principal (the original investment) in periodic coupons (payments). This is different from standard bonds, when the coupon is only an interest payment and the principal is paid back in a lump sum when the bond matures. Here, the periodic payments are made up of both principal as well as interest. These payments will not vary throughout the life of the bond, but the composition of the payments (the proportion of principal and interest) varies each month. For the asset service department each payment will need to be paid into two different accounts (capital and income) as it will affect the client's tax position.

Zero coupon bonds (ZCBs) do not pay interest; instead they are issued at a significant discount to their face (or nominal or par) value. The holder does not receive interest throughout the life of the bond but realises a profit when the bond matures. See Chapter 3, Section 3.2.

Capital Instruments and Transactions

Two common types of bond are government and corporate bonds. These are explained below:

- **Gilts**, or gilt-edged securities, are long-term UK **government bonds** issued to finance fiscal deficits or capital spending. They are seen as risk-free instruments because they carry the full credit backing and support of the state. For this reason they act as benchmarks against which corporate bonds are priced. They offer investors a high degree of safety but relatively low returns and are extremely liquid. They are fixed-interest instruments and normally pay interest semi-annually.
- **Corporate bonds** are long-term securities issued by companies (corporations) to raise capital for project financing, takeovers or restructuring. They typically offer investors a higher rate of return than government bonds. This higher rate reflects the additional cost of borrowing incurred by a company compared with a government, because of its higher potential for **default**. Potential for default is synonymous with the **credit risk** of a particular firm, reflected in its **credit rating**. The lower the credit rating, the higher the cost of borrowing. They are fixed-interest instruments and normally pay interest semi-annually. If they are issued in the issuer's home country and currency they are called domestic bonds; if they are issued in a different country from that of the issuer in the currency of that foreign country they are called foreign bonds (eg, a UK company issuing a yen bond in Japan); if they are issued and traded outside of the issuer's home country, and traded in a currency different from that of the country where they are issued, they are called eurobonds (eg, a UK company issues a sterling-, dollar- or euro-denominated bond in Japan).

Bonds may contain special provisions allowing early **redemption**, known as call or put provisions. These allow the issuer (call) or holder (put) to redeem the security before **maturity**. For instance, for convertible bonds (see Section 3.2) with a **call provision**, a firm may influence the decision to convert by exercising the call provision at a time when the market value of the common shares is greater than the call price of the bond.

3.1.2 Treasury Bills (T-Bills)

T-bills are short-term domestic securities, issued by governments to raise short-term finance. They are generally non-interest-bearing, issued at a discount to their face value, and with a term of anything from one month to a year.

3.1.3 Commercial Paper (CP)

Commercial paper (CP) is an unsecured, short-term **bearer security** issued by a company. It is not usually interest-bearing; instead, it is priced at a discount to the face value. The attractiveness of CP to investors depends entirely on the credit rating of the issuer.

A CP issued outside of the US has a maturity of one to 365 days (usually 30 and 180 days, in practice). This compares to domestic US CP that has a maturity of one to 270 days.

CP denominations are typically in the range of £1 million to £5 million. Issuance is generally to the professional or wholesale market and governed by local market regulations.

3.1.4 Certificates of Deposit (CDs)

Certificates of deposit (CDs) are unsecured, short-term, interest-bearing instruments. A CD represents a sum on a fixed-term deposit with a bank or building society. The interest is only paid at the end of the term. The investor can liquidate their investment prior to maturity by selling the CD in the market. It is a common form of collateral when borrowing securities.

CDs offer higher rates of return than most other comparable investments.

In the London wholesale money markets, CDs are usually only available in multiples of £100,000 or $100,000. In the US domestic markets, CDs are available in smaller amounts, from $1,000 upwards.

3.1.5 Floating-Rate Notes (FRNs)

Floating-rate notes (FRNs), also called floaters, are medium- to long-term securities issued by corporations or governments when the rate of each coupon period is reset at regular intervals. The reset rate is usually determined at the beginning of the coupon period itself, based on some relevant contractual short-term money market reference rate, for example, the London Interbank Offered Rate (LIBOR) or the Treasury bill (T-bill) rate.

3.1.6 Asset-Backed Securities (ABSs)

Asset-backed securities (ABSs) are securities that are backed by one or more particular assets. These assets are usually loans made by the originating institution, such as credit card receivables, mortgage loans or car loans.

An institution creates an ABS by setting up a separate company, called a **special purpose vehicle (SPV)**, to which the institution sells its loans. The SPV then issues securities, such as bonds or CP, and in turn sells them to institutional investors.

The interest and principal of ABSs are funded by the proceeds of the underlying loans, such as mortgage repayments. They are variable-dated instruments (ie, maturities commonly between three and 30 years) with interest payments that may be fixed or floating, with variable frequencies of payment.

The performance of the ABS is, therefore, dependent upon the performance of the underlying assets, as the cash flows from the underlying assets are the primary source of interest payments on the security.

The most common form of ABS results from repackaging mortgages (also called, more specifically, mortgage-backed securities). Mortgage-backed securities may redeem partially as each mortgage redeems. This will result in a pay-out made up of part interest and part capital. For the asset service department this will need to be paid into two different accounts (capital and income) as it will affect the client's tax position.

ABSs are designed to allow financial institutions to manage credit risk more effectively by removing loans from their balance sheet. This enables the institution to lend more money and also reduces the amount of capital provisioning that it is required to make. ABSs are now somewhat unfashionable, as the exponential growth of the market for these securities, and in particular the growth of the market for derivative instruments based upon them, was one of the major causes of the credit crunch of 2007/08.

3.2 Convertible Bonds

Learning Objective

1.2.2 Know the characteristics of a convertible bond in respect of: interest; term; basis of rights to convert

Firms issue convertible bonds in order to make them more desirable to investors. **Convertibility** gives the investor the right to exchange the bond for a set number of shares at a stated price. This price is usually significantly higher than the prevailing market price of the issuer's shares. If the market price exceeds the stated price during the life of the bond, the investor may wish to convert. If the price is lower, the bonds may be sold in the market, or held until their maturity.

Example

Bond Description

ABC plc £258 million 4% Senior Unsecured Convertible Bonds due 2010 that allowed the holder to convert the bonds into ABC ordinary shares at a cost of 145p per share, which represented a 48% premium over the reference price (ie, the current market price on the day that the bond was issued) of 98p.

Explanation

On 16 July 2008, the telecoms company, ABC plc, issued bonds with a total value of £258 million (the principal amount of the bond), which paid semi-annual coupons of 4% (on 16 January and 16 July) each year (the coupon date), until 16 July 2015 (the maturity date) when ABC plc repaid the proceeds of the bond to the investors. The bonds were issued at a price of 100%, ie, at face value.

Alternatively, at any time during the life of the bond, the investors could convert the bonds into equities issued by ABC plc at a price of £1.45 per share. Therefore, if the investor had bonds with a face value of £10,000, they would have been able to exchange these bonds for 6,896 shares (plus cash fractions) in ABC plc. At the time that these bonds were issued, ABC plc shares were trading at 98p per share, so obviously conversion was only worthwhile when, and if, the price of ABC plc shares rose to more than £1.45.

This type of bond offers the benefit to the borrower that they can pay a lower coupon rate, and is attractive to an investor who thinks that the price of shares is likely to rise during the lifetime of the bond, but in the meantime wants to have the benefit of the coupon income.

Conversion is a voluntary corporate action event that is explained in more detail in Chapter 4, Section 3.

3.3 Restrictions

Learning Objective

1.2.3 Understand the impact on a bond price (up, down, no change and indeterminable) in respect of each of the following events: interest distribution; removal of a restriction on transfer; conversion

3.3.1 Interest Distributions

When interest is paid to bondholders, the **clean price** does not change but the **dirty price** decreases by the amount of interest that has been distributed to the bondholder. Clean and dirty prices are explained in Chapter 3, Section 3.1.2.

3.3.2 Removal of Restrictions

In the US, restricted bonds are unregistered bonds acquired from the issuer in private placements. A private placement is a sale of new securities without an **initial public offering (IPO)**, usually to a small number of chosen private investors. Such issues, as a result, have restricted transferability for a certain period of time. During this time the holder is prevented from selling the bonds back to the issuer.

The price of restricted bonds is generally lower than that of unrestricted bonds. This allows for the reduced liquidity produced by the **restrictions**. For this reason, when a restriction is removed, the price of the bond would be expected to increase

For example, in the US, Securities and Exchange Commission (SEC) rule 144a covers such restrictions. These restrictions are not permanent and can be removed or changed. Specific restrictions on ownership can also be included in the terms of each bond issue.

3.3.3 Conversion

It is up to each individual bondholder to decide when and if to convert all or part of their holding into the underlying shares. The process of conversion is discussed in Chapter 4, Section 3.

When an investor converts their holding, then that holding ceases to exist, which makes the bond more scarce. This implies that the price of the bond should rise, but the extent to which it will rise is limited by the scope for **arbitrage**, which is explained in Chapter 2, Section 6.

4. Transaction Types

Learning Objective

1.3.1 Know the characteristics, uses and the impact on asset servicing of: repos/reverse repos; triparty repos; buy/sellbacks; stock lending/borrowing; synthetic products – contracts for difference and swaps

Capital instruments are transferable securities, with most transfers occurring as a result of trades. In some circumstances, however, securities are transferred in order to satisfy a **stock borrowing** requirement or else as collateral against a funding requirement (ie, a cash loan).

The transaction types that are used to facilitate lending activity are:

- repos/reverse repos
- triparty repos
- buy/sellbacks, and
- stock loans.

4.1 Repurchase Agreements (Repos)

A repurchase agreement or repo is an arrangement whereby one party (the repo seller) sells a security to another party (the repo buyer) and simultaneously agrees to repurchase the same security at a subsequent date at an agreed price. The repurchase date can be anything from one day to a few months' duration, and the security involved will generally have a high credit rating (such as a government bond).

Repos originated in the 1940s as a substitute for a short-term bank loan. In a repo, the seller is, in effect, the borrower of cash, in exchange for securities as collateral. Because the loan is collateralised, the interest rate is set slightly lower than the unsecured cash borrowing rate. This rate is reflected in the difference between the sale price and the repurchase price, the repurchase price being higher than the sale price.

The securities sold under a repo agreement become the legal property of the buyer. This means that the buyer will receive any interest payments accrued through the life of the arrangement. These will be reclaimed by the seller as a cash payment and, as such, are not included as **consideration** as part of the return leg.

A reverse repo is the same transaction viewed from the security buyer's perspective, ie, the arrangement is set up in order to receive securities as collateral for the cash that has been lent.

It is common for securities sold under a repo agreement to be sold on by the buyer to another party and then sold on further to set up a chain of transactions, all linked by the requirement to meet the above two conditions.

Similar transactions to repos and reverse repos are sell/buybacks and buy/sellbacks, respectively. The difference in these transactions is that:

- there is less documentation involved than in a repo
- there is no movement of cash due to coupon payments; these are instead reflected in the difference between the selling and buying price.

4.1.1 Triparty Repos

Triparty repos are transactions used for funding and investment purposes in which bonds and cash are delivered by the trading counterparties to an independent custodian bank or **clearing** house (the triparty custodian). The **custodian** is responsible for ensuring the maintenance of adequate collateral value, both at the outset of a trade and during its term. The triparty custodian marks the collateral to market on a daily basis and makes margin calls on either **counterparty**, as required.

Triparty repos reduce the operational and technological barriers to participating in the repo markets.

Financial institutions are increasingly using triparty repos as the preferred settlement method for the funding operations owing to the opportunity to benefit from increased efficiency and cost savings.

4.2 Stock Lending

The practice of stock (or securities) lending is the provision of securities to market participants in return for a fee. It is attractive to lenders because it allows them to enhance the revenue from their portfolios, and there is demand from borrowers in order to:

- allow short selling (ie, the deliberate selling of securities without owning them)
- meet settlement obligations if there is a lack of the security in the firm's inventory on the required settlement date, and
- support derivatives activities when a firm may be subjected to an options exercise.

Legal title of the loaned security passes to the borrower, although the lender retains beneficial rights. The lender's main rights are that:

- they can request the return of the security at any time during the loan period (an 'immediate recall' will be one settlement cycle in the market, to allow the borrower to buy stock and/or arrange a new loan), and
- they are entitled to all privileges of ownership (apart from voting rights) even though physical possession has been surrendered.

Securities lenders will only lend stock providing that the borrower supplies collateral. This collateral may be in the form of cash, other securities or a letter of credit.

Markets are encouraged to enable securities lending in order to improve the liquidity of stock in the market. The principle of perfect markets is that for every buyer there is a seller and for every seller there is a buyer. This means that, ideally, the market should always be able to support any requirement for a purchase or sale. If securities are simply held in custody, the market volume available to meet trading commitments is reduced. Lending is a means of returning held securities to the market while at the same time allowing the lender to earn a return in the form of a lending fee. The lender can thus enhance the return of their portfolio at the same time as supplying a market need.

Stock lending plays a key role in the stability of the international markets because of this increased liquidity. For this reason, it is actively encouraged by regulators.

4.3 Synthetic Products

4.3.1 Contracts for Difference (CFDs)

A contract for difference (CFD) is a contract between two parties, buyer and seller, stipulating that the seller will pay to the buyer the difference between the current value of an equity and its value at a future date. If the difference is negative, then the buyer pays instead to the seller. CFDs allow investors to speculate on share price movements without the need for ownership of the underlying shares.

CFDs allow investors to take long or short positions, and (unlike futures contracts) have no fixed **expiry date** or contract size. CFDs are often used by UK investors to gain exposure to the growth potential of an individual equity without the requirement to pay **stamp duty**.

CFDs are also referred to as spread bets.

The holder of a long position in a CFD is entitled to any dividend income or other event-related benefits from the underlying share (in exactly the same way that a holder of the underlying share has these entitlements). Conversely, the holder of a short position in a CFD will have to reimburse the trading counterparty for any such benefits.

4.3.2 Swaps

Swaps are types of over-the-counter (OTC) derivatives. OTC derivatives are complex instruments, and are not dealt with at length in this workbook. A more comprehensive explanation can be found in the CISI's *Introduction to Securities & Investment* workbook.

In asset servicing, we are most concerned with equity swaps.

Basically, all swaps are agreements whereby two parties agree to exchange a set of cash flows with each other. In an equity swap one party agrees to pay another the funds generated by holding a position in a given equity or group of equities (known as a basket) for a given period of time, while the other party agrees to pay the first party a rate of interest on the market value of the equities at the beginning of the period. The 'funds generated' by holding an equity position include any capital growth (or capital reduction if the market price falls during the life of the swap) as well as any dividend income and any benefits that arise from corporate actions. It therefore follows that if one of the parties to the swap will receive these benefits, the other party to the swap will have to pay them.

Equity swaps play a similar role in the market to CFDs. They are used by market participants to gain or reduce exposure to a particular stock or basket of stocks without purchasing the stocks themselves, or to reduce exposure without selling the stocks themselves.

Both CFDs and swaps are types of derivative instruments – ie, they are 'derived' from another instrument – the actual equity or equity index on which they are based. The instrument on which a derivative is based is known as the 'underlying' instrument.

4.3.3 The Impact of these Transaction Types on the Asset Servicing Process

Chapter 2 describes the life cycle of an event, and stage three of that life cycle is the calculation of event entitlement and notification to investors. If these transactions did not exist, then the only investors who would be concerned when a company announced a corporate event would be the holders of that company's shares, but the existence of these transactions broadens the scope of those participants affected. To take a very simple example, if a company announces that it will pay a dividend to stockholders on a given **record date**, then the following table shows the list of those investors affected:

The effect of lending and borrowing and synthetic transactions on entitlement	
Those entitled to receive the benefit	Those that have to pay the benefit
Holders of long positions in the stock concerned	Holders of short positions in the stock concerned
Lenders of the stock (including repo, but not buy/sellback participants)	Borrowers of the stock (including repo but not buy/sellback participants)
Holders of long positions in CFDs	Holders of short positions in CFDs
Holders of long positions in swaps	Holders of short positions in swaps

5. Depositary Receipts (DRs) and CREST Depositary Interests (CDIs)

Depositary receipts (DRs) are negotiable certificates that represent either a fractional or multiple number of foreign shares, apart from CREST Depositary Interests (CDIs) which are represented on a par. They are generally issued by commercial banks and traded on a local exchange that is different from the domicile of the issuing company. Their purpose is to allow a firm's stock to be traded abroad.

5.1 Types of DRs

Learning Objective

1.4.1 Know the definition of the following depositary receipts: American depositary receipts (ADRs); global depositary receipts (GDRs)

DRs can be issued in either a sponsored or an unsponsored form:

- A **sponsored DR** means that the security is issued by a **depository** appointed by the foreign issuer under a formal agreement (called the deposit agreement). This is the most common form of issue.
- An **unsponsored DR** is one when a depository issues the security without a formal agreement with the issuer. This may occur due to market demand.

Capital Instruments and Transactions

The two main categories of DR are the **American depositary receipt** (ADR) and the global depositary receipt (GDR).

5.1.1 American Depositary Receipts (ADRs)

ADRs were the original DRs and comprise all such securities traded on US markets. They were first introduced in 1927 in response to an increasing demand by US investors for non-US stocks.

ADRs settle through the Depository Trust & Clearing Corporation (DTCC). From a tax perspective, they take the tax status of the country of the underlying equity.

5.1.2 Global Depositary Receipts (GDRs)

GDRs (which are sometimes known as international depositary receipts or IDRs) are issued in non-US markets. They were first traded in 1990 and their use has seen rapid growth because of the expansion of emerging markets. Investors demand the ability to invest in these markets without the financial risks presented by local settlement conventions and immature markets.

GDRs settle through ICSDs, such as Euroclear Bank and Clearstream.

5.2 CREST Depositary Interests (CDIs)

Learning Objective

1.4.1 Know the definition of the following depositary receipts: CREST depositary interests (CDIs)

CREST holds all international stocks in a pool in a local depository, such as Clearstream for German stocks and DTC (Depository Trust Company) for US stocks. CREST then issues a CDI to each holder of the security, which can then be transferred in CREST, just like a UK equity. This is similar to the ADRs and GDRs discussed in prior paragraphs. A CDI is an electronic reflection of the underlying security held in the domestic (country of origin) market.

Taking the US as an example, if a shareholder holds electronic stock in the US they will hold their securities with a custodian who in turn will hold them as an electronic record at the DTC, so the custodian's nominee details will appear on the DTC register. This is known as holding stock in the 'domestic' market. Securities held this way can only be traded domestically, ie, in the market of the country of origin. If a shareholder wants to trade their securities outside of the US domestic market, they can instruct their custodian to transfer their securities to the CREST account in DTC, to allow trading in them.

Restrictions apply: only securities that are listed in CREST as CDIs can be transferred to CREST's DTC account. CREST is a member of DTC. So, once the securities have been transferred out of the original custodian's nominee name and into CREST's account in DTC, the securities will then have been 'cross-bordered' into the UK market as CDIs. They can then be traded in the UK market. Securities can be returned to the domestic market by effecting a reverse of the original 'cross-border'. In real terms this simply means the transfer from CREST's DTC account to that of the new beneficiary.

5.3 The Implications for Issuers and Investors of DRs

Learning Objective

1.4.2 Understand the implications for investors holding depositary receipts and the impact with regard to the following: income tax; withholding tax; voting rights; rights issues in regard to ADRs; bonus issues; income distributions; stock lending/borrowing

The benefits to the issuer of DRs are as follows:

- allow the issuer to raise finance from a much larger market, and
- enhance the corporate image by demonstrating a broad shareholder base outside the home country.

From the investor's perspective, the advantages are as follows:

- they allow investors to receive dividends in their native currency, thus avoiding the need to arrange additional foreign exchange (FX) transactions. The FX transactions become the responsibility of the party issuing the DR.
- they allow international investors to buy and sell shares in a company more easily than trading them on a local exchange.
- they are subject to the laws of the investor's country of residence, which may give the investor more confidence.
- they offer a simple and safe means of trading, especially if local markets carry considerably higher settlement risk (ie, the emerging markets) or if local markets use unfamiliar trading and settlement processes.
- they remove the need to open accounts in immature or highly regulated markets.

Potential drawbacks for investors are as follows:

- Depending on the wording of the legal documentation governing the DR, holders may not have any choice in what to do about certain corporate actions, such as rights issues, takeover bids or share buybacks. For example, the depository may be required to automatically sell all rights in the market and credit DR holders with the proceeds rather than taking up rights on their behalf.
- Income tax on DRs is dependent on the underlying stock and its country of inception; the tax is applied at the level of the country of issue on the ordinary share capital. In addition, investors may be subject to **withholding taxes** (explained in Chapter 6).
- Profits are denominated in local currency and then converted to the currency of the market on which the DRs trade. This conversion means that the investor is vulnerable to exchange rate risk.
- Voting rights of DR holders are limited by the standard terms of the deposit agreements or hindered by operational considerations.

DRs, just like any other security, may be borrowed and lent. Theoretically they may be used as the underlying instruments in more complex transactions such as CFDs and swaps, but it is more likely that the underlying equities would be used in these transactions.

6. Warrants

Learning Objective

1.5.1 Know the definition of a covered/uncovered warrant and the associated terms: call; put; exercise; strike price

1.5.2 Understand the main characteristics of the following warrants: puts; calls; index-linked; auto-expiring

An option gives you the right, but not the obligation, to buy (or sell) an underlying asset:

- at a point in the future (up to the expiry date of the option)
- at a predetermined price (the strike price).

This asset can be a variety of things. It can be a physical asset, such as a certain quantity or quality of a metal, or it can be another financial instrument such as shares.

Options are prefixed by the word 'call' or 'put':

- right to buy the underlying asset = call option
- right to sell the underlying asset = put option.

The amount the investor pays for the option is called the premium.

An option is an example of a financial instrument called a **derivative**, as its value is in part based on (or derived from) the price of the underlying asset.

A warrant is an option where the underlying asset is a share. Warrants can be attached to a new issue of bonds in order to make the bonds more attractive to investors. After the initial offering, warrants may, if detached, be bought and sold separately on exchanges in the same way as equities.

Additionally, they can be issued separately by a third party, such as a broker/dealer or investment bank. If the third party actually owns the underlying shares, it is known as a covered warrant, and, if they do not, then it is known as an uncovered warrant, and carries a far higher risk.

Investors buy warrants because they believe that a share price will move in a particular direction. Although they could buy the share itself, the warrant is a geared instrument that may potentially deliver a greater return on the investment. This is best illustrated by an example.

6.1 Call Warrants

Example

An investor buys a **call warrant** on a share in Company X at a strike price of £1 for a premium of 20p.

- If the warrant expires without the share price going above £1, the investor will make a loss of 20p (the premium). A call warrant is said to be out-of-the-money if the share price is lower than the strike price.
- If the share price rises above £1, the investor has the right to buy the shares at £1, sell them on the market at the higher price and keep the difference. A call warrant is said to be **in-the-money** if the share price is higher than the strike price.

Plotting profit/loss against share price gives:

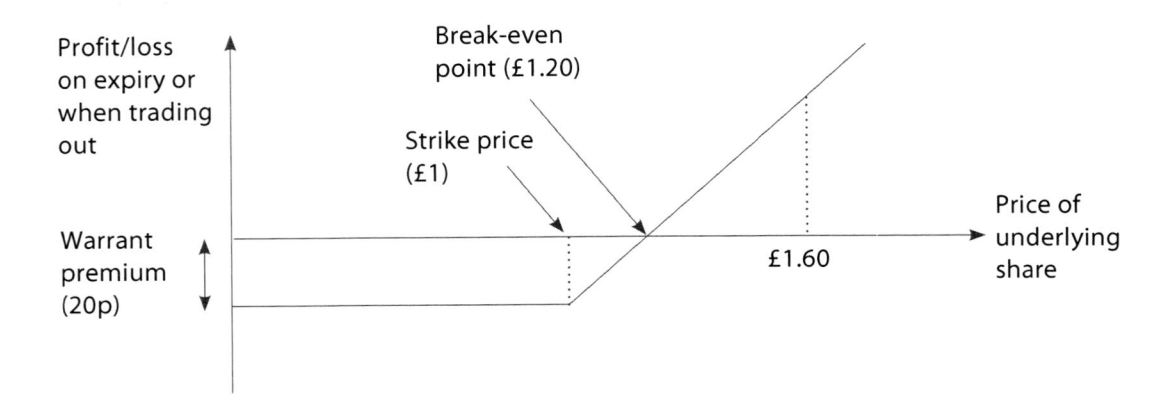

If the price of the shares goes up as far as £1.20, the investor will break even. They can buy the shares at £1 as per their warrant, and then sell them to the market at £1.20. They will make 20p on this transaction, which will offset the 20p they paid for the warrant.

Any further increase in the price of the share is profit. If the price rises as far as £1.60:

Profit per warrant = price of underlying share − strike price − warrant premium = £1.60 − £1 − 20p = 40p

The investor, therefore, has a limited loss (the 20p they paid) but an unlimited potential profit.

The price that the warrant trades at in the market will be related to the current share price, but also to the expectation of what the share price will do before the warrant expires.

If the share price does what the investor expects (ie, increases), then buying a warrant will realise a greater profit than if they had invested in the share directly.

Consider the percentage gain for the example above and if £1 had been invested in the share.

Example

Percentage gain	=	Profit/investment x 100
Warrant gain	=	40p/20p x 100
	=	200%
Share gain	=	(£1.60 – £1)/100p x 100
		60%

If the share had moved down to 80p:

Percentage loss	=	Loss/investment x 100
Warrant loss	=	20p/20p x 100
	=	100%
Share loss	=	20p/100p x 100
		20%

We can see that, although the warrants produce a bigger profit when the underlying price moves in the right direction, they also produce greater losses when the underlying price moves in the wrong direction, even to the extent of a complete loss of capital invested. This is one of the reasons why warrants are considered risky investments.

Note that since there is an expiry date on the warrant, it is important to keep track of whether the warrant is in- or **out-of-the-money**, especially as the expiry date approaches. If the warrant is not exercised before the expiry date it will be worthless. There are many ways that these can be tracked, from a simple paper diary through to complex securities systems that will warn of upcoming expiries.

6.2   Put Warrant

Example

An investor buys a put warrant on a share on Company Y at a strike price of £1 for a premium of 20p.

If the warrant expires without the share price falling below £1, the investor will make a loss of 20p – the premium.

If the share price falls below £1, the investor has the right to sell the shares to the warrant issuer for £1. For example, if Y's share price fell to 50p then the investor makes a profit of 30p per share, calculated as follows:

Exercise price	100p
Less premium	20p
Less market price at time of exercise	50p
Profit	30p

Plotting profit/loss against share price gives:

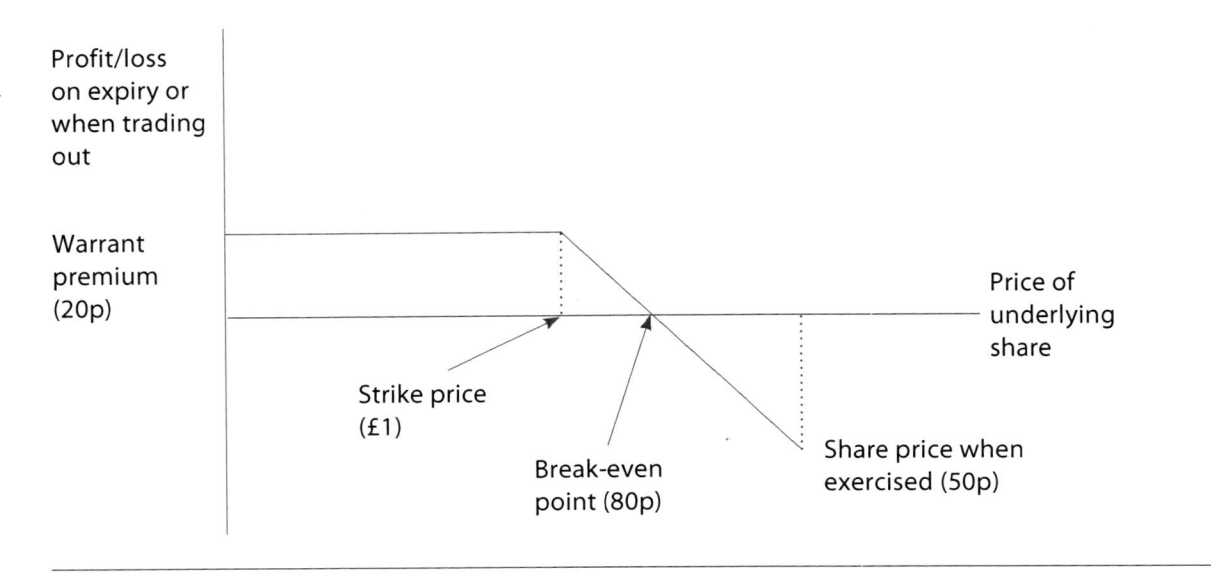

[Graph showing profit/loss against share price with labels: Profit/loss on expiry or when trading out; Warrant premium (20p); Strike price (£1); Break-even point (80p); Share price when exercised (50p); Price of underlying share]

6.3 Index Warrant

An index warrant is similar to a normal warrant but, instead of being based on the price of a single underlying share, is based on an index such as the FTSE 100.

These will be issued by third parties, such as broker/dealers or investment banks.

Example

The FTSE 100 warrant might be priced in pence such that each index point represents £1. So, buying a warrant on the FTSE 100 when it is at 4000 is like buying a warrant on a £4,000 security, eg, for a FTSE 100 call warrant with an exercise price of 4000, if the FTSE 100 expiry price is 4241, the amount paid on expiry = (4241 – 4000)/100 = 2.41 index points = £2.41 per warrant.

6.4 Auto-Expiring Warrant

As already stated, warrants have an expiry date after which they cannot be exercised. For in-the-money warrants, there is a danger that the investor will miss the expiry deadline and lose their profit.

To make a warrant more attractive to an investor, it can be issued as an auto-expiring warrant. If the warrant is in-the-money at the expiry date, the profit is automatically paid to the investor.

End of Chapter Questions

Think of an answer for each question and refer to the appropriate section for confirmation.

1. What is the difference between an ordinary and a preference share?
   Why might an investor choose one over another?
   Answer reference: Sections 2.1.1 and 2.1.2

2. What is the difference between authorised and issued share capital?
   Answer reference: Section 2.3

3. What is the meaning of ranking *pari passu*?
   Answer reference: Section 2.3.1

4. Give examples of two benefit distributions and two stock events.
   Answer reference: Section 2.4

5. What are the two common types of bond called and how is interest paid on each?
   Answer reference: Section 3.1.1

6. How does an institution create an ABS?
   Answer reference: Section 3.1.6

7. What is the definition of a repo?
   Answer reference: Section 4.1

8. Why is stock lending attractive to lenders?
   Answer reference: Section 4.2

9. What is the purpose of a depositary receipt?
   Answer reference: Section 5

10. Give two advantages for the firm issuing a depositary receipt.
    Answer reference: Section 5.3

11. Explain why investing in a call warrant is more risky than investing in the underlying share it is based on.
    Answer reference: Section 6.1

12. What risk does an auto-expiring warrant mitigate?
    Answer reference: Section 6.4

Chapter Two
The Life Cycle of an Event

1.	Overview of the Life Cycle	31
2.	Information-Gathering and Data	32
3.	Event Entitlement	39
4.	Response-Gathering and Instruction	45
5.	Payment, Claims and Post Payment Reconciliation	47
6.	Arbitrage	50

This syllabus area will provide approximately 6 of the 50 examination questions

1. Overview of the Life Cycle

Learning Objective

2.1.1 Understand the difference between: voluntary events; mandatory events; mandatory events with options

2.1.2 Know the key stages of the life cycle of an asset servicing event: market announcement; event data collection and validation; notification; election processing; payment/settlement of entitlement; reconciliation

There are many different types of corporate actions, as we will see in the following two chapters. It is possible to generalise to a degree and break down the events to some generic constituent parts.

As mentioned in Chapter 1, Section 2.4, at the highest level, asset servicing events (corporate actions) can be divided into voluntary events, mandatory events and mandatory events with options. Their characteristics are as follows.

- **Voluntary events** – as the name implies, with a voluntary event there is no obligation on the investor's part to take up any offer made to them, although an investment decision even to take no action still needs to be made. An example is a **warrant exercise**, when, throughout the lifetime of the warrant, or at set periods, the investor can elect to buy the underlying share at a predetermined price.
- **Mandatory events** – in contrast, a mandatory event will proceed regardless of the views of the investor. Investors have a say in the proposals when they are discussed and voted on during the company meeting, providing that they hold stock with voting rights. This is discussed in Chapter 5. One example of a mandatory event is a subdivision, where each share is split into a number of other shares, which reduces the market price of each share but with an increase to the number of shares in issue.
- **Mandatory events with options** – this event type is a mixture of the previous two. Elements of the event are mandatory and then, after this, the shareholder has an investment decision to make. An example is when a dividend is to be paid and the investor has the option of taking the dividend in cash or as additional shares. Each company decides a default method (cash or stock) of dividend payment. If no indication of preference is received from the investor within the period of response, they will receive the default.

1.1 Key Stages of the Life Cycle

The stages of the life cycle of an asset servicing event can be categorised as:

1. **market announcement** – a company is required to announce to the market details of its impending actions
2. **event data collection and validation** – this is the information-gathering stage
3. **calculation of event entitlement and notification to investors**
4. **response-gathering and instruction** (election processing)
5. **payment and claims**
6. **post-payment reconciliation** (event settlement and reconciliation).

In all corporate actions, there may be a significant amount of cash or stock involved when dealing with substantial holdings of securities. An event ignored when it should have been acted upon, a response deadline missed or an entitlement paid to the wrong party are all high-risk occurrences, and can all be costly to an asset servicing firm, damaging its reputation with its clients and in the market generally.

2. Information-Gathering and Data

Learning Objective

2.2.1 Understand the cycle of information-gathering from the company announcement

Data-gathering ensures that a firm is aware of events that are coming up and that it allows a sufficient amount of time to effect investment decisions on the event, or to get salesmen, traders, clients and fund managers to make their decisions. Information-gathering can be fragmented, as the information will come from a number of sources and will not always be consistent. The timing and methods of announcement are very important; firms will often use multiple sources to ensure all events are discovered.

The process of data-gathering can be described using the following diagram:

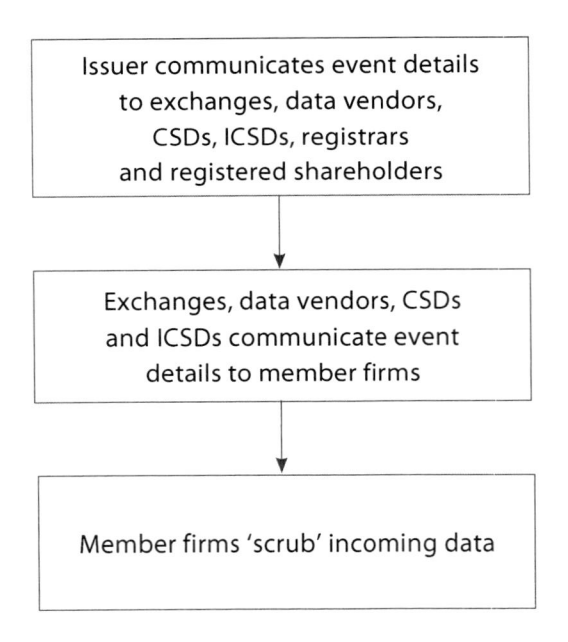

```
┌─────────────────────────────────────┐
│   Issuer communicates event details │
│      to exchanges, data vendors,    │
│        CSDs, ICSDs, registrars      │
│      and registered shareholders    │
└─────────────────────────────────────┘
                  │
                  ▼
┌─────────────────────────────────────┐
│  Exchanges, data vendors, CSDs      │
│   and ICSDs communicate event       │
│      details to member firms        │
└─────────────────────────────────────┘
                  │
                  ▼
┌─────────────────────────────────────┐
│  Member firms 'scrub' incoming data │
└─────────────────────────────────────┘
```

Issuers of securities inform the exchanges on which those securities are traded, and the central securities depositories (CSDs) where the trades are settled, on announcement date. These institutions then inform their clients. Because many securities are quoted on more than one exchange and/or are held by more than one CSD, this means that client firms may receive multiple notifications in different forms. The more common forms of notification are described in Section 2.3. This creates the need for data scrubbing (also known as data cleansing), which is described in Section 2.4.

The roles of CSDs are discussed in more detail in Chapter 7, Section 2.9.

2.1 Timing of Corporate Actions

In general, a company must announce, without delay, any major new developments in its sphere of activity which are not public knowledge which may:

- by virtue of the effect of these developments on the assets and liabilities, or on the financial position, or on the general course of the company business, lead to substantial movement in the price of its listed securities, or
- in the case of a company with debt securities listed, by virtue of the effect of these developments on the assets, liabilities or financial position or on the general course of the company business, lead to substantial movement in the price of its listed securities, or which may significantly affect its ability to meet its commitments.

Corporate actions fall under the above definitions.

There are no simple rules which dictate when a corporate action will occur, but there is a tendency for some types of corporate actions to cluster together, as shown in the examples below:

- A company's financial year end may be timed to coincide with the end of the tax year or the end of the calendar year. Dividends will be announced following the end-of-year calculation of profit (and potentially six-monthly or quarterly after that). As a result, a securities firm may have to cope with dividend events occurring on many of its holdings simultaneously.
- Mergers, takeovers and initial public offerings (IPOs) (ie, when a private firm first offers its shares for sale to the public on the market) are more frequent in a buoyant market, as the companies that instigate these events are less cautious and more optimistic. As a result, there may be a cyclical nature to such events: none are seen for months in a particular sector and then suddenly market conditions improve sufficiently for several companies to float, or purchase other companies at roughly the same time.
- Merger and acquisitions activity may also follow a cycle. A developing sector, such as financial services following deregulation, will fragment as new firms enter the market. As the market matures, it becomes more efficient to merge firms and reap the economies of scale. 'Merger mania' may follow in a particular sector, as all the firms decide that they must grow by merger or acquisition, rather than organically, in order to survive. There may also be a concurrent rights issue to fund or fight off the attempted acquisition.
- If a particular sector is struggling, there may be a clustering of rights issues to raise additional finance. Often, the first rights issue is the most successful, as the market can rapidly lose its appetite to pump additional funding into the sector.

Once a firm has decided upon a corporate action, there are a number of methods that it can use to notify the market of its intention and to collect responses. Some of the more common ones are listed in Sections 2.2 and 2.3.

2.2 The Prospectus

Learning Objective

2.2.2 Understand the purpose of a prospectus

When there is some form of public offering, companies publish all relevant information in a prospectus.

The prospectus is a document that sets out some of the history of the company, plus details of its financial health and its plans for the future. The prospectus has two purposes. Partly, it is a sales document whose intention is to persuade people to buy the shares when they become available, but secondly, because the content of a prospectus is generally regulated by the stock exchange on which it is seeking listing, it must be a fair representation of the company, its prospects and the terms of the offer.

A company may place an advert in the national press stating its intention to issue a security. Interested parties are invited to write for a prospectus or, more recently, register interest on a website and receive the prospectus in electronic format, via a download or email. Existing shareholders must, however, be sent a copy of the prospectus, and major market participants will generally receive documentation automatically.

If a company does not want to go to the expense of advertising and receiving applications from many small investors, it can opt for a private placement. In this case a prospectus is still produced, but it is only circulated to a list of clients of the investment bank that advised on the deal, or through a network of investment banks. Small investors have to purchase any stocks they want from this network. See also Chapter 8, Section 7.

If the application is public, an application form for the shares is again printed in the national press along with the terms and conditions of the offer. It will also be available via the internet.

For fixed-interest securities, the prospectus defines, *inter alia*:

- how interest and principal will be repaid
- conversion terms, if any
- the investor's position in the hierarchy of debt, ie, whether this particular bond issue is:
  - senior debt (ie, in the event of the issuer being wound up then investors in this issue have a high-priority claim), or
  - subordinated debt (ie, in the event of the company being wound up then investors in this issue have a low-priority claim), or
  - the debt has an equal claim on the issuer's assets with all other debt securities from this issuer
- what the borrower will do if it is unable to pay interest/repay principal
- how the issuer plans to use the money raised by this issue.

The Life Cycle of an Event

2.3 Market Announcements and Notifications

Learning Objective

2.2.3 Know the different types of market notification: Euroclear DACE (Deadlines and Corporate Events notice); LSE – stock situation notices including name changes; DTC; SWIFT

This section describes the major methods that exchanges and CSDs use to inform their member firms about forthcoming events.

In the main, the tools that are used are electronic and facilitate a high level of automated processing by the receiving firm. However, readers should be aware that such facilities are not universal. For example, Monte Titoli (the Italian CSD) currently advises its members about events using an MTAQ message, which is delivered electronically but is simply a scanned copy of the issuer's press release. It is difficult for participants to automate the processing of messages of this kind.

2.3.1 Stock Situation Notices (SSNs)

Stock Situation Notices (SSNs) are produced by an analytical team at the London Stock Exchange (LSE) and cover corporate actions on stock listed on the LSE, including AIM (the Alternative Investment Market).

A member can elect to access the notices online or receive them by email. There are around 5,000 SSNs produced each year, covering all of the types of corporate action. Typically, they will contain items such as:

- security name, ISIN and SEDOL references
- event type
- full terms and any ratios
- key dates
- details of how to make an election (for voluntary and mandatory issues with options)
- **registrar** details.

SSNs are generated both as notifications of new events, and updates to existing ones. In addition to providing information about corporate actions, the service also offers its users information about other events, such as stock name changes.

35

2.3.2 Euroclear Bank Deadlines and Corporate Events (DACE) System

Euroclear Bank has a standardised electronic way of notifying its participants of corporate events and deadlines for stock positions held, commonly known as **DACE (Deadlines and Corporate Events)**.

Again, they will vary in form depending on the type of event, but, as an example, here are the elements in an offer from Argentina to exchange old bonds for new global bonds:

Element	Example
Exchange ratio	How the exchange ratio will be calculated, when the issue price is announced, and how rounded amounts and unpaid coupons will be treated.
New bonds resulting from the offer	Global bonds due 31 October 2020. ISIN code GB123456789. Coupon rate to be fixed on (date). Issue price to be fixed on (date).
Competitive and non-competitive offers	How to submit either type of bid, and the range of competitive bids that will be considered.
Timing	The timetable of events from launch to settlement of the offer, including key deadline dates.
Contact details	How to obtain the full documentation for the offer.
Offer restrictions	Details of any legal restrictions linked to the event.
Summary	
Participation details	How to instruct either Euroclear or your lead manager if you wish them to do this on your behalf.

2.3.3 Depository Trust Company (DTC)

Depository Trust Company (DTC) is the CSD for the US. It provides a Global Corporate Actions Validation Service (GCA) to its members and also to any non-member firm that wishes to purchase this service.

How the Service Works

1. Customers submit a 'Securities of Interest' (SOI) file, which contains a list of all securities that they wish to receive corporate action information on. As and when new securities are issued, and old ones mature or are otherwise discontinued, the file needs to be updated. The service 'scrubs' and publishes the active corporate action events that take place on each security on the SOI file.
2. The data is enriched with desk research performed by experienced professionals in multiple service centres, which includes the review of source materials, such as the prospectus, letter of transmittal and press releases.
3. Customers receive publication files throughout the day that contain composite records for each corporate action event that matches the SOI file. Publication files are available in either the industry-standard **ISO 15022** format (see Section 2.3.4) or in a proprietary format.
4. As well as containing key dates and rates, the composite record also includes clear and comprehensive 'terms and restrictions' text that enables customers to pass the announcement record straight through to their investor clients or front-office trading desk.
5. Available as an option, a unique custodian verification feature compares and validates the composite records from the GCA against data received from the customers' custodian network.

2.3.4 SWIFT and ISO Standards in Relation to Corporate Events

Learning Objective

2.2.5 Know the SWIFT and other standards in relation to corporate events: MT564/Corporate Action Notification; MT565/Corporate Action Instruction; MT566/Corporate Action Confirmation; MT567/Corporate Action Status and Processing Advice; MT568/Corporate Action Narrative; ISO15022 and ISO20022

Some clients of custodians are not positioned to receive **SWIFT** messages, so may receive automated faxes instead. However, faxes can go astray and recipients can be away from the office, potentially leading to missed deadlines.

Using SWIFT messages means that delivery is guaranteed, **operational risk** is reduced, transmission is secure and there are messaging standards in place to ensure that all of the messages are concise and conform to the agreed industry standard.

The MT56X series of messages is used for corporate events under the SWIFT ISO 15022 standard, as follows:

- **MT564 – Corporate Action Notification** – sent by an agent or custodian to advise their client of the details of a forthcoming corporate action.
- **MT565 – Corporate Action Instruction** – sent by a client or custodian to advise the instruction for a corporate action.
- **MT566 – Corporate Action Confirmation** – sent by an agent or custodian to confirm that stock or cash has been debited from or credited to a client account.
- **MT567 – Corporate Action Status and Processing Advice** – used to advise the status, or a change in status, of a corporate action-related transaction previously instructed by, or executed on behalf of, the receiver.
- **MT568 – Corporate Action Narrative** – used to provide complex instructions or details relating to a corporate action event in narrative form. In other words, this message is used as a tag message to include narrative that does not fit into the restricted format of an MT564 message.

The MT56X series is used to process all common forms of corporate actions on both equity and debt securities. For a simple corporate action – such as a cash dividend payment – the agent will send an MT564 on record date, notifying their client that a dividend is due, and then, on payment date, will send an MT566 confirming the flow of cash. For a more complex action, the information sent on the MT564 may need to be supplemented by additional information on the MT568.

Since the introduction of ISO 15022 in November 2002, SWIFT has seen an increase in the volume of corporate action messages, and this growth is expected to continue as part of the wider drive for increased corporate-action-processing automation. This has also led to the growth in organisations investing in systems which will allow for the automated reading and interpretation of these messages, therefore allowing for greater **straight-through processing (STP)**.

2.3.5 Migration to New International Standards: ISO20022

Most national stock exchanges and national CSDs are, like SWIFT, currently sending and receiving corporate actions messages based on the ISO 15022 standard which is now over ten years old and based on somewhat dated technologies. However, the Depository Trust & Clearing Corporation (DTCC), which is the CSD for the US, has, since 2013, been offering its participant firms the opportunity to send and receive corporate actions messages based on the **ISO 20022** standard.

This standard, unlike its predecessor standard, is based on a central dictionary of business items used in financial communications. This allows communities of users and message development organisations to define message sets according to an internationally agreed approach using internationally agreed business semantics. The messages themselves are constructed using **XML** standards.

Although the DTCC was one of the first CSDs to make this standard available, many others are expected to follow in the near future.

2.3.6 Data Vendors and their Role

Learning Objective

2.2.4 Know the role of a data vendor

In addition to the notifications provided as a service by the exchanges, **data vendors**, such as Thomson Reuters, Interactive Data Corporation, Fidessa, Bloomberg and SIX Financial Information (formerly Telekurs), play a key role in providing the investment community with similar information for a fee. Their advantage is that they may cover various different markets, reducing the overall number of information-providers and also reducing the amount of duplication.

The market data services industry is competitive and constantly developing in terms of quality and automated delivery. For example, a number of vendors are involved in a pilot scheme to deliver elements of their data over the SWIFT network as opposed to their own proprietary delivery mechanism. As explained in the previous section, this would reduce operational risk and head count and allow for lower fees, therefore making the organisation more attractive to potential customers.

2.4 Data Scrubbing

Learning Objective

2.2.6 Understand the purpose of data scrubbing

So far, the information described in Section 2.3 seems straightforward. However, from the raw information that is gathered, there has to be a process of selecting the relevant information, known as data scrubbing. Data scrubbing must occur before the event details are entered into any system that plays a role in processing the event.

There are a number of possible situations that could be problematic:

- If a security is held with more than one custodian, the firm will receive notices from more than one place. Only one set of information needs to be recorded, although a comparison of all the information must be carried out.
- There will be a number of corporate actions on securities that the firm does not hold and which can therefore be ignored. Custodians should only notify their clients on stocks they hold with them.
- The reverse of this situation is that the firm acquires a security which it has not previously held and therefore may have ignored a corporate action notice that has already been received. The custodian must inform the client of this situation.

Ideally, there will be automated flows of this information such that duplicate notifications of events are ignored, likewise notices for securities not held. In this environment it is the responsibility of the asset servicing analyst to keep track of what is happening and to prioritise their work effectively, based on the proximity of the close date and the value of missing the event. The value can be a real cost, ie, being obliged to pay a client a benefit because the firm missed a deadline, or an opportunity cost, ie, a potential profit missed because a rights issue had not been subscribed.

3. Event Entitlement

For particular types of corporate action, entitlement to participate may be based on a characteristic of the instrument or when it was bought. For example:

- a holder of **non-voting shares** is not entitled to vote at the AGM
- a holder of preference shares may be entitled to a dividend whereas a holder of ordinary shares is not
- a holder of shares bought cum-dividend is entitled to a dividend whereas a holder of shares bought **ex-dividend** is not, and
- corporate actions, like dividends, have an **ex-date** and, therefore, holders of shares bought prior to the ex-date are entitled to participate in corporate actions, while holders of shares bought on or after the ex-date are not.

3.1 Term Definition

Learning Objective

2.3.1 Know the definition of: record date; ex-date; cum-entitlement; ex-entitlement; special-ex; special-cum; pay date

2.3.2 Understand the significance of ex-date in establishing contractual entitlement to benefits

2.3.3 Understand the significance of record date

2.3.8 Understand the impact of special-ex/special-cum on entitled positions

2.3.9 Be able to calculate an entitlement when a position is subject to special-ex/special-cum trading

There are a number of corporate actions which have similar characteristics in terms of their timing and when the benefits pass from seller to buyer. In general terms, these are best illustrated by the following diagram, where the benefit is a cash dividend. In other events the benefit may be an entitlement to take up an offer of additional shares.

```
Announcement          Ex-Date         Record          Pay Date
   Date                                Date
     │                   │               │               │
     ▼                   ▼               ▼               ▼
─────────────────────────────────────────────────────────────────
       ⟨──── Cum-Period ────⟩⟨── Ex-Period ──⟩⟨── Cum-Period for Next Dividend ──⟩
```

Cum-div trades (price includes right to dividend payment) Buyer receives dividend	Ex-div trades (price excludes right to dividend payment) Seller receives dividend

Special-ex trades Seller receives dividend	Special-cum trades Buyer receives dividend

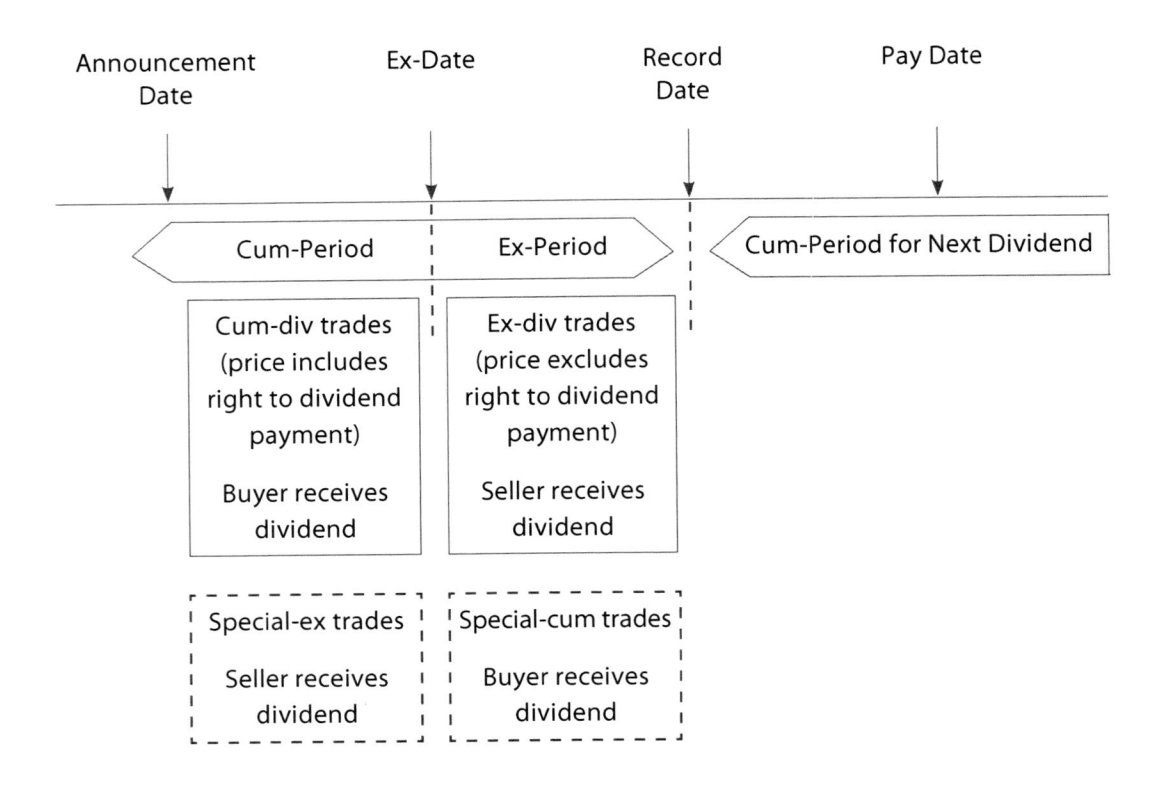

Announcement Date

On the announcement date, the directors of a company will announce whether the shareholders have voted to pay a dividend (quarterly, semi-annually or annually). They will also declare the type of dividend, the amount paid per share, the payable date and the record date.

Ex-Date

The ex-date is the date used to determine who is entitled to receive the benefits in respect of the securities being traded. There are two common options:

- Trades dealt prior to ex-date are dealt cum-entitlement or simply cum. That is, the purchaser will receive the benefit.
- Trades dealt on or following ex-date are dealt ex-entitlement or simply ex. That is, the seller will receive the benefit.

However, by mutual agreement between the two trading parties, it is possible to trade special-ex (ie, ex-dividend in the **cum-dividend** period) or special-cum (ie, cum-dividend in the ex-dividend period).

Record Date

Depending on the market, several days may be required to change stock ownership records following a sale. The registrar takes the stock ownership on record date, normally a few days, or a full settlement cycle, after ex-date, to determine who to pay the dividend or other benefit to.

Payment Date

On the payment date, the dividend is paid. The payment date can range from the record date (usually in bearer markets) through to several weeks or even months later in registered markets; the norm would be two to four weeks.

Special Transactions

In some cases, it is possible to trade a stock prior to ex-date, but only when the buyer agrees that they will not be entitled to the benefit. This is known as a special-ex transaction. The buyer would, of course, pay a lower price in recognition of this.

The reverse, when the buyer is entitled to the benefit on or after ex-date, is known as a special-cum transaction, and the buyer would, of course, pay a higher price.

Example

Firm A holds a fully settled position of 10,000 shares that are due to pay a dividend on 5 June. On 12 May A agrees to sell 2,000 shares to B on a special-ex basis. The trade settles on time on 15 May.

Date	Action	Firm A's settled position	Firm B's settled position
12 May	Opening balance	10,000	0
12 May	Trade date of special-ex sale to Firm B	10,000	0
15 May	Settlement date of special-ex sale to Firm B	8,000	2,000
17 May	Record date	8,000	2,000
5 June	Payment date	8,000	2,000

In this example, Firm B owes Firm A the dividend on 2,000 shares. In most markets, the depository has automated procedures to charge B and credit A with the benefit, but in other markets it may be necessary for Firm A to make a claim on Firm B.

3.2 Entitlement Calculations Including Stock on Loan

Learning Objective

2.3.4 Understand the impact of late booking and cancellation of trades on an entitled position

2.3.5 Be able to calculate an amended entitlement due to a late-booked or cancelled trade

2.3.6 Understand the impact of a stock loan/borrow on an entitlement position

2.3.7 Be able to calculate an entitlement when a position is subject to stock loan/borrow activity

The following example shows the effects of stock borrowing and lending, as well as failed trades, on the position that is entitled to the benefit:

Example

Consider a holding of BT shares. An interim dividend of 2p per share is announced. The record date is set as 14 January, with the payment date as 14 March. The ex-date, therefore, becomes 12 January. This allows for all cum-trades dealt with a normal settlement period to settle by close of business on the record date.

Consider the following stock record for a firm taken on the ex-date, minus 1. Trades dealt on the ex-date are ex-dividend.

The stock record is a snapshot of:

- trades that are open with the market, and
- stock loans and borrows.

Consider the following record of open transactions at close of business on 11 January, the day prior to ex-date. These are both open trades and stock lending and borrowing records.

The opening balance of the account at the custodian is 5,200 BT shares. These are settled trades.

	Trade type	Counterparty/book	Trade ref	Trade date	Value date	Sell	Buy	Comments
Trades	Sell	ABC Inv Man	123876	5 Jan	10 Jan	1,800		[1] Failed trade
	Sell	GET Securities	123895	10 Jan	13 Jan	300		[1] Pending trade
	Sell	XYZ Securities	123953	10 Jan	13 Jan	100		[1] Pending trade
	Sell	Good Inv ltd	123986	11 Jan	14 Jan	2,200		[1] Pending trade
	Buy	Best Co Inc	123999	11 Jan	14 Jan		2,200	[2] Pending trade
Stock	Borrow	Lender ABC	3004	18 Dec	17 Jan		12,000	[3] Open borrow for return 14 Jan
	Lend	Borrow DEF	3008	28 Nov	5 Feb	10,000		[4] Open lend for return 5 Feb

The Life Cycle of an Event

The theoretical stock balance resulting from the above transactions is:

Settled trade position	5,200
[1] Sell transactions	(4,400)
[2] Buy transactions	2,200
[3] Stock on loan from the market	(12,000)
[4] Stock being lent to the market	10,000
Balance	1,000

This theoretical position will only be turned into a settled position with the custodian once all the above transactions have been successfully settled and cleared.

- The firm is borrowing stock from a lender and, therefore, will have to pay part of the dividend received to the lender.
- Under a separate transaction the firm is lending stock to a borrower and will, therefore, receive the dividend from the borrower.

Consider the same position at close of business on 14 January, the record date. Three of the sell trades have settled so the lines of stock held at the custodian have been reduced.

Opening balance at custodian	5,200
Sell trade 123895	(300)
Sell trade 123953	(100)
Sell trade 123986	(2,200)
Closing balance at custodian	2,600

Another trade, 123999, fails because of incorrect settlement instructions. The table, therefore, looks like this:

	Trade type	Counterparty/book	Trade ref	Trade date	Value date	Sell	Buy	Comments
Trades	Sell	ABC Inv Man	123876	5 Jan	10 Jan	1,800		Failed trade
	Buy	Best Co Inc	123999	11 Jan	14 Jan		2,200	Failed trade
Stock	Borrow	Lender ABC	3004	18 Dec	17 Jan		12,000	Open borrow for return 14 Jan
	Lend	Borrow DEF	3008	28 Nov	5 Feb	10,000		Open lend for return 5 Feb

The impact on an entitlement is greatest when there are multiple loans and brokers involved for stock held by the same client. While each broker is contractually bound to protect the full entitlement on the positions held by them, there will, over the aggregation of the loans to various brokers, be more than one entitlement calculation. This can lead to a client losing out on one or more shares due to fractional roundings.

Example

Rights issue in the UK registered market
Ratio 5:8

Client x
Loan 1
150,000 shares to Broker A
150,000/8 x 5 = 93,750 no fraction

Loan 2
27,530 shares to Broker B
27,530/8 x 5 = 17,206 fraction 0.25

Loan 3
253,454 shares to Broker C
253,454/8 x 5 = 158,408 fraction 0.75

If this had been one position, then the fractions would add up to one additional share.

The borrowing brokers may, in turn, have lent the shares on, in differing amounts to multiple entities, creating further fractional losses of entitlement. Each borrowing counterparty is obliged to return an entitlement as derived from the actual position borrowed, regardless of whether onward lending has resulted in further lost fractions. In such cases, additional shares may have to be purchased in order to satisfy such obligations.

The situation is the same for the custodian for the stock split between the custody accounts and the stock on loan, as again each position carries its own entitlement; however, in this case there is no requirement to purchase the lost fractions, as the client will receive the full entitlement for each position.

3.3 Transformations

Learning Objective

2.3.10 Understand the concept of the transformation process

The transformation process in the UK is carried out within the CREST system. This allows trades that are in flight to be transformed into the entitlement and delivered on to the counterparty.

For mandatory issues without an option the transformation is carried out automatically. For mandatory issues with options and voluntary events, the parties to the trade enter the option required as a protection measure as an ACON message. If CREST does not receive an ACON message for a mandatory issue with options, the trade will transform into the default option.

4. Response-Gathering and Instruction

Learning Objective

2.4.1 Know the definitions of the following terms in relation to a mandatory event with options and a voluntary event: issuer deadline; agent deadline; market deadline (for elections); deposit date (protect deadline)

2.4.2 Understand the concept of broker-to-broker buyer protection and protection through the CCP in relation to late/failed trading and stock loan activity

2.4.3 Understand the implications of deadlines in relation to an event

For voluntary events or mandatory events with options, the owner of the shares is required to make a decision, eg, to take a dividend as cash or as shares. Normally, the custodian or other agent will collate the decisions made by all of its clients and then forward these to the CSD, which will inform the company by relaying to the registrar or **paying agent**.

There are, therefore, a number of deadlines.

- The **agent deadline** – each agent will require some time to collate and forward the responses to the registrar, and so will set a discretionary deadline, which is earlier than the market deadline, in order to allow sufficient time to complete required tasks.
- The **issuer deadline** – this will normally coincide with the market deadline, but is specifically set by the issuer.
- The **market deadline** – this is the final time by which the company or its representative (registrar) must receive their responses.
- The **deposit deadline** – if stock has to be lodged in a particular account for an event to occur, eg, for a rights issue or conversion, the deadline is often referred to as a deposit deadline. This deadline is usually a time during the day rather than just the day itself. This means that the custodian must ensure that the deadline date and time are met.
- The **buyer protect deadline** – this is defined as the last date by which a 'buying counterparty' that has the legal right to choose a particular event option but does not yet hold the securities (such as a party in an unsettled transaction or the lender of securities) may instruct its counterparty to deliver the specified option.

These deadlines are key within the world of asset servicing, since missing them can mean that benefits due to the shareholders are lost and the cost has to be covered by the entity that missed the deadline. Therefore, adherence to these deadlines is critical to processing corporate actions.

If the asset servicing analyst has to elicit responses from many people, such as salesmen and clients, they should work towards the agent deadline.

In a worst-case scenario, the client making the decision may be several steps away from the CSD.

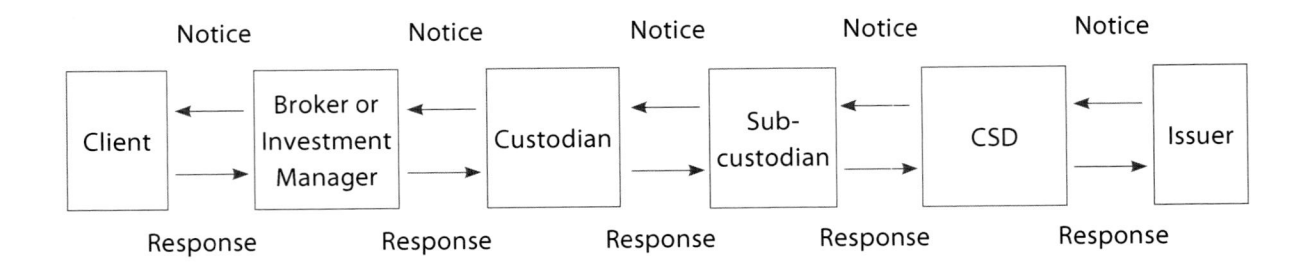

```
Notice        Notice        Notice        Notice        Notice
  ←            ←             ←             ←             ←
Client → Broker or → Custodian → Sub- → CSD → Issuer
         Investment              custodian
         Manager
  →            →             →             →             →
Response    Response      Response      Response      Response
```

In this case, there will be a chain of deadlines.

There are competing drivers which affect the efficiency of the process:

- The end client, whether a private client or a market trader, may wish to wait until as late as possible so that their decision on whether to accept the offer is based on the most current market price of the shares. If a decision is made too early, and the market falls rapidly, the client may make a loss.
- Any entity which has to collate responses and pass them on to the next stage will want to receive the responses as early as possible.

For certain open transactions when a trade fails to settle, a client who has bought the shares may not be registered in time to take up any option due to them. The trading firm acting on their behalf will normally only take up an option on an express instruction from a client. This is known as a buyer protection instruction. The instruction will request that the option is elected on behalf of the new owner. In the UK it is necessary within the CREST system to send an ACON message. This is an instruction, linked to the open trade for which a claim will be generated, stating which option the buyer wished to elect for.

However, in the UK, if an open transaction in nil-paid rights is not going to settle prior to the acceptance deadline, the seller will automatically protect the buyer, that is, take up the rights on their behalf. They will do this unless they receive a lapse instruction (also via ACON) from the buyer, indicating that they do not wish to take up the rights. This default action is covered in the rules of the LSE.

Often, when a firm is acting for a client, it will work on 'reasonable endeavours'. This phrase is a legal expression. It means that, although the firm will do everything it could reasonably be expected to do to meet a deadline on behalf of its client, it is not responsible for any financial impact should it fail to do so if the instruction was passed on later than the client deadline.

5. Payment, Claims and Post-Payment Reconciliation

Learning Objective

2.5.1 Understand how to validate a claim for the following transactions: repo; buy/sellback; sell/buyback; stock loan; failed trade

2.5.2 Understand the implication of pay/effective date in relation to an event

2.5.3 Understand the implication of failing to settle a claim for nil-paid rights prior to the deadline for acceptance in the UK market

2.5.4 Know the definition of auto-depository compensation

2.5.5 Understand how the transformation process may generate claims

5.1 The Payment Process

The payment process can be split into the corporate actions that can be handled by a firm's systems and those that need to be handled manually. They may differ in the amount of authorisation that is required to release messages to SWIFT or other payment systems.

Generally, most securities processing systems have a limited corporate actions functionality that will generate payment messages when a dividend is due to be paid out to a client and receipt messages when a dividend is due to be received in. To reduce the risk associated with this payment process, many brokers will not pay out a dividend to a client until they have received it. This may require manual intervention to suspend payments to clients if funds are not received.

For other payments, such as a subscription to a rights offer, the payment will need to be raised and authorised according to a firm's internal procedures. This should mean a segregation of duties to reduce the opportunity for fraudulent payments. An example may be that payment instructions (sometimes referred to as a payment ticket) can only be raised by the front office and must be authorised by a supervisor in operations before it can be released as a payment message into the SWIFT (or other) system.

For cash payments, ie, dividends or coupons, the date on which the cash movement takes place is known as the pay date. For other types of corporate actions where there may be a movement of stock, ie, a bonus issue, the date on which the stock movement takes place is known as the effective date or certs due date.

5.2 Claims

There are a number of situations where the entity that is entitled to the benefit will not automatically receive it. This can be for a number of reasons, for example:

- If a trade dealt cum-dividend is unsettled as at close of business on record date. The buyer is entitled to the benefit, but the seller is on the register. The buyer will claim the benefit back from the seller.
- If stock is subject to a repurchase agreement. In a repo, the buyer of the repo becomes the legal owner and so any benefit will be paid to them and has to be reclaimed by the seller, if detailed as such under the terms of the repo.
- If a benefit is distributed while stock is out on loan, a readjustment of the stock and the collateral held against it will need to be made; the benefit may be returned to the lender or form part of an adjusted loan.
- CREST claims generated automatically on loans and open trades at record date.

If a trade has been netted at an exchange or clearing house and is the subject of a claim, the exchange will need to create a number of claims to move the cash or benefits between the parties correctly. For a firm that has netted trades with several clients, it needs to be able to divide the overall claim so that each client receives what is due to them. If two counterparties have a number of claims against each other, they may be able to net them to reduce the overall movement of cash or stock and the risk. If the claim is processed via an exchange, the exchange may do this automatically. In other cases, it is up to the two parties to agree bilaterally to net.

Finally, it is worth noting that it is common practice to raise a claim for everything that a firm believes that it is owed, even when the trade documentation indicates that the claim should be paid automatically by the party being claimed from.

On rights issues in the UK, when the buyer fails to make an election it is the market practice default for the seller, as the registered holder, to subscribe to the rights and to deliver the fully paid shares to the counterparty against consideration for the subscription price.

5.3 Cash and Stock Reconciliations

With a few exceptions, eg, a change of legal name of the issuer, corporate actions will have an impact on either the stock or cash ledgers of a firm, or both. As an example, a dividend will be recorded as a receipt of cash on the firm's ledger. This amount will be calculated from the announced dividend and the ex-date holding. The actual cash is received in the firm's bank account and will appear on its bank statement. In the same way that high street banks take deposit of people's cash, custodians take deposit of both securities and cash for corporations and other financial institutions. Depository (depot) accounts contain securities and nostro accounts contain cash.

The statement will be reconciled with the firm's ledger to ensure that all expected movements of stock and cash have taken place. Depending on the booking and settlement process, some firms will also need to ensure that any changes are reflected in the trading systems at the same time as the settlement systems. When this happens it becomes a three-way reconciliation:

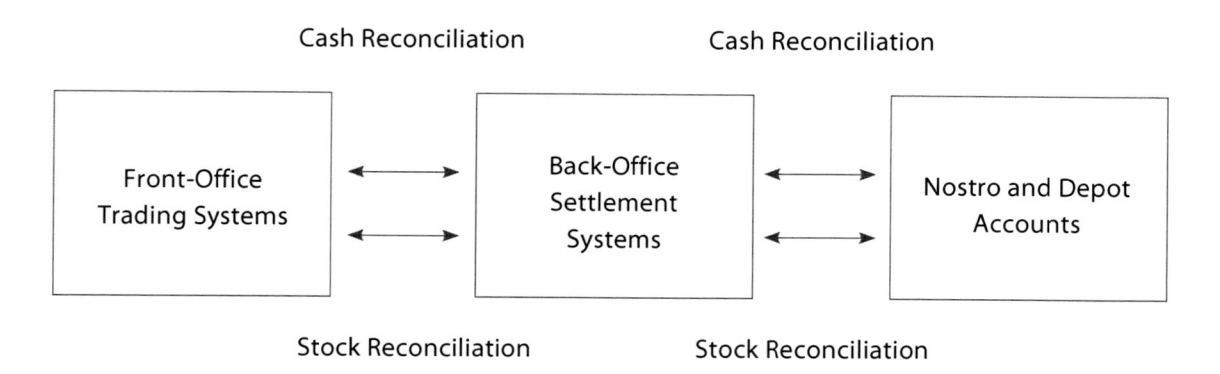

```
           Cash Reconciliation           Cash Reconciliation

   ┌──────────────┐        ┌──────────────┐        ┌──────────────┐
   │ Front-Office │ ←────→ │  Back-Office │ ←────→ │   Nostro and │
   │   Trading    │        │  Settlement  │        │     Depot    │
   │   Systems    │ ←────→ │   Systems    │ ←────→ │   Accounts   │
   └──────────────┘        └──────────────┘        └──────────────┘

          Stock Reconciliation          Stock Reconciliation
```

Corporate actions can cause reconciliation breaks for a number of reasons. Some examples are:

- a delay in payment or receipt of funds or stock, for example due to late instruction
- a subdivision or **consolidation** that has changed the number of shares held at the depository, but which has not yet been reflected in the firm's system
- the recording of a corporate action in the firm's systems that did not in fact occur, or
- the recording of a dividend receipt as cash when it was received as stock, or vice versa.

A firm may have a separate control function to perform these reconciliations and it may be more familiar with day-to-day trading reasons for reconciliation breaks than those attributable to corporate actions. The corporate actions analyst should be able to identify the reason for each break and the course of action to correct it, ie, for the final item above, cancel the cash receipt and rebook it as a receipt of stock.

5.4 Auto-Depository Compensation

Learning Objective

2.5.4 Know the definition of auto-depository compensation

For rights issues, bonus issues and dividends, there will be situations following failed or delayed settlement where the buyer is entitled to a benefit, either in cash or stock. Depending on the agreement, the depository will automatically raise a claim for the additional benefit from the seller. This is known as **auto-depository compensation** or, in the UK, claims processing.

6. Arbitrage

Learning Objective

2.6.1 Understand the concept of arbitrage

2.6.2 Understand the impact on transaction processing

2.6.3 Understand the impact on entitlement and reconciliation

6.1 Arbitrage Definition and Examples

Arbitrage is defined as the simultaneous purchase and sale of substantially identical assets in order to profit from a price difference between the two assets.

As a hypothetical example, if General Electric **common stock** trades at $16 on the New York Stock Exchange (NYSE) and at £10.20 on the LSE, and the exchange rate is $1.5 to the pound, an investor could guarantee a profit by purchasing the stock on the LSE and simultaneously selling the same amount of stock on the NYSE. Of course, the price difference must be sufficiently great as to offset commissions, any other charges and administration costs.

Arbitrage may be employed by using various instrument combinations such as:

- buying convertible bonds and selling the underlying shares, or vice versa
- buying warrants and selling the underlying shares, or vice versa
- buying individual stock futures or options, and selling the underlying shares, or vice versa
- buying equity index options and selling the underlying shares in the proportions that they are reflected in the index, or vice versa. This is known as basket trading.

Corporate action arbitrage is slightly different from the above examples. For example, an issuer may offer investors a choice of taking their benefits as cash or securities. The holder might want cash, but another investor might want securities. In this form of arbitrage, the holder lends the securities to the other investor who chooses the stock option, pays the cash benefit to the borrower, and sells the resulting shares. The borrower is assuming that the proceeds from selling the shares will be greater than the cash option proceeds it has to pay to the lender.

6.2 The Impact of Arbitrage on Transaction Processing, Entitlement and Reconciliation

Let us consider the case of an investor who has decided to buy convertible bonds and sell the underlying equity. An example of a convertible bond is provided in Section 3.2 of Chapter 1.

There are four key issues involved in processing arbitrage transactions involving convertible bonds:

1. The purchase of the bonds and the sale of the underlying equities need to be truly simultaneous. If there is a delay in executing one of the transactions, then the price difference may evaporate or be reversed.

2. At some point in time, the convertible bond needs to be converted into the underlying shares so that the short position can be closed out. The conversion process may be thought of as an investor-initiated corporate action. This means that the normal notifications from exchanges and CSDs that were discussed in Section 2 of this chapter are not received – it is up to the investor to recognise the need for, and the terms of, conversion. The bond's prospectus will provide details of the conversion terms. In the example bond shown in Chapter 1, conversion may take place at any time during the life of the bond, but some issues have a restricted conversion period; for example, conversion may only take place during the last three years of the life of the bond. The process of issuing conversion instructions is dealt with in Section 3 of Chapter 4.
3. Because the investor is running a short position in the underlying equity, the investor will need to borrow stock in order to make delivery while the conversion is being processed. Stock lending and borrowing was discussed in Section 4.2 of Chapter 1.
4. It is important to remember that as soon as the bond is converted it ceases to exist. This means that the holder of the convertible bond loses the right to all future coupon payments as soon as the bond is converted. The ABC bond shown in Chapter 1 paid 4% coupons on 16 January and 16 July each year. This meant that a holder who instructed the **conversion agent** to convert £100,000 face value of bonds on 15 January would lose the coupon of £2,000 that is to be paid one day later. If, however, conversion were instructed for 17 January, then the loss would be only one day's coupon for the new period.

Because any delays in executing or settling the purchases and sales, stock loans and/or bond conversion can have a significant profit and loss (P&L) impact, it is necessary to reconcile all open arbitrage transactions on a daily basis, and chase any transactions that are not being executed or settled on the due date.

The principles described above apply equally to conversion of warrants into their underlying equity, with the exception that, as warrants do not usually pay interest, there is less need to be concerned about the timing of the exercise of the warrant.

End of Chapter Questions

Think of an answer for each question and refer to the appropriate section for confirmation.

1. Give the six stages of the life cycle of an asset servicing event in their correct order.
   Answer reference: Section 1.1

2. Give reasons why the following events may cluster together:

   A. Dividend payments
   B. Mergers
   C. Initial public offerings
   D. Rights issues

   Answer reference: Section 2.1

3. What is the common method of advising of initial public offerings?
   Answer reference: Section 2.2

4. What is a Stock Situation Notice and who would produce one?
   Answer reference: Section 2.3.1

5. What is a DACE and who would produce one?
   Answer reference: Section 2.3.2

6. What is the SWIFT messaging standard introduced in 2002, and what is the series of messages used for corporate actions?
   Answer reference: Section 2.3.4

7. Give three examples of situations that require data scrubbing.
   Answer reference: Section 2.4

8. Describe these four dates related to an event entitlement:

   A. Announcement date
   B. Record date
   C. Ex-date
   D. Payment date

   Answer reference: Section 3.1

9. What is the difference between an agent deadline and a market deadline?
   Answer reference: Section 4

10. Why would the end client wish to wait until as late as possible before deciding whether or not to take up a rights issue?
    Answer reference: Section 4

11. What is the purpose of a protection instruction?
    Answer reference: Section 4

12. What three-way reconciliation must be performed to ensure that corporate actions have been correctly reflected in all books and records?
    Answer reference: Section 5.3

Chapter Three
Mandatory Events

1. Introduction	57
2. Equity Events	57
3. Bond Events	69
4. Liquidation	78
5. Redenomination	81
6. Market Report	81

This syllabus area will provide approximately 9 of the 50 examination questions

1. Introduction

As discussed in the last chapter, a mandatory event is a corporate action that takes place following shareholder approval at a shareholder meeting, but which does not require an active investor participation thereafter. This is distinct from a voluntary event, which requires the shareholder to make an investment decision, even if it is to take no action or 'lapse' these issues; these will be discussed in the next chapter.

A custodian's asset servicing department is responsible for the efficient processing of mandatory events and for ensuring that the investor is notified and compensated as appropriate.

The main mandatory events which are discussed in this chapter are:

- dividends
- bonus issues
- subdivisions
- consolidations
- mergers and demergers
- capital repayments
- coupons
- maturity and redemptions
- delayed/defaulting securities
- liquidations
- redenominations.

2. Equity Events

2.1 Dividends

Learning Objective

3.1.1 Understand that a dividend is paid from realised profits

3.1.2 Know the frequency of dividends and the payment timetable for UK, US, Japan and Italy: ex-dividend date; record dates; special-ex; special-cum; pay date

3.1.3 Understand the impact of a dividend on the share price

A dividend is a distribution of profits to the shareholders of a company. The key facts are:

- Dividends are paid on a periodic basis, determined by market convention and the ability of the company to pay them. Payments are usually made on a quarterly, semi-annual or annual basis depending on the type of asset involved. For example, most UK companies pay dividends semi-annually, while most US corporations pay dividends quarterly.

- Generally, dividends are stated as a monetary amount, although preference share dividends are sometimes stated as a percentage of the **par value** of the share.
- Dividends must be paid to preference shareholders before any other shareholders are paid.
- If a company's earnings are insufficient to pay dividends, the dividend is normally cancelled for ordinary shares, but cumulative preference shareholders will have the payment accumulated and deferred until funds are available.
- Dividends become payable once they are declared by the board of directors. The record and payment date of the dividend are also set by the company. The exchange will then set the ex-date, which determines whether shares are traded cum-dividend or ex-dividend.
- If the security has been purchased on the ex-date, the seller is entitled to the dividend. So, a fall in the share price, proportionate to the value of the dividend, is expected on the ex-date.
- The terms 'realised' and 'unrealised' profits are typically used within a fund accounting function. In some situations, for tax or reporting reasons, funds have to recognise income which at a point of time has not been received but on paper has been earned. For example, a fund's financial year ends on March 31. If one of its holdings declares a dividend on March 28, but the dividend is not paid until April 4, the fund might wish to treat this dividend as income of the year just ended, in which case the fund accountant makes an **accrual** for the amount of the dividend.

The asset service analyst needs to be aware of upcoming dividend payments and of the dividend timetable for all relevant shares to ensure that disbursements are made to clients correctly and in a timely manner. The guiding principle is that the Financial Conduct Authority's (FCA's) Client Money Rules stipulate that dividend proceeds must be credited to customers' accounts within 24 hours of receipt, which would normally be on pay date unless there was a claim involved on another party such as a stock borrower.

See Section 6 for the payment timetable in relation to Japan, Italy and the US.

2.1.1 Scrip Dividends (Subscription Reinvestment Plan)

Learning Objective

3.1.5 Be able to calculate a scrip dividend entitlement given a cash dividend, a reference price for the shares and a record holding date

A scrip dividend option is when a company offers investors the choice of payment of a dividend in shares rather than cash. This is a mandatory event with options. If the shareholder does not make an election, they will still receive the default as set by the company.

A scrip dividend is an issue of new shares to the exchange from a company's **authorised share capital** (see Chapter 1, Section 2.3). Sufficient reserves of authorised share capital must exist to cover the terms of the scrip issue, or must otherwise be sought at an extraordinary general meeting (EGM) or annual general meeting (AGM) prior to announcement.

The dividend will be declared with a monetary value per share. The share entitlement is then calculated by placing a valuation on each new share. This will generally be an average of the traded share price over a one-week period before the announcement, and is known as the scrip reference price.

Mandatory Events

From the issuer's point of view, a scrip dividend improves the cash flow because new shares are being created rather than cash being paid out.

From the investor's point of view, it allows the accrual of new shares without paying a broker's commission. Depending on the market, there may be tax implications.

$$\text{Number of new shares received} = \frac{\text{number of shares owned} \times \text{dividend amount}}{\text{scrip reference price}}$$

In extreme circumstances, when market volatility negatively impacts the value of stock between the market election deadline and payment date, a company may reserve the right to cancel the scrip issue in the interests of its shareholders. A negative swing of 15% between the reference and market price is generally the trigger for such action, with exact details/terms of cancellation being defined within the issue prospectus.

Example

ABC ltd shares are trading at £1.80 when it declares a dividend of 8p per share. Shareholders are given the option of payment by cash or in the form of a scrip dividend.

If an investor with a holding of one million shares decides to receive a scrip dividend, how many new shares will they receive, assuming that the share price is unchanged on payment date?

Cash value of dividend = 1,000,000 × 0.08 = £80,000

Number of new shares received = (1,000,000 × 0.08)/1.80 = 44,444

The value of the new shares = 44,444 × 1.80 = £79,999.20

Because it is not possible to receive fractional shares as a result of a scrip issue, the remaining 80p will be either paid in cash, held over until the next dividend or, if the investor has given permission, donated to charity.

2.1.2 Dividend Reinvestment Plan (DRIP) Dividends

Learning Objective

3.1.4 Know the distinction between scrip dividends and dividend reinvestment schemes

Some companies offer **dividend reinvestment plans (DRIPs)** whereby actual payment of cash due from the declared dividend is withheld, and used to buy shares of the company on the open market. There is generally no predetermined reference price, so elections are 'blind' – a shareholder does not know the entitlement they will receive at the point they actually make the election. The dividend cash due to shareholders who have elected for DRIP shares is combined and used to purchase shares on the open market, by the company-appointed broker, generally over a one-week period. The reference price is then derived as the mean market price achieved in the purchase of shares over the defined purchase period. Shares purchased under a DRIP scheme are subject to standard market tariff, ie, in the UK are subject to stamp duty and broker's commission.

From the issuing company's point of view, DRIPs have no real effect on cash flow, as the cash that would have been paid is used in the purchase of shares that already exist in the open market – no new issue of shares occurs.

There is little, if any, benefit to major shareholders in electing for a DRIP, as all standard purchase fees still apply and the stock price is beyond discretion. However, small shareholders may benefit due to the elimination of minimum broker fees, and so can accrue small additional shareholdings at a realistic price.

2.1.3 Scrip versus DRIP

The table below outlines the major differences between the scrip and DRIP schemes:

Perspective	Scrip	DRIP
Security issuer	The issuer does not have to pay the dividend; it retains the cash	The issuer has to pay the dividend, so does not save cash
Security issuer	The issuer increases the number of shares in issue, therefore increasing the cost of future dividends and benefits	No new shares are created, therefore the cost of future benefits remains unchanged
Investor	Does not have to pay stamp duty or stamp duty reserve tax (SDRT) when new shares are created	Has to pay stamp duty or SDRT when shares are purchased in the market
Investor	Has price certainty in advance	Does not have price certainty in advance of the market transaction

The effect on the share price of a reinvested dividend is exactly the same as with a dividend; in theory, the share price would drop by the value of the dividend.

2.1.4 Evergreen Options

Evergreen options are facilities provided by registrars which allow for the shareholder to apply (by way of a mandate) for a DRIP or scrip election for all future dividend payments.

2.1.5 Dividend Access Plans

Learning Objective

3.1.6 Understand the concept of dividend access plans

In recent years, a number of large companies have changed the domicile of their parent company from the UK to another country with a more favourable corporate tax regime.

Such changes of domicile are designed to reduce the amount of tax paid by the company and possibly also by the end investor.

Under such a plan, shareholders may choose whether they receive their dividends from a company resident for tax purposes in the UK or from the company that issued the shares, which is resident for tax purposes outside the UK.

2.2 Bonus Issues

Learning Objective

3.2.1 Know the definition of a bonus issue

3.2.2 Understand the reasons for initiating a bonus issue

A bonus issue, which is a benefit distribution, is a free issue of new shares to existing shareholders at a ratio set by the issuing company in proportion to the shareholders' existing holdings. The shareholder does not pay for the new shares, there is no transfer of funds between the company and its shareholders, and the company does not raise any capital, nor is there any change to the par value of the shares.

A firm may initiate a bonus issue to:

- bring the share capital in line with current business needs
- reduce the share price in order to make the shares more marketable
- increase the liquidity of the shares by increasing the number of them in circulation
- replace a cash dividend.

The issue is carried out by transferring some of the reserves to the share capital account within the firm's balance sheet.

Bonus issues are also known as scrip issues or capitalisation issues.

2.2.1 Bonus Rights

Learning Objective

3.2.3 Know the difference between a bonus issue and a bonus issue with rights

Rather than just issuing new shares, issuers sometimes issue bonus rights. These are tradeable and can be converted to shares at a set date. These mainly occur in bearer markets.

Example

Telefonica issues one bonus right for every one share held. The rights can be converted back to ordinary shares at a ratio of one new share for every ten rights, free of payment. So, if Telefonica is trading at €10 per share with rights, the price will reduce to €9.09 on the ex-date. The rights will subsequently trade at 91 cents each. The rights price will then track the ordinary price.

The reason for issuing bonus rights is to remove fractional entitlements. In the example above, if the bonus issue were converted directly into equity at a ratio of 1:10 then any shareholders not holding an exact multiple of 10 would end up with fractions. By issuing tradeable rights, the company allows its shareholders to round up or down before converting back to ordinary shares, or, if the shareholder does not wish to maintain their current level of investment, they can sell out of the rights.

2.2.2 'B' and 'C' Share Bonus Issues

Learning Objective

3.2.4 Understand the reasons for initiating a 'B' share bonus issue

3.2.5 Understand the reasons for initiating a 'C' share bonus issue

Certain companies, including Rolls-Royce, McBride, Betfair, Persimmon and Booker Group, have previously chosen to distribute some of their income by means of a capitalisation/bonus issue instead of paying an increased dividend. This has typically taken the form of a distribution of 'B' shares at a pre-advised ratio (the bonus) in lieu of a cash dividend. The issued 'B' shares then have options attached, at shareholder discretion, and effected by election:

- Redeem the 'B' shares for cash to the value per ordinary share, being the equivalent of the cash dividend – and further elect the cash as either a dividend or capital distribution.
- Elect to convert them into ordinary shares at a pre-set conversion share value.
- Retain the 'B' shares.

Rolls-Royce has taken a decision that moves this one step further. The following is an extract of an announcement that this firm made in 2008:

> C shares: The directors have announced their intention to create a new class of shares to be called C shares, which will be redeemable for cash, and the directors intend that payments thereafter will be made by the issue of C shares, commencing with the 2008 interim payment to shareholders. The main difference between B shares and C shares is that the C shares will not carry an option to convert into ordinary shares. The company plans to arrange with its registrar for a scheme to enable shareholders to reinvest their payments in a market purchase of ordinary shares. For those shareholders who retain their C shares, a C share dividend at a rate of 75% of the London InterBank Offered Rate will be payable half-yearly in arrears. Full details of this proposal, and a resolution seeking shareholder approval, will be included in the Notice convening the 2008 Annual General Meeting.

Bonus issues may be attractive to investors because they are an alternative to dividends, which are taxed differently. If there is a bonus issue there is no immediate liability to **capital gains tax (CGT)** when the shareholder receives the bonus shares, but there may be a CGT liability when the shares are sold.

There may be further adaptation to this concept in the future due to changes in tax credits in the UK.

2.3 Subdivisions and Consolidations

Learning Objective

3.3.1 Understand the reasons why a company may subdivide or consolidate its shares

3.3.3 Understand the impact of subdivisions and consolidations on the share price

3.3.4 Be able to calculate the impact of subdivisions and consolidations on the share price

2.3.1 Subdivision or Stock Split

A subdivision (also known as a stock split) is a decision taken by the company's board of directors to increase the number of shares that are outstanding by issuing more shares to current shareholders. A subdivision occurs after the board of directors authorises the split and it is voted through at the AGM by the shareholders. In a 2-for-1 subdivision, every shareholder with one stock is given an additional share, thus doubling the total number of shares that the company has issued.

A subdivision is sometimes a course decided upon by a company when their share price has increased to levels that are unsustainable against comparable companies in the same industry sector. The primary motive is to increase liquidity in the stock by making individual shares more affordable, even though the underlying value of the company has not changed. The market value of the company remains static, so the total value of all shares prior to the subdivision must equal the total value of all shares after the subdivision.

The price of a share is also affected by a subdivision. After a subdivision, the stock price will be reduced since the number of shares that are outstanding is increased. In the example of a 2-for-1 subdivision, the stock price will be halved.

Example

If an investor owns 100 shares of ABC ltd with a market value of £10 per share, they will have a total holding worth £1,000. If the company affects a 4-for-1 subdivision, they will consequently own 400 shares with a value of £2.50 per share. While the share price has dropped to reflect the increased number of shares outstanding, the total holding will remain at £1,000.

Note the par value of the shares will also reduce in a corresponding way, ie, from Ord £1 to Ord 25p shares.

Many subdivisions take place solely for the liquidity reason described above, but subdivisions sometimes occur as part of the spin-off or demerger activities described in Section 2.5 of this chapter. There may also be a cash component involved in order to provide shareholders with an equitable value at the conclusion of the issue compared to the position that they held prior to it.

Subdivisions related to spin-offs might involve the division of the issued share capital into two lines of stock, one of them possibly being an alternative instrument such as a convertible bond, a loan note or a deferred line. The latter may then, subject to receiving shareholder, regulatory and court approval, be cancelled. A more complex subdivision could involve the parent line dividing into multiple lines of new stock of varying instrument types including, but not limited to, different types of equities in different subsidiary parts of the parent corporation, which may also be inclusive of a cash equalisation element.

An example of this could be a company which over the years has acquired other companies in different markets and now has decided to divest itself of some of these companies as they are of sufficient standing to warrant a listing in their own right. This listing may not be in the country of the parent company, or the company may decide to allow the shareholders to decide which market they wish to hold the subdivided stock in, as it could be listed in multiple markets, such as the US, the UK and Switzerland.

The listing would take place on either a par value or no par value stock, and this will affect the overall package offered to the shareholders.

If a stock is trading at $10 and the company decides to subdivide the parent line into three lines and gives each one a value of $3, then the cash component would be expected to be around $1 per share.

Although these are mandatory issues, once approved by the shareholders they still have an elective element, in that the shareholder can decide in what market to hold the resultant stock.

Difference Between a Subdivision and a Bonus Issue

Learning Objective

3.3.2 Know the difference between a subdivision and a bonus issue

Subdivisions and bonus issues are seemingly similar in as much as, under both, the investor ends up with a greater number of shares without having to increase the investment to pay for the additional shares. There is a vital difference, however. In a bonus issue, the paid-up share capital of the company increases. For example, if it is a 1:1 bonus, the paid-up share capital would double, but in a subdivision the paid-up share capital remains as it is, with the number of shares alone undergoing an increase or decrease – the described par value of the security would be divided by the factor of the subdivision.

2.3.2 Consolidation or Reverse Split

A consolidation, which can be known as a reverse split, is when the outstanding shares are consolidated so that the total number is decreased. It is typical of stocks with lower than expected share prices that would like to increase their share prices either to gain more respectability in the market, or to prevent the company from being de-listed from the stock exchange – most stock exchanges will de-list stocks if they fall below a certain price per share.

Although the price will vary from market to market, in a 1-for-2 consolidation each shareholder would lose one share, but the value of each share would double, so that the value of the shareholding is not decreased.

A consolidation could be on a 1-for-5 or 1-for-10 basis, so a shareholder is left with 10% or 20% of the original number of shares.

A consolidation, just like a subdivision, requires shareholder approval.

Example

Company XYZ announces a 1-for-10 consolidation.

Shareholder A owns 100 shares at £10 per share. After the consolidation they will consequently own ten shares at £100 per share.

The share price increases to reflect the reduced number of shares outstanding but, again, the total value of the investment remains at £1,000. The par value of the shares will also increase correspondingly, ie, from Ord 10p shares to Ord £1 shares.

A consolidation can also be used to offload a part of the company that has failed to make a profit and has had an untoward effect on the company as a whole. In this instance the company will place a value on this part, consolidate the remainder of the company around the profitable parts of the company, and write off from the books the loss-making element. This is often referred to as 'returning to its core business'.

A consolidation can also be used by a company to facilitate a restructure, for example if it is in debt and unable to make payment in cash to its creditors. The company can negotiate with its creditors to issue stock in lieu of the debt; this requires the agreement of both the creditors and the regulatory bodies. If this type of consolidation means that the control of the company passes out of the hands of the current board of directors and the company ownership passes to a new person or company, then shareholder approval is also required.

2.4 Mergers

Learning Objective

3.10.1 Understand the reasons for initiating a merger

3.10.2 Be able to calculate the effect on book value of a merger

Mergers are the joining together, by mutual consent, of two or more organisations of all or part of their operations. They are often motivated by the desire of two companies, whose products and services complement each other in some way, to pool their resources into a single business. In this case, shareholders of both pre-merger companies have a share in the ownership of the post-merged business, with the top management of both companies sharing the top management positions in the new company.

The characteristics of a merger are:

- neither company is publicly portrayed as the acquirer or acquired, although one company may be seen as dominant
- the original companies cease to exist as corporate entities
- both parties participate in establishing the management structure of the combined business
- both companies are of sufficiently similar size that one does not dominate the other when combined, and
- all or most of the consideration involves a share swap rather than a cash payment.

Mergers can also be motivated by the desire of one company to take over and control another. In this case, top management positions will be filled by the acquiring company. These are more usually termed takeovers or acquisitions and are covered in more detail in the next chapter.

From an asset servicing perspective, knowledge of and information access to merger activity is required to ensure that clients are kept informed, and especially to allow them to register their vote on these issues within the required timescales at company meetings. This process is covered in more general terms in Chapter 5, Corporate Governance.

As a merger is usually an agreed deal between the two parties, albeit subject to shareholder approval, they are usually a meeting of minds and the share price of the newly merged entity may increase during the first few days of trading. However, if the merger is not well received by the press and the market, the share price can be talked down; as such, there is not an agreed formula that can be used to indicate the price of the stock.

2.5 Demergers (Spin-Offs)

Learning Objective

3.4.1 Understand the reasons for initiating a demerger

3.4.2 Be able to calculate the effect on book value of a demerger

A demerger, which is also known as a spin-off, is a distribution by the parent company of shares in one or more of its subsidiaries to current shareholders. Thus the subsidiary company becomes an independent listed company in its own right. The shares will be issued to parent company shareholders in proportion to their current holdings, with the subsidiary becoming a separate legal entity.

A company may initiate a spin-off because of a desire to divest part of its business. For instance, the main business of ABC ltd is long-haul airline travel. It also owns a subsidiary (XYZ ltd) that specialises in low-cost, short-haul flights. As part of a rationalisation strategy that requires ABC to concentrate on core business, it may decide to spin off XYZ.

A demerger may also be initiated as part of a management buy-out in which management and venture capitalists seek to unlock the value hidden in the subsidiary, or because the subsidiary is so well viewed that it makes the parent company a target for a takeover.

The cost of shares in the resulting company is the actual cost of investment in the demerged company; this is divided by the net worth, multiplied by the net book value of the assets being transferred. Once the calculation has been completed, and the cost of shares in the resulting company determined, the net asset value (NAV) of the shareholder across the new and the parent company remains at the value of the original investment.

Please note that spin-off events are sometimes accompanied by subdivision events. See Section 2.3 of this chapter for more information.

Example

On 2 February 2013, Mr Jones bought 1,000 shares of ABC plc for £1.00. On 4 July 2016, a demerger takes place whereby, for every ten ABC shares held, he will receive one share of the demerged DEF plc.

Therefore, he now holds 1,000 ABC and 100 DEF shares.

On the first day of trading, ABC trades at £4.00 per share and DEF at £3.00 per share.

His old holding originally cost £1,000 (ie, 1,000 shares x £1.00) and is now worth £4,300 (ie, 1,000 ABC shares at £4.00 plus 100 DEF shares at £3.00).

ABC acquisition cost = £1,000 x £4,000/£4,300 = £930.23.

DEF acquisition cost = £1,000 x £300/£4,300 = £69.77.

2.6 Capital Repayments

Learning Objective

3.5.1 Know the definition of a capital repayment

3.5.2 Understand the reasons for initiating a capital repayment

3.5.3 Know the following methods of achieving a capital repayment: redeemable bonus issue; renominalisation; repayment

A capital repayment is when a company pays back part of the issued share capital to its shareholders. A company may decide to do this if it has an excess of cash that it has no immediate need for.

For any form of capital repayment, shareholder approval at an AGM or EGM is required.

Renominalisation (sometimes described as par value change) describes the process of a change in the nominal or the quoted par value of a share, resulting in new tradeable units after a conversion. The nominal value of a share is reduced and the excess funds are paid to the shareholder.

It is possible that a company with shares issued at par value £0.25 may wish to make a payment to shareholders, other than a dividend, without reducing the share price or using its reserves. In this case, it could renominalise the par value to £0.15 and pay £0.10 per share to shareholders; however, it is more common that deferred shares are issued and subsequently cancelled by the issuer under the terms of the event.

In certain countries, eg, the US, most shares are issued with no par value and therefore cannot be renominalised.

3. Bond Events

3.1 Coupons

Learning Objective

3.6.1 Know the definition of a coupon

A coupon is the common term for the rate of interest paid on the nominal value (face value) of a bond. It derives its name from bearer bond certificates (ie, when an issuer does not maintain a register of legal ownership and so bond ownership is evidenced by ownership of a certificate). In order to claim any interest owing on the bond, the owner of the certificate would present a physical coupon to the issuer or their paying agent and in return the owner would receive the interest payment for the last interest-bearing period (the coupon period). The coupons were attached to the certificate, with each coupon representing a specific interest payment due at a given point in the life of the bond.

By contrast, for registered bonds the issuer automatically arranges for the interest payment to be sent to the bondholders who appear on the issuer's register as at a given record date. It is the name on the register that confers legal ownership.

Despite the inception of electronic bookkeeping, and with bonds existing as electronic records, the word 'coupon' continues to relate to the interest payment, even though there is no longer the requirement to process the paper coupons. 'Coupon' has become a generic term to refer to the interest payment on a fixed-interest security, irrespective of whether it is bearer, registered or dematerialised stock.

A coupon can be paid monthly, quarterly, semi-annually or annually, and the price of a bond including the interest (known as the dirty price, see Section 3.1.2) will fall immediately following a coupon payment by the same amount as the interest payment.

To the issuer the coupon represents the cost of borrowing, and to the investor it represents the return on investment, the measure of the return being the bond's **yield**. There are several definitions of and calculations used to measure bond yield, one of the most common of which is known as redemption yield or yield to maturity (YTM). YTM is best defined as the return an investor would earn if a bond were purchased when issued and held continually through to its maturity. It includes the coupon payments plus any gain or loss on the capital at maturity.

Usually, the longer the term of a bond, the higher the interest rate that is paid to the holder; this compensates the bondholder for the inflation risk of having money tied up for a long time.

If interest rates change while a bond is being held, it will be worth more or less on the open market than when it was first issued. If the current interest rates are higher, investors could get a better return by buying bonds sold at that current interest rate, so an older bond will be sold at less than face value, at a discounted price. If the current interest rates are lower, an older bond could be sold at more than face value, at a premium to its issued price.

Bond yields are inversely correlated with stock prices. Higher bond yields mean lower returns for other types of investments.

A company with a high credit rating may expect to pay a lower coupon than a company with a lower credit rating. This difference in coupon represents the extra credit risk – that is, the risk of the issuer defaulting on its payments – that an investor is exposed to when investing in a company with a lower credit rating.

The reference point for setting the coupon of a bond is the risk-free rate of borrowing, which is reflected in the more mature markets by the cost of government borrowing – the rate that the government issues its own bonds. The following will also affect coupon payments:

- **interest rate conventions**
- clean/dirty prices
- zero coupon bonds (ZCBs)
- **stripping**, and
- first long/first **short coupons**.

3.1.1 Interest Rate Conventions

Learning Objective

3.6.2 Be able to calculate bond interest using the following methods: (30/360; Actual/360; Actual/365; Actual/Actual)

There are four common methods of calculating the interest payable on interest bearing bonds. These are called interest rate conventions. They are:

- Actual/360-day convention
- Actual/365-day convention
- 30/360-day convention, and
- Actual/Actual convention.

Each convention differs slightly in the assumptions about the calculation of the period over which interest is payable. The conventions change depending on the market, for instance:

- UK corporate bonds pay interest based on Actual/365-day convention
- US corporate bonds pay interest based on Actual/360-day convention
- eurobonds generally pay interest based on the 30/360-day convention, and
- most government bonds pay interest based on the Actual/Actual convention.

Each convention is defined below:

Actual/360-Day Convention

This case assumes and bases the calculation on a 360-day year.

$$\text{Interest payable} = \text{nominal value} \times \text{annual coupon (\%)} \times \frac{\text{actual days in period}}{360}$$

Mandatory Events

Actual/365-Day Convention

This case assumes and bases the calculation on a 365-day year:

Interest payable = nominal value x annual coupon (%) x $\dfrac{\text{actual days in period}}{365}$

30/360-Day Convention

This case assumes and bases the calculation on there being 30 days in each and every month and 360 days in a year.

Interest payable = nominal value x annual coupon (%) x $\dfrac{\text{days in period (assuming 30 days in month)}}{360}$

Actual/Actual Convention

This convention has been defined by the International Capital Market Association (ICMA) and assumes the number of days in the year is equal to the calendar days in the interest period, multiplied by the number of interest periods in the year.

Interest payable =

nominal value x annual coupon (%) x $\dfrac{\text{calendar days in period}}{(\text{calendar days in period}) \times (\text{number of interest periods in year})}$

Example

Question

Investor X holds £1 million corporate bonds of ABC ltd with a coupon of 6%. Interest is paid quarterly and the interest periods are:

- 1 January to 31 March
- 1 April to 30 June
- 1 July to 30 September
- 1 October to 31 December.

Calculate the amount received by the investor per period and in total for each of the four interest rate conventions.

Answer

The interest rate periods are 90 days, 91 days, 92 days and 92 days respectively.

Actual/360-Day Convention

Q1: Interest paid = £1m x 0.06 x 90/360 = £15,000

Q2: Interest paid = £1m x 0.06 x 91/360 = £15,166.67

Q3: Interest paid = £1m x 0.06 x 92/360 = £15,333.33

Q4: Interest paid = £1m x 0.06 x 92/360 = £15,333.33

Total interest received = £60,833.33

Actual/365-Day Convention

Q1: Interest paid = £1m x 0.06 x 90/365 = £14,794.52

Q2: Interest paid = £1m x 0.06 x 91/365 = £14,958.90

Q3: Interest paid = £1m x 0.06 x 92/365 = £15,123.29

Q4: Interest paid = £1m x 0.06 x 92/365 = £15,123.29

Total interest received = £60,000.00

30/360-Day Convention

Q1: Interest paid = £1m x 0.06 x (3x30)/360 = £15,000

Q2: Interest paid = £1m x 0.06 x (3x30)/360 = £15,000

Q3: Interest paid = £1m x 0.06 x (3x30)/360 = £15,000

Q4: Interest paid = £1m x 0.06 x (3x30)/360 = £15,000

Total interest received = £60,000.00

Actual/Actual Convention

Q1: Interest paid = £1m x 0.06 x 90/(90x4) = £15,000

Q2: Interest paid = £1m x 0.06 x 91/(91x4) = £15,000

Q3: Interest paid = £1m x 0.06 x 92/(92x4) = £15,000

Q4: Interest paid = £1m x 0.06 x 92/(92x4) = £15,000

Total interest received = £60,000.00

3.1.2 Clean and Dirty Prices

Learning Objective

3.6.3 Know the difference between 'clean' and 'dirty' prices

3.6.6 Understand how an early record date impacts a coupon calculation

When analysing bond prices, investors need to be able to compare different bonds on a like-for-like basis. This is more difficult when a bond price includes **accrued interest**.

Accrued interest is the amount of interest that has been earned on a bond but not yet paid to the bondholder as the payment is made on set dates. So, if interest is paid six-monthly, interest will accrue for up to six months before it is paid. For this reason, the value of the bond increases between one payment date and the next. Therefore, if a bond is sold part-way through the accrual period, this will be factored into the price.

Because accounting for accrued interest makes it difficult to compare bonds, prices are quoted excluding this figure. This is the clean price.

Generally, when a bond is sold, it is sold at its clean price. The final price paid by the buyer, including the accrued interest, is called the dirty price.

Record date and pay date are the key dates used to derive interest entitlement. Interest usually accrues from pay date to pay date and receipt is based on a record date. Record date is normally the day before pay date. This is because, historically, the interest payment was the physical coupon attached to the certificate and when it was clipped the bond traded without the interest. However, the record date can be at any time before the pay date. If it is longer than one day before the pay date, it is called an early record date.

The interest is actually paid to the holder of record. Anyone who buys bonds between the record date and pay date will be entitled to the interest, if they paid the accrued interest on the trade, but they have to claim the interest from the seller. These are commonly known as interim trades.

Example

Question

On 22 July, purchaser X buys £100,000 bonds at 98.125% from seller Y. These bonds have a coupon of 6%, which is paid semi-annually on 1 April and 1 October. Interest is calculated on Actual/365-day convention basis.

What is the total amount payable to seller Y, assuming that the trade settles on a T+3 basis and that accrued interest is calculated up to the day prior to settlement date?

Answer

Clean price = 98.125%, therefore the principal amount is £98,125.00

On settlement date minus one (24 July) the bonds have accrued 115 days' interest since the last payment date of 1 April (30 days in April, 31 in May, 30 in June and 24 in July).

Accrued interest = £100,000 x 6% x 115/365 = £1,890.41

Total amount payable = £98,125.00 + £1,890.41 = £100,015.41

So the total amount payable is £100,015.41

Therefore the dirty price is 100.01541%

3.1.3 Zero Coupon Bonds (ZCBs)

A zero coupon bond (ZCB) does not pay interest; instead it is issued at a significant discount to its face value (par). The holder does not receive interest throughout the life of the bond but realises a profit when the bond matures. The discount is calculated to provide a similar rate of return to the investor as might be expected from the payment of periodic interest.

For example, a five-year bond may be issued with a par value of £100 and a coupon of £10. If income tax is 20% then the investor will receive net income of £40 over the five-year period. A ZCB discounted to £60 would, if held to maturity, produce the same net income.

The advantages of ZCBs are:

- the investor does not incur through-life processing costs to service interest payments
- they represent an alternative investment choice for the investor to the receipt of periodic payments by realising profit in terms of capital gain rather than income, which has different tax implications
- in international bond markets, there is the additional benefit that the exchange rate risk associated with converting proceeds from a foreign currency to base currency is limited to a single conversion of the redemption value rather than multiple conversions of periodic payments.

3.1.4 Stripping

Learning Objective

3.6.4 Understand that a bond may be stripped to meet investor requirements

A stripped bond is a normal bond that has had its coupons removed. The coupons are then sold separately, with a face value and maturity equal to each interest payment. This is called stripping. Both the coupons and the original bond then become ZCBs.

Stripping is used as a tool to change the characteristics of the original bond in order to provide greater flexibility to the investor.

In most markets, stripping is carried out by the central securities depository (CSD), which breaks the security into its components and delivers them back to the investor. The role of the CSD is examined in more detail in Chapter 7, Section 2.10.

Example

An example would be a bond that has a maturity of five years, a face value of £5 million and annual interest payments of 10%. This could be stripped to produce a five-year ZCB with a face value of £5 million, plus five smaller ZCBs with a face value of £0.5 million and a maturity of between one and five years. This would depend on when the interest rate payment was due.

Stripping of US Treasuries first occurred in 1982 and of UK government bonds in 1997. It is now common in international markets.

3.1.5 First Long/First Short Coupon

Learning Objective

3.6.5 Know the definition of 'first long' and 'first short' coupon

A bond does not have to be issued at the beginning of a coupon period. If it is issued at some point between two coupon dates, the first payment will be paid on either:

- the first coupon date, and be equivalent to an amount less than the whole coupon. This is called a short coupon, or
- the second coupon date, and be equivalent to an amount greater than the whole coupon. This is called a long coupon.

The intention to pay a short or long coupon will be stated in the bond's prospectus and will form part of the source data held by corporate action information vendors.

3.2 Bond Maturity

Learning Objective

3.7.1 Understand the following terms: redemption (maturity); partial redemption; early redemption; drawing; lottery

3.7.2 Understand the options available to a convertible bondholder when a company redeems a bond

The maturity of a bond is the period of time from issuance to redemption. This can be expressed with respect to the:

- original maturity, ie, the term to redemption at the time of issue, or
- current maturity, ie, the remaining time to redemption for bonds already in issue.

A bond is redeemed when the issuer repays the principal amount of the debt to the bondholder at maturity. Most bonds are redeemed by single lump sum payments. These are called **bullet redemptions**.

Example

XYZ Bond 3.5% 31/12/24

Nominal value held by the investor £1,000,000

Current market price £96

In the above situation, the investor will receive an income of 3.5% per annum calculated on their holding of £1,000,000 for the period until maturity, ie, 31 December 2024, assuming the bond is held until that date. More importantly, for this example, the current market value of the bond would be £1,000,000 x £96 = £960,000, representing a discount to the nominal value. If the investor purchases the bond at this price and holds it to redemption, the investor will receive a capital repayment of £1,000,000, resulting in a capital profit of £40,000.

Some issues allow for early redemption, ie, the payment of the principal prior to the published maturity date. The various methods are described below. Note that call options and **put options** are usually described as early redemptions, but **drawings** are usually described as methods of **partial redemption**.

If an early redemption is announced by the issuer of a convertible bond, the holder of a convertible bond may have the right to take up the conversion prior to redemption, depending on the terms and conditions of the bond.

3.2.1 Call Option

A **call option** gives the issuer the right to redeem bonds prior to the maturity date. These bonds are callable bonds. Redemption will usually be at a premium, that is to say a price above the face value of the bonds. This premium will fall as the bonds approach maturity.

Call options offer the issuer protection against a fall in interest rates. This allows it to refinance its funding requirements and issue new bonds at a lower coupon. Early redemptions may also be employed by firms wishing to reduce their debt burden.

3.2.2 Put Option

A put option gives the holder the right to request an early redemption. It is a voluntary event rather than a mandatory event. It is included here for ease of reference. In these cases, the redemption will usually be at a discounted price and include a minimum holding period.

This choice is attractive to investors as it protects them from the opportunity cost of holding bonds that have a lower coupon than the prevailing market interest rates. It will also provide protection against possible restructuring events that may damage the price or liquidity of their assets.

3.2.3 Drawing

For certain bonds, a situation occurs when some, but not all, capital is repaid to bondholders. This can be achieved in two ways:

- in a pro rata manner where each investor receives a payment in proportion to the value of their holdings, or
- as the result of a lottery when actual bond numbers are drawn by the issuer in order to qualify for the payment. This process is known as drawing. As the bonds are usually **dematerialised**, the custodian will perform another lottery to determine who receives the funds.

Drawings are more common on Danish and US bonds.

3.3 Delayed/Defaulting Securities

Learning Objective

3.8.1 Know the definition of an issuer default on the servicing of interest and principal payments on bonds

3.8.2 Know the difference between sovereign debt default and corporate debt default

3.8.3 Understand the reasons why an issuer may delay interest payments on bonds

3.3.1 Default

Default occurs when a debtor has not met their legal obligations according to the debt contract, eg, they have not made a scheduled coupon or redemption payment, or have violated a loan covenant (condition) of the debt contract. Default may occur if the debtor is either unwilling or unable to pay their debt.

Default can be of two types: debt service default and technical default.

- **Debt service default** occurs when the borrower has not made a scheduled payment of interest or principal.
- **Technical default** occurs when an affirmative or a negative covenant is violated.
    - **Affirmative covenants** are clauses in debt contracts that require firms to maintain certain levels of capital or financial ratios. The most commonly violated restrictions in affirmative covenants are tangible net worth, working capital/short-term liquidity, and debt service coverage.
    - **Negative covenants** are clauses in debt contracts that limit or prohibit corporate actions (eg, sale of assets, payment of dividends) that could impair the position of creditors.

3.3.2 Sovereign Default

Sovereign (government) borrowers are not subject to bankruptcy courts in their own jurisdiction, and thus may be able to default without legal consequences. The most recent example of sovereign default was Greece in March 2012. The Greek government negotiated the biggest sovereign debt restructuring in history with its creditor bondholders, which allowed Greece to wipe some €100 billion from its debts of around €350 billion. This type of negotiated default is known as orderly default.

Holders of €152 billion of the €177 billion of sovereign bonds issued under Greek law signed up to the swap. The rest – those who did not respond to the bond-exchange offer, or the holders of around €9 billion of bonds who opposed it – were forced to accept the deal. The Greek government then invoked a recently enacted law that bound all private bondholders to the bond-swap if more than two thirds of them consented to it. Holders of around €20 billion of the €29 billion of Greek bonds included under foreign law also agreed to the swap.

The practical consequences for asset servicing institutions of this orderly default were that current bonds were redeemed early, and exchanged for new securities with lower face values and/or interest rates. This had the effect of creating large numbers of corporate action transactions.

3.3.3 Corporate Default

Corporate defaults can give the bondholder the right to demand that the company be placed in receivership. It can also lead to the complete liquidation of a company's assets to pay creditors. To do this, the holders declare the bonds due and payable before a court.

Defaults have a major impact on a company's health and its future outlook. Its credit rating would likely be lowered, which would increase its future cost of borrowing. Its share price would also fall, reflecting the loss of confidence as shareholders seek to offset any future losses by selling their positions. Alternatively, it may be possible to negotiate an orderly default with bondholders. The types of processes that can be negotiated are discussed in Section 7 of Chapter 4.

3.3.4 Delayed Interest

As part of an orderly default, interest payments can be delayed. This tactic of delaying interest will result in extended bonds, which are bonds with delayed principal repayments. Collateral normally stays the same. Often, extension terms are stamped on the front of the bonds. Occasionally companies issue extended debt certificates instead of stamping original bonds.

4. Liquidation

4.1 Voluntary and Compulsory Liquidation

Learning Objective

3.9.1 Know the difference between voluntary and compulsory liquidation on equities

Liquidation is the termination of a business. The process can be initiated by a company's:

- shareholders
- directors, or
- creditors.

Voluntary liquidation is when the company initiates the process. Compulsory (or involuntary) liquidation is when the company's creditors initiate the process.

The liquidation value of a company is the estimated net value of its assets, including property, stock, equipment and contracts, less any obligations that must be satisfied under the terms of the liquidation.

Those with a claim include tax authorities, other creditors and ordinary shareholders (who are bottom of the list, as they share in the risks and rewards of the company).

The priority of each security is best understood by looking at what happens when a company goes into liquidation. Shareholders are last in line behind other creditors, such as tax authorities and suppliers of goods and services who have not been paid. During insolvency proceedings it is the creditors who get priority on the company's assets to settle their outstanding debt, followed by (for US stocks) **debenture** holders, who hold stock which is backed purely by the integrity of the company, followed by bondholders, then by the preference shareholders, and finally the ordinary shareholders.

This hierarchy is formed according to the 'principle of absolute priority'.

Preference Shares/Preferred Stock

Unlike ordinary shares (common stock in the US), holders of preference shares (preferred stock) have some rights and are higher up the pecking order when the assets are liquidated.

Ordinary Shares/Common Stock and Deferred Shares

The lowest level of stock in a corporation is known as ordinary shares in the UK, and common stock in the US. The rights relating to these securities depend, in part, on the company's articles of association and the by-laws of the corporation. In general, when a company goes into liquidation, owners of these securities are the last in line to receive a distribution of the corporation's assets when they are liquidated. Some corporations may, however, have classes of stock such as deferred shares which rank lower than common stocks.

4.2 Contrasting Treatments in the US and the UK

Learning Objective

3.9.2 Understand the stages of liquidation in the following markets: UK; US

4.2.1 US

In the US, businesses are liquidated under the provisions of Chapter 7 of the Federal Bankruptcy Code.

When a business is unable to service its debt or pay its creditors, it may file (or be forced by its creditors to file) for bankruptcy in a federal court under Chapter 7. A Chapter 7 filing means that the business ceases operations unless continued by the Chapter 7 trustee. The trustee generally sells all the assets and distributes the proceeds to the creditors.

Fully secured creditors, such as collateralised bondholders or mortgage lenders, have a legally enforceable right to the collateral securing their loans or to the equivalent value, a right which cannot be defeated by bankruptcy. A creditor is fully secured if the value of the collateral for its loan to the debtor equals or exceeds the amount of the debt. For this reason, however, fully secured creditors are not entitled to participate in any distribution of liquidated assets that the bankruptcy trustee might make. If there are any assets remaining after the secured creditors have been paid, there may be a distribution to common stockholders.

Chapter 11 of the Federal Bankruptcy Code provides an alternative to the final closure of the business that is the result of Chapter 7. Chapter 11 usually results in reorganisation of the debtor's assets and debts, but can also be used as a mechanism for liquidation. Debtors may 'emerge' from a Chapter 11 bankruptcy within a few months or within several years, depending on the size and complexity of the bankruptcy. The Bankruptcy Code accomplishes this objective through the use of a bankruptcy plan. With some exceptions, the plan may be proposed by any party in interest. Interested creditors then vote for a plan. Upon its confirmation, the plan becomes binding and identifies the treatment of debts and operations of the business for the duration of the plan.

Debtors in Chapter 11 have the exclusive right to propose a plan of reorganisation for a period of time (in most cases 120 days). After that time has elapsed, creditors may also propose plans. Plans must satisfy a number of criteria in order to be 'confirmed' by the bankruptcy court. Among other things, creditors must vote to approve the plan of reorganisation. If a plan cannot be confirmed, the court may either convert the case to a liquidation under Chapter 7, or, if in the best interests of the creditors and the estate, the case may be dismissed, resulting in a return to the status quo before bankruptcy. If the case is dismissed, creditors will look to non-bankruptcy law in order to satisfy their claims.

4.2.2 UK

UK law also provides two alternative forms of dealing with insolvent companies. UK law is based on the Insolvency Act 1986, as amended by the Enterprise Act 2002. The UK equivalent of Chapter 7 is known as 'liquidation'. A company that simply wishes to cease trading will enter the process known as voluntary liquidation; a company that is unable to pay its debts may be the subject of compulsory liquidation. In a compulsory liquidation, a liquidator is appointed.

This individual is the equivalent of the trustee in US law, and the liquidator will attempt to sell the assets of the company and then distribute them in the following order:

1. The liquidator's fees are paid out of the company's remaining assets.
2. The preferential creditors (such as debenture holders) under applicable law are paid.
3. The claims of the holders of a floating charge will be paid; some other claims may also fit into this layer.
4. If there is anything left, the unsecured creditors are paid out in accordance with their claims.
5. In the instances where the unsecured creditors are repaid in full, any surplus assets are distributed to ordinary shareholders in accordance with their entitlements, usually nominal distributions per share held. There may be several distributions over a period of years, as all credit liabilities are satisfied.

UK law also provides an alternative to liquidation, in the form of administration. An **administrator** can be appointed by the holder of a floating charge, or by the company or by its directors. Other creditors must petition the court to appoint an administrator. The administrator must act in the interests of all the creditors and attempt to rescue the company as a going concern. If this proves impossible, they must work to maximise the recovery of the creditors as a whole. Only then may the administrator attempt to realise property in favour of one or more secured creditor. Administration is analogous to going into Chapter 11 in the US.

5. Redenomination

Learning Objective

3.3.5 Understand why a redenomination will occur and how it is achieved

Redenomination is the process whereby a new unit of value replaces the existing unit. This process occurs for currencies, and also affects fixed-interest bonds denominated in that currency.

There are two main reasons why a currency may be redenominated:

- **Inflation** – owing to inflation, the same amount of monetary units have continuously decreasing purchasing power. In other words, prices of the same products or services must be expressed in higher numbers. When prices reach a certain point, the high numbers can impede the well-being of daily transactions because of the risk and inconvenience of carrying stacks of bills, the strain on systems, eg, automatic teller machines (ATMs), and because human psychology does not handle large numbers well. To address this problem, authorities can alleviate it through the process of redenomination. If inflation is the reason for redenomination, this ratio will be some number larger than one, usually a positive integer power of ten like 100, 1,000 or one million. In recent years, examples of currency redenomination have occurred in Turkey and Zimbabwe. During a redenomination process, the new unit is often the same as the old unit, with the addition of the word 'new'. The word 'new' may or may not be dropped a few years after the change. Sometimes the new unit is a completely new name, or a 'recycled' name from previous redenomination or from ancient times.
- **Monetary union** – when countries form a monetary union, as with the euro, redenomination may be required and the conversion ratio is often not a nice even number, or even less than one.

6. Market Report

Learning Objective

3.1.2 Know the frequency of dividends and the payment timetable for UK, US, Japan and Italy

6.1 Japan

Dividends

Dividend entitlements are calculated based on the settled positions held in the Japan Securities Depository Center (JASDEC) and registered holdings for physical shares as of the record date which generally falls on two dates: 30 September and 31 March, respectively. Dividends are usually paid within three months of the record date, interim dividends are paid in December and final dividends are distributed in June.

Most companies pay dividends electronically via the Zengin system on payment date, even though some companies still pay entitlements by cheque mailed to the registered holder. JASDEC is required to notify issuing companies on the record dates of the names of the beneficial shareholders, based on information received from participants. The companies pay income entitlements to the participants' accounts on behalf of the investor for further credit to the clients' accounts. For physical holdings, including securities subject to foreign ownership limit, companies credit dividends directly to the registered holders' accounts.

Interest

Interest on most fixed-income instruments is paid semi-annually, although some corporate issuers may pay on an annual basis. Interest on Japan Government Bonds (JGBs) is paid semi-annually, usually on 20 March and 20 September, or 20 June and 20 December. For every issue, the issuer must appoint a paying bank and the interest proceeds are generally paid by electronic transfer.

Most Japanese bonds, including JGBs, have bullet maturities. Corporate bonds have either bullet maturities or are redeemable in equal instalments through a sinking fund. Redemption proceeds are usually paid by electronic transfer.

Corporate Actions

The most common corporate actions are bonus issues. The ex-date falls two business days before the record date. Entitlements are record-date-driven and calculated based on settled positions held in JASDEC and registered positions for physical shares. For securities held in JASDEC, the participants (including the local custodian) provide details of the **beneficial owners** and the standing proxy (ie, the local custodian) as of record date to JASDEC. JASDEC then forwards this information to the companies, which pay corporate actions entitlements to the participants' accounts held at JASDEC on behalf of the investor for further credit to the clients' accounts. For physical holdings, including securities subject to foreign ownership limit, companies credit corporate action entitlements directly to the registered holders' accounts.

Bonus issues are announced about four weeks before the record date. Entitlements are calculated based on settled positions for securities held in JASDEC and registered positions for physical shares. New shares are issued eight to ten weeks after the record date and usually rank *pari passu* with the existing shares when issued.

6.2   Italy

Dividends

Italian companies pay dividends annually, within one month of their AGM, which is usually held within four months from the closure of their fiscal year (normally 31 December). These four months can be extended to six months if the company statutes foresee this and if the company must issue consolidated group annual statements. The bulk of the dividends are paid between the end of March and the end of July.

All companies are legally obliged to announce dividend distributions. They are announced to the Italian Stock Exchange and the announcement date is usually one month before payment date.

Provisional entitlements are calculated on traded positions as from ex-date up to ex-date+2. Final entitlements are calculated on settled positions at close of ex-date+2.

Record date is the day before payment date. Payment date is three days after the ex-date.

The distribution of dividends involves the issuing company, the paying agent, the CSD Monte Titoli, and local custodians.

Interest

Interest on debt instruments is usually paid twice a year, although there are cases of annual or quarterly payments.

Italian government bonds issued after the introduction of the euro have an interest calculation based on 365 days.

Interest is credited on payment date based on settled holdings on close of business on pay date − 1. Interest is distributed by Monte Titoli in the same way as dividends. Interest is paid directly to the participants' accounts at the central bank. Monte Titoli credits interest to its participants on a gross basis, ie, without any tax deduction. The Italian local custodian banks act as withholding agents.

The coupon date is the interest payment date for both government debt securities and listed corporate bonds. The payment date for unlisted corporate bonds depends on the company.

Corporate Actions

Companies approve corporate actions during their AGM or EGM and must then inform Monte Titoli. In turn, Monte Titoli announces corporate actions to its participants. Information on corporate actions is distributed through the Italian Stock Exchange (for listed companies), issuing companies, Monte Titoli and in the local financial press.

The most common actions are bonus issues. Demergers, subdivisions, rights issues and mergers are also known in the market.

The corporate action peak season is from April to July, but they can be processed throughout the year, depending on the issuing company.

6.3 US

Dividends

Dividends are commonly declared quarterly. They are paid gross by cash, stock or a combination of both. Domestic investors receive the proceeds gross of tax, but foreign investors are paid less 30% withholding tax (WHT). (See Chapter 6 for more information.)

Dividends originate with the directors of the issuing corporation making a declaration as to the type and amount of dividend, the payment date, record date, and ex-dividend date (ex-date). Entitlement is based on the settled position as of record date. Normally, the ex-date is set two business days before the record date. Record date may precede payment date by at least one week or up to a month.

Interest

- **Registered bonds** – interest on bonds is usually paid on a semi-annual basis. However, some bonds may pay monthly, quarterly or annually. The payment frequency is fixed at the time the bond is issued. Holders of fully registered bonds will receive all payments automatically. Entitlement is based on the settled position as of record date.
- **Bearer bonds** – interest coupons are clipped from bearer bonds and presented to the paying agent. On payment date, the paying agent disburses funds to the collection agent who credits the accounts of beneficial owners. Accrued interest on US issues is usually calculated on the Actual/360-day basis. The interest accrues from the previous payment date (inclusive) to the settlement date (exclusive). The dollar amount of the accrual is computed by dividing the number of days accrued by the number of days in the period, multiplied by the annual interest rate.
- **Dividend/interest claims** – if an expected payment is not received, or is thought to be incorrect, a dividend or interest claim can be initiated. A confirmation is obtained from the transfer or paying agent of the record date holdings (number of shares or units) of the registered shareholder or bondholder. Once the record date holdings are verified, the proper claim can be established and payment made.

Corporate Actions

Common forms of mandatory actions in the US market include mergers, liquidations, bankruptcies, subdivisions and stock distributions.

Voluntary corporate actions, such as tender offers, conversions, **class actions** and redemptions, include an effective date, which is when solicitations may legally begin; and an expiration date, which is when solicitations may cease. There is generally no fixed pattern when voluntary corporate actions are announced. Most mandatory corporate actions carry an effective date and are announced within approximately 48 hours of the effective date.

End of Chapter Questions

Think of an answer for each question and refer to the appropriate section for confirmation.

1. What is the main reason why mandatory events are called as such?
   Answer reference: Section 1

2. What is a scrip dividend?
   Answer reference: Section 2.1.1

3. What are the two other terms that are synonymous with bonus issue?
   Answer reference: Section 2.2

4. Why might a firm initiate a bonus issue?
   Answer reference: Section 2.2

5. How does the total value of all shares change as a result of a subdivision and what is its effect on the share price?
   Answer reference: Section 2.3.1

6. What are the characteristics of a merger?
   Answer reference: Section 2.4

7. What is a capital repayment, and why might a company decide this course of action?
   Answer reference: Section 2.6

8. What is the formula for Actual/365-day convention?
   Answer reference: Section 3.1.1

9. What is accrued interest and what is its effect on the value of a bond?
   Answer reference: Section 3.1.2

10. What are the advantages of zero coupon bonds?
    Answer reference: Section 3.1.3

11. What is the term describing the removal from a bond and separate sale of coupons?
    Answer reference: Section 3.1.4

12. What is the difference between a bullet redemption and a redemption with call optionality?
    Answer reference: Sections 3.2 and 3.2.1

13. Who can initiate the process of liquidating a company?
    Answer reference: Section 4

14. What are the two main triggers for a redenomination?
    Answer reference: Section 5

Chapter Four
Voluntary Events

1.	**Overview of Voluntary Events**	89
2.	**Rights Issues**	89
3.	**Conversions**	98
4.	**Warrants**	101
5.	**Takeovers and Exchanges**	103
6.	**Tenders**	106
7.	**Debt Exchange Offers**	108
8.	**Class Actions**	109
9.	**Market Report**	110

This syllabus area will provide approximately 16 of the 50 examination questions

1. Overview of Voluntary Events

Following on from the description of the life cycle of a mandatory asset servicing event, this chapter provides a detailed description of voluntary events.

From the asset servicing analyst's point of view, voluntary events carry a higher degree of risk than mandatory events as, if deadlines are missed or if the event has not been fully understood or researched, there is frequently a financial penalty and loss of reputation for the custodian or other entity on behalf of its clients. As voluntary events have deadlines, it is vital to track the various stages of the event.

As was stated in Chapter 2, with a voluntary event there is no obligation on the investor to take up any offer made to them. Some of these events, such as a rights issue, have a limited period of validity and it is up to the investor to inform the company if they wish to take up the offer. Other events, such as conversions, may be built into the characteristics of the instrument, an example being a convertible bond that can be converted at any point during the lifetime of the bond, with a decision only being required on the final conversion date.

The events that this chapter will cover are:

- rights issues
- conversions
- warrants
- takeovers
- exchanges
- tenders
- debt exchange offers
- class actions.

2. Rights Issues

Although a rights issue is categorised as a voluntary event, from a processing point of view it is perhaps more accurately described as a multi-faceted event and is, therefore, a mandatory event with options. This is because different stages of the rights issue have different categories, both voluntary and mandatory. A rights issue only becomes a voluntary event when the company deadline to subscribe is reached. If at that point the shareholder declines to make an election then their holding remains unchanged, although the net asset value (NAV) of their holding would will be reduced if any other shareholders do subscribe, as there would then be more shares issued.

2.1 Reasons for Rights Issues

Learning Objective

4.1.2 Understand the reasons for rights issues and the options available to the shareholder

A company often wants or needs to raise cash; this can be for a number of reasons ranging from investing in a new project to either funding or setting up a war chest to fight off a takeover.

Generally, a company will have a number of options available to it when it is raising finance. It can issue **bonds**, take out a loan from a bank, or issue shares. For industries such as manufacturing, raising capital in the form of fixed-interest bonds may be the best option, as the cash flows can be predicted from day one, and can be matched with the income from whatever project the bonds have gone to finance. Conversely, in a service industry that may have a lower capital requirement, it may make more sense for the company to raise the finance through short-term variable rate loans and overdrafts, rather than tie in to longer commitments.

If a company is having difficulty raising finance via the bond market or the overdraft market, it may decide its only option is to raise the finance from its shareholders. When this happens, the rights issue may be viewed by the market as a sign of a weak company. Conversely, if a company is stocking a war chest so that it can take over a competing company, a rights issue may be seen as a positive move and will be well received.

2.2 Shareholders' Options

In such circumstances, it is common for a company to approach its existing shareholders with a cash call – they have already bought some shares in the company, so would they like to buy some more?

UK company law gives a series of protections to existing shareholders. As already stated, they have pre-emptive rights – the right to buy shares so that their proportionate holding is not diluted. A rights issue can be defined as an offer of new shares to existing shareholders, pro rata to their initial holdings. It is because it is an offer and the shareholders have a choice that this aspect of a right issues is an example of a 'mandatory with options' type of corporate action.

As an example of a rights issue, the company might offer shareholders the right that, for every four shares owned, they can buy one more at a specified price that is at a discount to the current market price. Each shareholder is given choices as to how to proceed following a rights issue. They could:

- Take up the rights, by paying the discounted price and increasing their holding to five shares.
- Sell the rights on to another investor. The rights entitlement is transferable (often described as 'renounceable') and will have a value because it enables the purchase of a share at the discounted price.
- Do nothing. If the investor chooses this option, the company's advisers will usually sell the rights at the best available price and pass on the proceeds (after charges) to the shareholder. These proceeds are known as 'lapsed rights proceeds'.
- Alternatively, the investor could sell enough of the rights to raise cash and use this to take up the rest (see Section 2.4.2).

Underwriters of a share issue agree, for a fee, to buy any portion of the issue not taken up in the market at the issue price. The underwriters then sell the shares they have bought when market conditions seem opportune to them, and may make a gain or a loss on this sale. The underwriters agree to buy the shares if no one else will, and the company's investment bank will probably underwrite some of the issue itself.

2.3 The Impact of Rights Issues on Share Prices

Learning Objective

4.1.3 Understand the impact of rights issues on the share price and shareholding

4.1.4 Be able to calculate a theoretical ex-rights price and a nil-paid rights price given a cum-rights price, a nil-paid rights issue ratio, and a subscription price

The company and its investment banking advisers will have to consider the numbers carefully. If the price at which new shares are offered is too high, the cash call might flop. This would be embarrassing – and potentially costly for any institution that has underwritten the issue.

The initial response to the announcement of a planned rights issue will reflect the market's view of the scheme. If it is to finance expansion, and the strategy makes sense to the investors, the share price could well rise. If investors have a very negative view of why a rights issue is being made and what it says for the future of the company, the share price can fall substantially. This was seen with HBOS and RBS, when the price of shares on the open market fell below the discounted rights issue price. The rights issues were flops and the underwriters ended up having to take up all unsubscribed new shares.

Example

ABC plc has 100 million shares in issue, currently trading at £4.00 each.

To raise finance for expansion, it decides to offer its existing shareholders the right to buy one new share for every four previously held. This would be described as a 1 for 4 rights issue.

The price of the rights would be set at a discount to the prevailing market price, at say £2.00.

The share price of the investor's existing shares will also adjust to reflect the additional shares that are being issued. So, if the investor originally had four shares priced at £4.00 each, worth £16.00, they can acquire one new share at £2.00. On taking the rights up, the investor will have five shares worth £18.00 or £3.60 each. The share price will therefore change to reflect the effect of the rights issue once the shares go ex-rights. The adjusted share price of £3.60 is known as the **theoretical ex-rights price** – it is theoretical because the actual price will be determined by demand and supply.

The rights can be sold and the price is known as the premium. In the example above, if the theoretical ex-rights price is £3.60 and a new share can be acquired for £2.00, then the right to do so has a value. That value is the premium and would be £1.60, although again the actual price would depend upon demand and supply.

Example

An investor holds 3,000 shares in a stock that is priced at £2.00 per share. The company subsequently makes a 2-for-3 rights issue at £1.50, such that each ordinary shareholder has a right, but not an obligation, to purchase two new shares at this price for every three existing shares that it holds.

The investor decides to subscribe to the rights issue. Consequently, it purchases a further 2,000 shares through the rights issue at £1.50, to supplement its existing holding of 3,000 shares each worth £2.00.

Hence, the total value of the investor's shares will be:

$$(3{,}000 \times 2.00) + (2{,}000 \times 1.50)$$
$$= 6{,}000 + 3{,}000$$
$$= £9{,}000$$

The investor now holds 5,000 shares in total:

$$\text{Price per share} = \frac{9{,}000}{5{,}000} = £1.80$$

Hence, the price per share after the rights issue would be expected to adjust to £1.80 (the theoretical ex-rights price). Note that this is a theoretical price because stock market conditions and level of investor demand will dictate that the share price will be constantly fluctuating for tradeable securities, so the price may rapidly move away from this predicted level.

To estimate the capital gain that the investor may secure by selling the rights, an approximate value may be calculated as follows:

Nil-paid rights = theoretical ex-rights price – rights issue price

= £1.80 – £1.50

= £0.30

So we would expect the nil-paid rights to be worth £0.30 per share.

2.4 Mechanics of the Issue

Learning Objective

4.1.1 Understand the stages involved in a rights issue

4.1.5 Be able to calculate a split rights entitlement

4.1.6 Understand the principles of oversubscription

4.1.8 Know the difference between renounceable and non-renounceable rights

4.1.9 Know the meaning of open offers in the UK

4.1.10 Understand the meaning of lapsed rights proceeds

The order of events is as follows:

1. The company makes the announcement of the issue via the stock exchange or local regulatory body, depending on the market.
2. Registered market entitlement calculation – in a registered market, the rights are delivered at the ratio and then subscribed on a 1-for-1 basis with your entitlement.
3. Bearer market entitlement calculation – in markets where bearer shares are common (such as some continental European countries), the number of rights received is, generally, on a 1-for-1 basis with your holding. The company will issue rights as a ratio to the current shares held. For example, in a 1:1 rights issue the shareholder will receive a right for each share held; in a 3:1 rights issue the shareholder will receive three rights for each share held.

For both bearer and registered securities, the rights are issued as a **nil-paid security** (each nil-paid security = a right to buy an ordinary share in the issuing company at the offer price) which has its own ISIN; this is different from the ISIN for the ordinary shares of the company. The company registrar will act on the company's behalf and sends out the offer documents. If the shares are dematerialised, the nil-paid rights will be electronically transferred to the shareholder's account. If the shares are physical, the company issues the nil-paid rights in physical format; for custodians this may mean splitting the rights into individual shareholder positions as they will receive one **allotment letter** per market account and may have an omnibus account structure on their books and records.

All shareholders will receive the nil-paid rights. This is the mandatory stage.

Example: Registered Market

You hold 100 shares in a registered security and a 5-for-12 issue is announced.

You will receive 41 rights to 41 additional shares. (Divide 100 by 12, multiply by 5, and discard the fraction.)

You can either use these 41 rights to subscribe to the additional 41 shares or sell/lapse the 41 rights.

Example: Bearer Market

You hold 100 shares and a 5-for-12 issue is announced.

You will receive 100 rights to 40 shares. (Divide 100 by 12, discard the fraction, and multiply by 5.)

You can either use 96 rights (entitlement divided by 5, multiplied by 12) to subscribe to the additional 40 shares (you will automatically receive fractional sale proceeds on the remaining four rights) or sell/lapse the 100 rights.

The agent receives market allotment letters. The agent will need to split these into individual shapes. This may cause a delay in the settlement of rights trades.

---

4. If the shareholder wishes to take up or subscribe to the offer, they will return the nil-paid rights together with the payment for the subscription to the **receiving agent** (see Chapter 7). They are now known as **fully paid rights**, as the shareholder has transferred the full cash amount. This must be done by the deadline stated in the offer document. The last date is known as the **acceptance date**. This is the voluntary stage.
5. For an investor who has acquired fully paid rights in the market, they must register their holding by the renunciation date (ie, the latest date on which the seller can renounce their rights to the new shares); otherwise the issuer will send the new shares to the shareholder who was allocated the nil-paid rights.

It has become a common practice in the UK for all aspects of a rights issue to be processed electronically in CREST. Rights (technically nil-paid shares) are eligible for settlement in CREST. Rights are generally tradeable for a period of two to three weeks starting on the ex-date and ending on the day before the final subscription date (the payment date). Rights that are not exercised as of payment date lapse; a company will sell the lapsed rights on the market, and distribute the proceeds to relevant shareholders as lapsed rights proceeds.

If rights are not CREST-eligible, then they are physical rights, and the rights letter of allotment is issued by the registrar per registered account. This may require the custodian requesting that the letter of allotment be split into the individual clients' shapes, which will allow the client to trade their rights position. Trading of physical rights is enacted in the same way as any other physical trading, but on a T+1 basis.

All rights have a **call date** by which the subscription cost must be paid; if it is not paid, then the rights lapse. For a pending trade in rights, it is market practice that the person actually holding the rights as of the call payment date makes the **call payment** and, thereby, protects the entitlement of the buyer. For an open trade in the nil-paid rights, CREST automatically transforms the transactions from the nil-paid to the fully paid ISIN and increases the consideration to reflect the call payments paid by the seller to protect the buyer.

Should the buyer wish to lapse the rights, it will input an ACON instruction to notify the CREST system to transform the transaction into the lapsed security. (The ISIN changes to an assented – non-settling – ISIN representing the lapsed rights; the quantity stays the same, as does the consideration.)

2.4.1 Renounceable and Non-Renounceable Rights

If the issue is renounceable, the rights can be freely traded and a shareholder can sell their nil-paid rights on to another investor who can then subscribe to the issue in the same way as the shareholder. Conversely, the shareholder can increase their rights holding by purchasing additional rights, and an investor who does not hold the stock can purchase rights in the market. There may be a market in nil-paid rights up until the subscription deadline.

Non-renounceable rights cannot be traded, and the right is not transferable in any way, although the entitlement may be transferred if it is the subject of a valid market claim as described in Chapter 2, Section 5.2.

2.4.2 Splitting Entitlement

Most countries have converted to scripless trading. This means that securities are held electronically or in dematerialised form. In countries that are still holding securities in physical form, allotment letters are issued to eligible holders. Provisional allotment letters provide the confirmation of the allocation of the right to the holder.

On occasion, shareholders may issue partial instructions, using all of the combinations of options. They can sell part, take up part and lapse part of their holding. In these circumstances the allotment letter has to be returned to the registrar for splitting, which requires the registrar to reissue two (or more) allotment letters, one for the number of shares to be sold, one for the number of shares to be taken up and another for those to be lapsed.

In particular, private investors often issue instructions for what is known as 'tail-swallowing'. This is the name that has been given to the process of selling some proportion of the rights in order to take up another proportion, without the investor having to pay any cash. For example, if the new shares cost £1, and the rights are trading at 10p, the sale of ten rights securities enables the investor to buy one new share without any cash outlay.

2.4.3 Oversubscription

In some rights issues, where the terms and conditions of the offer allow, it is possible to subscribe to more newly issued shares than the holder has rights to buy.

An application for oversubscription is usually made at the point of exercising the rights held. Generally there is no ratio, or other restriction, made on the number of additional shares which may be applied for in this manner; although there may be conditions applied on a per event basis.

In case there are more shares being additionally subscribed to (oversubscription) than there are available through the rights issue, a pro rata allotment will be applied. The total number of shares which may be available through the oversubscription mechanism is entirely dependent upon any current shareholders deciding not to accept any of the rights to which they are eligible. These unsubscribed rights become available to the rest of the shareholders at a predetermined ratio (eg, the right to purchase 0.25 shares for every existing share held), based upon the total number of unsubscribed shares and the level of oversubscription applications.

There will be a maximum number of rights or warrants available on the whole and, should there be more subscription demand than supply available, whatever is left over will be allocated on a pro-rata basis to those who pick up their oversubscription privilege. This rate of allocation is known as the scaleback ratio.

There may be various combinations of conditions applied in ultimately determining eligibility and level of allotment to oversubscribed shares, such as reference to the original level of shareholding in determining the ratio. When administering any event where an oversubscription option is available, any administrator should ensure they are fully cognisant of the conditions and requirements.

Example

A shareholder holds a 2% stake in a company.

The company issues 100,000 new shares.

The shareholder will receive an amount of rights that would entitle them to subscribe to 2,000 new shares (2% of 100,000).

The shareholder exercises all their rights and subscribes to 2,000 new shares and gives instruction to oversubscribe to 1,000 new shares.

After the event is finished, the agent establishes that 95% of the shares were subscribed to by normal means of exercising rights (this would leave 5,000 new shares available for oversubscription).

The agent has received instructions to oversubscribe to a total of 10,000 shares.

The scale-back ratio on oversubscription in this case is 50% (5,000/10,000)

The shareholder in this example will receive and pay for 2,000 + 500 (oversubscription after scale-back) = 2,500 new shares.

2.4.4 Open Offer

Open offers are very similar to rights issues. The key difference is that the rights are non-tradeable and non-transferable.

An open offer, which can also be known as either a share offer, a subscription offer or non-renounceable offer, takes place for similar reasons as a rights issue, ie, when a company wishes to raise capital for the purpose of, for example, major investment, debt repayment, takeovers and bids.

The number of shares available is, as with a rights issue, determined by a ratio applied to investors' existing holdings at a specified date, again similar to rights issues – the record date for the registrar to determine allocation and ex-date to determine shareholder eligibility.

In some cases, and as with rights issues, holders may be able to subscribe to additional shares in excess of their guaranteed entitlement; this is also known as oversubscription and, similarly, the allocation may be subject to scaling down under the terms of the offer.

It should be noted that lapsed rights proceeds do not normally apply to an open offer event.

2.4.5 Lapsed Rights Proceeds

Rights issues are usually underwritten by a third party who, in cases where shareholders do not take up their total entitlements of rights, will take up (underwrite) the remaining rights and then sell all the new ordinary shares received.

Any premium (positive difference) over the sale price of the ordinary shares, less commissions/costs, and the take-up price will then be distributed to those shareholders who did not either sell or take up their rights.

If no premium was attained during the sale of new ordinary shares sold by the underwriters, no lapsed rights proceeds will be distributed and nil-paid shares will be removed from clients' accounts with no associated value.

Open offer events do not normally benefit from lapsed rights proceeds, although conditions of an event may facilitate such a feature.

2.4.6 Rights to Ordinary

The mechanical sequence of achieving a listing in ordinary shares from a rights issue is generally as follows:

1. **Nil-paid rights** – the rights in their issued/allocated form, giving the right to ultimately purchase ordinary shares. These nil-paid rights have their own unique **security identification number** and are traded independently of the ordinary line. They have a limited lifespan; the trading period, which will usually be the ex-date (date of issue) until market deadline minus one day (last day to be able to trade and settle within the nil-paid rights life cycle). All subscribed, paid-for, nil-paid rights will be transformed into fully paid rights.
2. **Fully paid rights** – a transitory mechanism between nil-paid and ordinary. These fully paid rights have their own unique security identification number and are traded independently of the ordinary line. Often the transitory period is non-existent (ie, the transfer from nil-paid, to fully paid to ordinary happens in a single sequence at the same time). However, fully paid rights may exist for a period of time if the newly issued shares are restricted in any way, such as not ranking for a dividend due to be declared. When the restricted period has elapsed, the fully paid shares will then transfer to the ordinary share line against which they will rank pari passu.
3. **Ordinary shares** – rank alongside existing ordinary shares, equal in every way; they rank pari passu.

3. Conversions

Learning Objective

4.2.1 Understand the reasons for initiating conversions

4.2.2 Understand the methodology of the following conversions: convertible bonds ⇔ equities; 144a ⇔ Reg S; 144a ⇔ unrestricted (registered) line; preference ⇔ ordinary

4.2.3 Understand the process for converting underlying local shares to ADRs/GDRs or vice versa

Conversions are used in some cases to transform the characteristics of a financial instrument to that of a different instrument entirely. The five conversions that are examined in this section are:

- convertible bonds to shares
- treatment of shares in the US under Rule 144a to/or from under Reg S
- Rule 144a to unrestricted (registered) line
- locally held shares to depositary receipts (DRs), and
- convertible preference shares to ordinary shares.

One important point to note about the conversions described in this chapter is that they do not normally involve the investor paying or receiving cash; one security is simply exchanged for another.

3.1 Convertible Bonds to Shares

When an investor buys a convertible bond it is usually as a long-term investment with an eye to converting it into a share at a later date. The decision is based on the belief that the conversion to the share will produce a higher return than that on the bond. There are many factors that will affect the return on each of them, such as the prediction of what will happen to interest rates and the prospects for growth of the company.

The mechanics of the conversion in the following outline are based on Euroclear Bank:

1. A conversion notice is completed and returned to a conversion agent with details of where to deliver the shares. (The role of a conversion agent is explained in Chapter 7, Section 2.11.)
2. Euroclear Bank is instructed to deliver the bonds to the conversion agent.
3. If the shares are Euroclear Bank-eligible, an instruction to Euroclear to receive the shares may also be sent. This is at the discretion of the shareholder, as they may hold equities directly in the local market. If the shares are not Euroclear Bank-eligible, another custodian will need to be instructed.

In theory, the bonds will be delivered and some time later, usually a few days, the shares will be received. As the decision to convert bonds to shares will be based on their relative prices, there may be a sudden rush to convert large quantities of bonds once conditions are right. For this reason, the conversion agent will often state in the prospectus a period during which they will convert the bonds so they can cope with a sudden volume. This may be several weeks, during which time neither the shares nor the bonds will be available.

3.2 Rule 144a to Regulation S

In general, trading in the US requires instruments to be registered with the Securities and Exchange Commission (SEC) (see Chapter 8, Section 13.3).

- Rule 144a permits **qualified institutional buyers (QIBs)** to trade privately placed securities without the two- to three-year holding requirements (see Chapter 8, Section 7 for more details).
- Regulation S clarifies the conditions under which offers and sales of securities outside the US are exempt from SEC registration requirements.

If a firm wishes to trade Regulation S shares inside the US, or Rule 144a shares outside, then it is possible to convert them from one type to another. This is completed via a conversion agent, usually a US bank. The procedure is as follows:

1. The conversion agent will provide legal documentation that must be completed and returned with duly authorised signatories. The document will state that the shares will only be sold on to other QIBs (if under Rule 144a) or that they will only be traded outside the US (if under Regulation S). This form is then medallion-guaranteed by the custodian or US representative; this means that a stamp is applied authenticating the signatures.
2. Two messages need to be sent to the custodian. One is to deliver the securities **free of payment** to the depository account of the conversion agent, and the other to receive the new securities back into the depository account free of payment.

The Regulation S instruments will be deposited and Rule 144a instruments will be received or vice versa.

3.3 Rule 144a to Unrestricted (Registered) Line

Sometimes a security that was only traded in the US under Rule 144a becomes unrestricted; ie, it can be bought and sold by any investor. This will occur when the issuer has decided to register the security with the SEC. This conversion follows similar procedures to those described in the previous section. A conversion notice is filled in specifying the transfer details, name of agent, etc. This needs to be signed by the converting securities holder. On receipt of the form, the securities are then converted to unrestricted, with all the benefits that this entails.

3.4 Local Shares to DRs

In this case, local shares refer to shares in a market where the investor does not reside and DRs refer to receipts in the investor's country of residence.

By converting the local shares to DRs, the investor gains a number of advantages (detailed in Chapter 1). The main benefits are as follows:

- The investor receives dividends in their native or base currency and does not have to arrange additional foreign exchange (FX) transactions. The FX transactions become the responsibility of the party issuing the DR.
- The purchase and sale of the DRs are under the laws of their country of residence.
- The trading and settlement process of the DRs will be more familiar to the investor and may be more robust than trading in the local market.

The mechanism is as follows (in this example the conversion is from a UK share to an American depositary receipt (ADR):

1. An instruction is sent to a conversion agent who will cancel the local shares and reissue them as DRs. In the case of ADRs this is usually a US bank.
2. Two instruction messages need to be sent to the custodian. One is to deliver the shares free of payment to the UK depository account of the American bank, and the second is to receive the ADRs into the depository account free of payment.
3. The American bank will normally charge a fee for this and **stamp duty reserve tax (SDRT)** will also be payable at the higher rate of 1.5% (only on creation of the ADR) as shares are entering a clearing system.

The shares are moved out of the depository account and are replaced by ADRs. For other markets the procedures will be similar, but the tax situation may be different.

Holders of the ADRs have a different set of entitlements and rights from shareholders:

- Dividends will be converted into dollars and paid to the ADR holder by the conversion agent.
- When there is a bonus issue, the conversion ratio of the ADR is amended. So, if prior to a 1:1 bonus issue an ADR represented ten local shares, after the issue it would represent 20 shares. The ratio is normally changed rather than additional ADRs being issued.
- Typically, ADR holders are not able to participate in rights issues due to legislative restrictions on domicile. If they are not eligible to participate, they will receive a cash payment in respect of the rights that they cannot take up. This cash payment respresents action whereby the depository bank sells the nil-paid rights on the open market and credits the ADR holders with the net proceeds received. Distribution of proceeds is proportionate to the number of rights held for each ADR holder for the average price achieved during the sale process.
- Holders of ADRs do not usually have voting rights.

3.5 Preference Shares to Ordinary Shares

Preference shares normally receive a fixed dividend before ordinary shareholders receive their variable dividend. This may be attractive to an investor in the early life of a company, in that if anyone is paid a dividend they will receive one. As a company becomes more mature, and the dividend stream becomes more secure, they may prefer the higher return of the ordinary shareholder rather than their existing fixed return.

The mechanism will be similar to that for convertible bonds to shares. The only significant difference is that a preference to ordinary share conversion normally has limited opportunities to convert during the course of a year. This is set out in the prospectus or on the certificate, and is not publicised by the company.

If a custodian fails to meet the market cut-off for the conversion instruction, the liability for obtaining the converted stock lies with them. This may prove very costly, as the conversion price is likely to be below the market price for the stock and the client would only be liable for the conversion they would have paid.

4. Warrants

Learning Objective

4.3.1   Understand how to exercise warrants

4.3.2   Be able to calculate the profit or loss as a result of the exercise of a warrant given the premium paid by the investor, the strike price and the underlying share price

4.3.3   Know the meaning of in-the-money, at-the-money and out-of-the-money

4.3.4   Understand the implications for investors if in-the-money warrants are not exercised on expiry

4.3.5   Know the definition of lapsed warrants proceeds

4.3.6   Be able to calculate the profit or loss as a result of the exercise of an uncovered warrant given the premium paid by the investor, the strike price and the underlying share price

A warrant issued by a company provides the holder with the right to acquire shares in that company at a predetermined price and ratio, at or on a future date. See Chapter 1, Section 6 for examples of profit and loss calculation.

Warrants are often issued by companies as an inducement to investors to invest in a new bond issue by the company. The prospect of a large return from holding a warrant obtained without cost can make a marginally attractive bond issue more palatable to the investor.

The warrant holder is not obliged to exercise the warrant and can sell it before the expiry date as they can be traded on the major exchanges.

Warrants can be exercised during the lifetime of the warrant on a basis as stipulated in the original terms of the warrant, usually six-monthly or annually.

Warrants can be issued completely separately by a third party, ie, a broker/dealer or investment bank. If the third party owns the underlying shares, it is known as a covered warrant, and if they do not, then it is known as an uncovered warrant, and carries a much greater risk to the issuer.

Warrants come from the same sources as equities: they are issued as part of an initial public offering (IPO) or a corporate action. Warrants are usually a freely tradeable instrument in their own right and carry their own ISIN. A holding in warrants can be added to beyond the original issue, or warrants can be invested into, as with any issued instrument.

In all cases, to calculate the profit or loss on exercising the warrants, the original price paid has to be taken into account.

The warrants carry a conversion cost known as the strike price. This is a predetermined price at which the warrants can be converted into the underlying stock and is set at their point of issue.

The current underlying stock price has to be included in the calculation along with any upcoming cash dividends. In some cases, although a loss may be made on the conversion, an upcoming corporate action may be attractive enough for the investor to swallow the initial loss.

The calculation can date back years to the original investments, as warrants can have a long timespan.

A = the premium paid to purchase the warrants, plus the strike price to convert, equals the total investment (note, if the warrants were issued as a bonus from a previous corporate action, the premium will be zero).

B = the current share price, plus the possibility of a cash dividend or a corporate action equals the true real-time market value.

Profit or loss = B − A

4.1 The Mechanics of Conversion

The holder of the warrant can exercise it at any point, in accordance with the terms of the warrant, and buy the underlying shares. Whether this is done or not, the timing of the conversion depends on the current price at which the underlying share is trading and what the expectations of the share movements will be up to the expiry date of the warrant.

For example, the warrant holder may believe that a higher profit may be realised by waiting. If the warrant can be exercised and the share bought at less than the current market price, the warrant is said to be in-the-money. Conversely, if exercising a warrant would mean paying more for the share than the current market value then it is said to be out-of-the-money. **At-the-money** is when the market and strike prices match exactly. Note that when calculating whether a warrant is or is not 'in-the-money', the premium is ignored.

Example: Conversion of Warrants

An investor pays a premium of 5p per warrant for 4,000 warrants, with a strike price of 560p.

Their outlay is, therefore, 4,000 x 5p = £200.

Two months later, the shares are trading at 580p and they exercise the warrants. They receive:

(580p − 560p) x 4,000 = 20p x 4,000 = £800

Their profit is therefore £800 − £200 = £600

Alternatively, if after two months the shares are trading at 520p and on that day the warrant is due to expire, the same investor will not exercise the warrant, since they can buy the shares at a lower price in the market than the strike price.

If the warrant is in physical form, then the form on the warrant must be completed and sent off with payment to the registrar or firm's agent, who will then return the shares. In dematerialised markets, the conversion is completed electronically.

If a warrant is auto-expiring and it reaches the expiry date, the investor will be automatically paid if the warrant is in-the-money. This payment is the lapsed warrant proceeds and is referred to as lazy money, reflecting the lack of effort on the investor's part.

If a warrant is not auto-expiring and the investor fails to instruct for the conversion of warrants by the due date, the warrants will expire and any in-the-money position will be lost.

5. Takeovers and Exchanges

Learning Objective

4.4.1 Know the definition of a takeover

4.4.2 Understand the impact of a takeover on share value and shareholding

A takeover is similar to a merger: it is simply the acquisition of one company by another. The motivation for a takeover is usually to improve the performance and profitability of the target company by, *inter alia*:

- gaining market share
- reducing competition
- realising efficiency gains by merging the two organisations
- acquiring teams of talented staff
- believing that it they can run the target company more efficiently, and
- selling off the assets of the target company in order to make a profit (this is known as **asset stripping**).

A takeover is a voluntary event in which a bidding company attempts to acquire a controlling interest in another company. It can be a hostile takeover, in which the board of the target company may attempt to dissuade the shareholders from accepting the bidding company's offer. The board will issue a **defence** document stating why it does not agree. Alternatively, if the board of the target company is favourable to the approach, then it will endorse the offer to its shareholders. This is known as a recommended takeover. Some recent examples of hostile takeovers in the UK include the acquisition of Cadbury plc by Kraft Foods Inc in 2010 (which was successful) and the attempt by Northstream plc to acquire Forth Posts in the same year, which was successfully defended by the target company. In the US, target companies often use **poison pill rights** issues to defend themselves against unwanted bidders, and this topic is discussed in Section 9.3.

The bidding company will offer the following in exchange for shares in the target company:

- shares, or other securities such as debt instruments, issued by the bidding company, or a mixture of shares and debt
- cash, or
- a combination of cash and securities.

Ultimately, the bidding company will always have a basic offer upon which any options to the bid itself will be built. If the bidding company is offering a choice of cash or new securities, it may be possible (if the offer terms allow) for the investor to elect to take an increased amount of cash for, say, 50% of their existing shareholding, and new securities for the remaining 50%, when the basic offer is, for example, at 25% cash and 75% shares. Such an election would be known as a mix and match decision with any election, for enhanced receipt of any element, offset by the actions of other shareholders. Such elections are subject to scale-back. For example, if all shareholders elect for the maximum cash option of a mix and match, there will be no offset for the cash distribution, as no holders had elected for enhanced stock. If one holder elected maximum stock, they would receive their desired election with their cash element being distributed pro rata on a shareholding basis to the maximum cash electors.

An exchange offer is a specific case when no cash changes hands; it is purely an exchange of shares.

In a takeover situation, shareholders would expect to be offered a premium to the share price as an incentive to give up their shares. When a takeover is rumoured or announced, the share price usually rises to a value close to the expected takeover price, and so the market capitalisation converges with the takeover value.

5.1 The Mechanics of Takeovers

Learning Objective

4.4.3 Know the process involved for 'acceptance' and 'no action' in the UK market

4.4.4 Know what is meant by a Section 979 notice in relation to a UK takeover

4.4.5 Know that buyer protection and bargain transformation will apply in respect of open transactions in a security subject to a takeover in the UK

4.4.6 Know the key dates in the takeover timetable in the UK: offer details to target; posting of first defence; earliest closing date; last date for target company announcement; last date for predator to revise offer; final closing date for offer

4.4.7 Understand what a dissenting shareholder is

In the UK, the terms of the offer, together with acceptance forms, are distributed to the shareholders of the target company, who have between 21 and 60 days to respond. Some other important dates in the takeover process include:

- posting of first defence – day 14
- offer details to target – day 28 (28 days to issue formal offer document from announcement of firm bid)
- last date for target company announcement – day 39
- last date for predator to revise offer – day 46.

Certificated shareholders who wish to take up the offer send the form of acceptance, together with their share certificates, to the offeror's receiving agent by the deadline.

In the event of an open market claim or failed delivery, the buyer will have to protect their entitlement with the counterparty. This involves the buyer instructing the counterparty as to which option they wish to take. The counterparty then acts on the instruction and, on receipt of the consideration, passes this on to the buyer. Such protection will normally only occur if an option is to be withdrawn at a certain point or at the final stages.

For dematerialised shareholders in the UK who are CREST members, the shares can be transferred to an escrow account via a CREST Transfer To Escrow (TTE) message which effectively passes control of the shares over to the offeror. There will be a different escrow account for each option that the bidding company has offered. This type of automation has largely done away with paper acceptance forms within the UK and other dematerialised markets.

If, when the offer closes, the bidding company has achieved the required percentage of the target company's shares as specified in the offer document (usually 80%), the offer becomes unconditional. The agent acting for the offeror then moves the shares out of the escrow account and into the offeror's account.

The shareholders can withdraw acceptance of the offer by transferring the stock back out of the escrow account, normally after day 42 of the offer if it is not unconditional.

During the course of a takeover offer, securities which are tendered under the terms of the offer are termed assented securities. Such securities are transferred to an escrow account in CREST, and they remain at escrow until the offer is declared wholly unconditional, at which point CREST will release either the cash or securities proceeds resulting from the takeover or, if the conditions of the takeover have not been met and the offer lapses, the original securities are returned from escrow.

The London Stock Exchange (LSE) allows trading in assented securities during the escrow period and assigns a temporary security code to such securities. Each option of the offer has its own assented security, an example being an offer with a cash and a stock option, where the assented assets will be assented for cash and assented for stock so that it is clear to the buyer what they are purchasing. This also facilitates the systemic payment of cash and/or allocation of stock as a result of the transformation process.

Once the offer has been declared wholly unconditional, possibly at 80% acceptance, the shareholders who elected to take up the offer will receive their cash or shares within six days. If the offeror acquires 90% +1 share of the target company's shares, under a 979 notice, it can undertake a compulsory purchase of the remainder of the shares. By issuing a 979 notice, any shareholders who still do not accept the offer become **dissenting shareholders**. A 979 notice is usually valid for a period of six weeks from issue, after which all shares that have not been accepted to the offer will be compulsorily acquired under the basic terms of the offer. Dissenting shareholders remain on their own dissenting shareholders' register. If cash formed the terms of the takeover event, such cash entitlements are placed in a trust account until acceptance. Stock is similarly placed and is entitled to any dividend or other benefits income until eventual acceptance.

Following the takeover, the target company may remain as a separate legal entity, operating as a subsidiary but owned by the bidding company. Alternatively, the bidding company may enrol the company into its own legal entity.

In the situation of a transaction which is open (has not settled) at the effective date of the offer, the deal would be transformed into an entitlement and a claim would be made. A very similar process for tender offers takes place, the exception on tender offers being that once tendered the shares are transferred to escrow and cannot be traded.

Taking 'no action' on a takeover will, at the early stage, have the same effect as not accepting any of the offers. This could, in theory, prevent the company from reaching the unconditional stage and prevent the issue going any further. In effect, the investor is abstaining from the issue.

Certain types of investors can only take action in the later stages of the takeover. For example, tracker funds are under obligation to reflect the percentages of the quoted companies that are covered within the remit of the fund. This is usually the main exchange such as the FTSE 100. Once the takeover reaches the wholly unconditional stage, then tracker funds accept the offer.

6. Tenders

Learning Objective

4.5.1 Know the definition of a tender offer

4.5.2 Know the difference between a tender offer and a Dutch auction

4.5.3 Understand the meaning of an odd lot offer/mini tender offer

4.5.4 Know the process involved for 'acceptance' and 'no action'

4.5.5 Understand the concept of oversubscription

4.5.6 Understand the concept of scale-back

A tender is an offer by the issuing company, or by another company, to buy a set amount of its issued share capital or its outstanding debt over a given period of time. Shareholders are asked to tender and surrender their holdings for a stated value, usually at a premium to the current market price. This is usually subject to the tendering of a minimum and maximum number of shares.

A tender offer is said to be oversubscribed if, for example, the issuer has announced that it will buy back 10 million shares and shareholders submit bids for 20 million shares. In such a case the issuer has to apportion the shares that it intends to repurchase between the investors who have tendered.

The offer may be based on purchasing all the shares at a single price, in which case, if the offer were oversubscribed, each investor would be able to sell 50% of their holding back to the company. Alternatively the tender offer might take the form of a Dutch auction.

A Dutch auction has similarities to a tender acceptance in that the company offers to purchase its ordinary shares at an amount between two prices. The company details the price range at notification and the increment of acceptance, eg, you can tender between €120 and €150 and can accept in lots of €5 (€120, €125, €130, etc, up to €150). An option of strike price is normally offered whereby a shareholder can accept the final price determined by the company whatever it may be between the price range – in this example, somewhere between €120 and €150. In the event of a Dutch auction being oversubscribed, the company will fill its required number of shares, starting with the lowest prices accepted and working up, including the strike price elections, until it has the required amount.

An odd lot is a quantity of shares which is less than the normal trading unit, not an exact multiple of a **board lot**. These will often be traded at a disadvantageous price to a board lot. Certain companies offer shareholders the opportunity to sell their shares back to the company or in the market at a specified price, free of commission and dealing costs. These offers are usually only available to holders of a low number of shares. Any purchase or sale of less than 100 shares is considered an odd lot. By doing this, the company reduces the cost when dividends are paid, as most small shareholders are private individuals who receive their dividends by cheque.

The final outcome of some of the events described above can be dependent on the number of holders participating and the number of shares that they offer. It may be the case that a company determines the ratio or ratios at which security or cash benefits will be paid only after all elections have been received (Dutch auctions). In some cases the final ratio or ratios will be less than the estimated ratios given when the corporate action event was announced; in other cases, the ratio actually paid out may be dependent on the size of a shareholding, with large holdings typically receiving a lower ratio than small holdings.

If a tender deadline is missed by a custodian, the client may be left with stock that they no longer want. In the case of a tracker fund, they may then have a disproportionate holding. In these circumstances, if the liability for the missed deadline lies with the custodian then it would be obliged to purchase the shares from the client at the price the client paid, and then dispose of them as soon as possible, thus exposing itself to the risk that the market price may have fallen in the meantime. The offer may be subject to proration (sometimes known as scale-back), where there may have been a surplus of shares tendered.

6.1 Open Market Share Buybacks

Learning Objective

4.5.7 Understand the reason for initiating an open market share buyback

An open market share buyback is an alternative to a tender offer. It is the most common share repurchase method in the US, representing almost 95% of all repurchases.

A firm announces that it will repurchase some shares in the open market from time to time, as market conditions dictate, and maintains the option of deciding whether, when, and how much to repurchase. Unlike tender offers, which have a fixed timetable, open market repurchases can span months or even years.

Before the company can take this action, it may have to seek shareholder approval in principle at an annual general meeting (AGM) or extraordinary general meeting (EGM), but once it has this approval it has a great deal of flexibility. However, as part of the 'approval in principle' process there may be daily buyback limits that restrict the amount of stock that can be bought over a particular time interval, to prevent price volatility. The price at which the shares are repurchased will be the market price on the day of the transaction.

From the point of view of the investor, an open market transaction is just the same as any other sale transaction; it is not processed as a corporate action as such.

From the issuer's point of view, the benefits of the open market method as compared to the tender and Dutch auction method transaction are as follows:

1. Open market programmes are very easy to set up. The issuer can just effect trades in the market as and when it sees fit.
2. Consequently, there is no need to set up a special programme with, for example, deadlines for investor responses.

7. Debt Exchange Offers

Learning Objective

4.6.1 Understand the meaning of a debt exchange offer

4.6.2 Understand the stages of a debt exchange

4.6.3 Know the process involved for 'acceptance' and 'no action'

4.6.4 Understand the concept of scale-back

Debt exchange offers occur when issuers ask bondholders to turn their notes in for new debt at a discount to the face value, usually as part of an orderly default process (see Chapter 3, Section 3.3). This type of action is usually taken because the issuer is having problems meeting its debt repayment and/or interest payment obligations.

Exchange offers reduce the company's debt, and often extend the maturities, but frequently at the expense of debtholders. Such offers may require the issuer to send out a consent solicitation or hold a bondholders meeting. These topics are discussed in Chapter 5, Section 6.

7.1 Competitive Bids

This is a process in which bondholders may submit competitive bids for debt exchange programmes to the issuer and the issuer selects the best price from the aggregated pool.

These requests are not guaranteed. Any failed requests may result in bonds continuing to be blocked until the exchange agent reconciles their books and confirms that relevant shapes can be unblocked and made available for trading.

This may not apply if a **lead manager** has taken an instruction directly, as sometimes a separate blocking deadline is set after the results of the exchange have been announced. At this stage the bondholder will know if their competitive bid has been accepted and whether a block is therefore required.

7.2 Non-Competitive Bids

Bondholders accept the basic offer at the rate set by the issuer. Acceptance is usually guaranteed; however, some bids may be subject to proration if the amount tendered exceeds the amount that the

Voluntary Events

issuer wishes to exchange. In such a case, the stock that is not being exchanged is either placed back on to the client's account, or in some cases accepted as the company's default for a cash buyback.

If a market cut-off is not met, the client could just receive the company or government's default and suffer a financial loss.

7.3 The Exchange Offer Process

Typically there are four dates that are important in an exchange offer.

On announcement date, the borrower makes the offer to all the holders of record on a given record date. The announcement spells out the details of the existing securities affected, the new securities that will be created, and any other relevant information such as the existence of consent solicitations or notice of a bondholders meeting. The offer also specifies an expiration date, ie, the latest date on which holders can accept the offer, and an exchange date which is the date when the old securities will be exchanged for the new securities.

7.4 Scale-Back

It is possible for the issuer to make an offer that only applies to a proportion of the outstanding debt, eg, if there is a particular bond issue with a face value of USD 100 million outstanding, the issuer could offer to exchange USD 50 million. In such a case, if USD 75 million were offered by investors then each respondent would only have bids accepted for two thirds of the amount tendered for exchange.

8. Class Actions

Learning Objective

4.7.1 Know the definition of a class action

A class action is a legal device that permits shareholders to group together and seek to bring legal proceedings against a company when the issues in dispute are common to all members of the class and the persons affected are so numerous as to make it impractical to bring them all before the court.

Shareholder class actions involve litigation brought against a firm and/or its directors by a group of shareholders who believe that the firm has violated aspects of the local law and regulations, or has committed malfeasance (defined as an act which the firm has no right to do).

They enable many small shareholders to litigate related claims that would be prohibitively expensive for an individual or a few of them to prosecute alone. They are often brought by shareholders who believe that they have been fraudulently misled about the future prospects and share price of a company.

Although historically these have been restricted to the US, they are becoming more prevalent in other countries, including the UK, Australia and the Netherlands.

9. Market Report

9.1 Japan

The most common voluntary corporate actions are rights issues. The ex-date falls two business days before the record date.

Entitlements are record-date-driven and calculated based on settled positions held in the Japan Securities Depository Center (JASDEC) and registered positions for physical shares.

Companies announce rights issues one to two months before the record date. The subscription period is about ten days and starts four to five weeks after the record date. Rights are not usually tradeable. Payment is usually made on the last day of the subscription period. New shares are available for trading about two months after the subscription date. The new shares are identified with a separate ISIN code and only rank *pari passu* with the existing issue as of record date of the next dividend payment. Both ISIN codes are merged as soon as the shares rank *pari passu*.

9.2 Italy

Learning Objective

4.1.7 Know the difference between the distribution and the exercise ratios of rights in the UK and Italy

Corporate Actions

Companies approve corporate actions during their AGM or EGM and must then inform Monte Titoli (the Italian central securities depository (CSD)). In turn, Monte Titoli announces corporate actions to its participants.

Information on corporate actions is distributed through the Italian Stock Exchange (for listed companies), issuing companies, Monte Titoli and in the local financial press.

The most common voluntary corporate actions are rights issues and tender offers. Exchange offers, warrant exercises and mergers are also known in the market.

The corporate action peak season has traditionally been from April to July, but they can be processed throughout the year, depending on the issuing company.

Rights Issues

Rights entitlements are calculated on ex-date. There are two possible ex-dates each month for rights issues: the first business day following either the first or the third Friday of each calendar month. Ex-date is the first day on which the shares are no longer traded with the rights attached.

Shareholders receive the rights they are entitled to on the *'scorporo'* day (detachment day), three working days after the ex-date. However, shareholders can already sell rights starting from the ex-date, because entitlements are defined on the ex-date.

In Italy, rights will always be distributed at a 1:1 ratio (one right received for every one share held) and then exercised at the specified exercise ratio announced for the rights issue. The UK market works in reverse, and the rights will always be distributed at the specified ratio (for example, five rights received for every eight shares held) and then exercised on a 1:1 ratio (one new share received for every one right exercised).

Ex-date is usually followed by an official trading period for the rights. Rights can be traded up to three working days before the subscription date. Subscription date is at least 15 calendar days after ex-date. The Italian exchange recommends issuing companies make financial instruments deriving from rights offerings available within ten business days starting from the end of the subscription period.

New shares may have regular ranking (*pari passu* with ordinary shares) or non-regular ranking. In the latter case, they will rank *pari passu* with ordinary shares following the payment of the next dividend.

Tender Offers

As per Law 19/92, amended by the Law Decree 58/98, a tender offer is generally irrevocable. Suspensive conditions may occur based on the answer from the public. Once the tender offer has been accepted, the shares, which have been tendered, are blocked and cannot be sold. Offer periods last from 15 to 45 business days. Entitlements for a tender offer may be on **trade date** or on settlement date upon the bidder's choice.

9.3 US

Learning Objective

4.1.11 Understand the meaning of poison pill rights in the US

Common forms of corporate actions in the US market include tender offers, exchanges, maturities, rights and warrants. The most commonly used sources for corporate action information are Depository Trust & Clearing Corporation (DTCC) depository notices, the *Wall Street Journal*, the *New York Times*, the New York Stock Exchange (NYSE) and letters from the offering company or agent.

Voluntary corporate actions, such as tender offers and **voluntary redemptions**, include an effective date which is when solicitations may legally begin, and an expiration date which is when solicitations cease. There is generally no fixed pattern when voluntary corporate actions are announced.

The term poison pill describes a strategy used by corporations in the US to discourage a hostile takeover. By using this technique the target company makes its stock less attractive to the bidder by making the takeover prohibitively expensive.

A poison pill allows existing shareholders, with the exception of the acquiring company, to purchase more shares in the target company at a discount. The target issues a large number of new securities which usually have severe redemption provisions, such as allowing holders (other than the acquirer) to convert the securities into a large number of common shares if a takeover occurs. This immediately dilutes the percentage of the target owned by the acquirer, and makes it more expensive to acquire the required percentage of stock to make the offer unconditional.

Although the US market has rights issues they are processed in two parts: firstly, as a mandatory event – a spin-off when the rights are spun off from the parent holding and available to trade (this is on ex-date); and then as a conversion, when the rights can be converted at cost into the new shares.

End of Chapter Questions

Think of an answer for each question and refer to the appropriate section for confirmation.

1. Give three methods that a firm could use to raise finance.
   Answer reference: Section 2.1

2. In respect of the company making the issue, under what circumstances is a rights issue viewed as:

   A. a positive move?
   B. a negative move?
   Answer reference: Section 2.1

3. What is:

   A. a nil-paid security?
   B. the call date?
   C. the renunciation date?
   D. a renounceable right?
   Answer reference: Sections 2.4 and 2.4.1

4. List five instances where one financial instrument might be converted to another.
   Answer reference: Section 3

5. When can a warrant be exercised?
   Answer reference: Section 4

6. Give three reasons how a company would increase its performance by taking over another company.
   Answer reference: Section 5

7. What is asset-stripping?
   Answer reference: Section 5

8. In a takeover, what percentage of shares are required for:

   A. the offer to go unconditional?
   B. compulsory purchase?
   Answer reference: Section 5.1

9. What is the CREST mechanism for accepting a takeover bid?
   Answer reference: Section 5.1

10. What is the definition of an odd lot?
    Answer reference: Section 6

11. What is a debt exchange offer?
    Answer reference: Section 7

12. How does the poison pill strategy discourage a hostile takeover?
    Answer reference: Section 9.3

Chapter Five
Corporate Governance

1.	Introduction	117
2.	Voting Rights and Obligations	117
3.	Company Meetings	118
4.	Proxy Voting	120
5.	International Markets	124
6.	Debt Securities	125

This syllabus area will provide approximately 4 of the 50 examination questions

1. Introduction

Corporate governance is defined as the set of processes, customs, policies and laws that affect the way a company is directed, administered, managed or controlled. The basic concepts apply to the directors and management of the companies concerned as well as to shareholders and other stakeholders such as debt holders, trade creditors, suppliers, customers and communities affected by the corporation's activities. Internal stakeholders are the board of directors, executives, and other employees.

Corporate governance is a highly topical issue in this century after corporate collapses such as Enron and AIG, and the controversy surrounding the activities of the UK subsidiaries of News Corporation.

In this chapter we are primarily concerned with those corporate governance issues that affect shareholders, such as company meetings and the way that shareholders use their voting power to influence management.

2. Voting Rights and Obligations

It is the responsibility of all shareholders, as part-owners of the publicly traded companies, to take an active interest in the running of the companies and to make their views known to the management of the businesses.

Approximately 70% of all stock in the UK is now held through institutions.

Fund managers and pension funds have taken an increasingly active role; in part, these funds are themselves under greater scrutiny and need to evidence that they have undertaken the correct corporate governance in connection with their investments. Shareholders have also realised that increased participation can influence the way a company is run and that they can steer it in the direction in which the managers see greater profit potential, and make sure that the company does not do anything unethical that could lead to financial difficulty, as happened to Enron, Parmalat, etc.

An obvious way of taking interest is through active voting at company meetings such as the annual general meeting (AGM).

Investors' holdings (and, therefore, their voting rights) are established with reference to a record date, usually two days before the meeting. The settled holdings at close of business on the record date determine the right to attend and vote at the general meeting. This right remains with the seller if shares are traded after the record date and before the meeting.

If securities are held with a depository or custodian they will generally be registered in the name of a nominee fund. In this instance, the beneficial owner holds the voting rights. Because the nominee fund is the holder of record, there may be delays in transmitting and receiving proxy information between depository, custodian and beneficial owner. A beneficial owner may have grounds for litigation against a depository or custodian if the investment or holdings were adversely affected by a decision made at a general meeting and the owner was not given the opportunity to vote due to transmission delays beyond their control.

2.1 Share Ownership

Learning Objective

5.4.1 Understand the purpose of Section 793 of the Companies Act 2006

5.3.1 Know who is entitled to vote for stock lending and repos

Section 793 of the Companies Act 2006 allows a company to investigate who currently owns its shares, or who has recently owned them. A company might use these powers if it were the subject of an actual or probable takeover bid, or if it were concerned about a lack of transparency over who was controlling it.

Companies use this power by sending a written 793 notice to any person or company whom they have reasonable cause to believe has, or had, an interest that is defined as owning, controlling or having certain rights over shares in their relevant share capital at some time during the three years immediately preceding the date of issue of the 793 notice. The Companies Act does not specify a set format for such notices. The Bank for International Settlements (BIS) has listed a standard one which companies adapt for their own purposes.

For stock on loan and repos, the stock borrower is the entity with the voting rights.

A company may appoint an agent (other than its registrar) to act on its behalf in the issuance of 793 notices and collation of subsequent data received. Due to the very sensitive nature of such information, it would be prudent of any recipient to a 793 notice from a third-party agent to verify the request with the company secretary of the issuing company.

3. Company Meetings

Learning Objective

5.1.1 Know the timescales for a company calling a meeting across the selected markets

5.1.2 Know the reasons for convening the annual general meeting and the extraordinary general meeting

5.1.3 Know the rights of shareholders to request an extraordinary general meeting and the timescales

5.1.4 Know the difference between 'abstaining' and 'taking no action'

5.1.5 Know the difference between an ordinary resolution and a special resolution

There are three main types of company meetings at which shareholders can vote in person or by proxy. These are the AGM, the extraordinary general meeting (EGM) and the bondholders meeting. Different markets will have different notification periods for meetings set by law. In the UK, shareholder meetings must be announced at least 21 days before the meeting. The notices are sent by the issuing company or its registrar via postal mail together with a meeting agenda. For international markets, see Section 5.

3.1 Annual General Meeting (AGM)

There is a legal requirement for public companies to hold AGMs in the UK within 15 months of the previous meeting, and to have one meeting in each calendar year. All of the registered shareholders must be informed of AGMs and must receive the agenda of the meeting and the annual report, usually 21 days before the date of the meeting. The notice must state the meeting agenda.

The ordinary business transacted at an AGM will include:

- receipt of the directors' reports
- appointment of an auditor
- approval of the company's accounts
- election/re-election of directors
- remuneration of directors, and
- agreement of dividend payments.

There may also be special business to discuss, such as investor approval to:

- issue new shares
- implement pension provisions
- waive pre-emptive rights (these are rights that allow investors to purchase additional shares of a new issue before they are offered to the general public)
- perform share buybacks, and
- change the company's constitution.

All business, ordinary and special, will form the resolutions of the meeting.

Notification of all meetings is through company websites, newspapers and regulatory news service announcements and by mail to registered shareholders. In the UK, a proportionately higher number of meetings have historically been held in March and April, to coincide with the tax year.

Beneficial owners can vote either by physical attendance, by mailing a **proxy voting** card or by appointing a proxy to attend the meeting (see Section 4). The entitlement date is the date on which a person needs to be entered on the register of the security to be entitled to vote. UK and Irish regulations also allow issuers to specify a time (not more than 48 hours before the meeting). This may cause problems if the nominee company has multiple clients who wish to vote in different ways. See Section 4.2 for a fuller explanation of the issues. The issuer's agent has the right to disregard any changes made to the register after this time.

If the beneficial owner's shares are registered in a nominee name, the vote must be lodged by the nominee company. Should the beneficial owners wish to vote through physical presence at the meeting, they must instruct the nominee company of their wish to attend. The nominee company will then lodge a corporate letter of representation nominating the beneficial owners to vote at the meeting. In some markets, further documentation is required.

By abstaining, the shareholder's vote is included in the count, so they have fulfilled their corporate governance duty but have not declared an intention to vote for or against any item. This should not be confused with taking no action. Here, the right to vote is ignored by the investor and, if no proxy vote is received prior to the meeting, it will be assumed that the investor wishes to take no action and therefore the vote will not be included in the count.

3.2 Extraordinary General Meeting (EGM)

An EGM may be convened by the company's directors if some business of special importance has arisen that requires investors' involvement and agreement. An EGM may also be convened at the request of members holding a certain percentage of voting power; in the UK, this is set at 10%. The request must state the meeting agenda, be signed by those requisitioning and be deposited at the registered office of the company.

Under UK law, the company's directors must issue a notice of intention to convene an EGM within 21 days of receipt of the request from a quorum of shareholders. The meeting itself must occur within 28 days of the notice. The term 'EGM' can also be used for a special general meeting (SGM).

There is no legal obligation for a company to publish the results of AGMs and EGMs, but it is common for most companies to make this information available through Companies House.

4. Proxy Voting

Learning Objective

5.2.1 Understand who is entitled to appoint a proxy and who is eligible to be a proxy for the selected markets

5.2.2 Know the different methods of appointing a proxy in selected markets

As just explained, most shareholders, depending upon the nature and rights of the shares they hold, have the right to attend, speak and vote at company general meetings. They may exercise this right personally, send in a postal vote if they cannot or do not wish to attend the meeting, or appoint a representative, or proxy, to act on their behalf. The proxy is a named individual to whom the voting rights are transferred. By appointing a proxy, the investor is granting power of attorney to the proxy to be an authorised substitute. The main reason for proxy votes is to allow an investor to vote at a company meeting without attending.

Under Section 324 of the Companies Act 1989 (updated 2006), a shareholder has the right to appoint a person to act for them and attend the meeting in person, to vote by way of a 'corporate letter of representation'. This is separate from appointing a custodian bank to vote as a proxy.

Minority investors, or the issuing company itself, can organise proxy groups to solicit other investors to vote on a certain issue in a desired way.

Proxy voting is defined as follows:

> *The exercise of the voting rights of an investor in shares, bonds and similar instruments through a third party, based on a legally valid authorisation and in conformity with the investor's instructions.*

There are few restrictions on who is eligible to cast a proxy vote. An investor basically can appoint any person as its proxy and either authorise the proxy to vote in a particular way or to use their discretion. It is common practice for companies to issue proxy cards together with AGM notices that allow investors to appoint the chairperson of the meeting as their proxy.

Also see Section 5 for Italy, the US and Japan.

4.1 The Role of the Proxy Voting Agent

Learning Objective

5.2.3 Know the role played by the proxy voting agent also in relation to voting service providers (VSPs)

5.3.3 Know the purpose of using a proxy to vote

Globally, more than 85,000 investor meetings are held each year, relating to more than $100 trillion in global assets. In the current environment, there is increasing regulatory pressure to improve investor participation in, and transparency of, the corporate governance process. Proxy voting allows investors, through their asset servicers and agents, to vote in these meetings without attendance in person.

The expansion of international investment is adding a new layer of complexity to the proxy voting function, driving the need for, and volumes of, cross-border proxy participation in shareholders' meetings.

Institutional investors such as pension funds and mutual funds often delegate their investment decisions to fund managers, and it is fund managers that are charged with voting their clients' holdings at company meetings. When they vote, they have to take into account whether the issue on which they are voting is affected by any corporate governance rules imposed on them by law, by regulation or by the explicit or implicit requirements of their client. For example, if the client were an ethical investment fund and the company were a food processor, the client would almost certainly require them to vote against any proposal to acquire a tobacco-grower.

Deciding how to vote can be complex if the legal residence of the client is different from that of the company in which it is invested, and/or if the information the company has provided is in a different language from their own or that of their investor client.

For these reasons, many fund managers use specialist firms to perform some, or all, of the following corporate governance functions:

- Researching into the issues that require a vote, and conformity with objectives set by the fund manager and its clients.
- Translation of relevant documents and presentation of the key points of the issues requiring a vote in a standard form. (Essentially this is the same process as 'data scrubbing', which was described in Chapter 2, Section 2.4.)
- Attendance at the meeting, including tabling questions and casting the vote.
- Specialist firms that provide the full range of services are known as voting service providers (VSPs). A firm or individual who simply votes according to their client's instructions is known as a 'proxy voting agent'.

4.2 The Proxy Instruction Process

Learning Objective

5.3.2 Know the meaning of a corporate letter of representation

A proxy document must be issued to all holders of record by the company at the same time as the notice for a general meeting. This document will detail the voting options (these are for, against and to abstain) and is used as evidence of the investors' preferences. It must be signed by the investor and returned to the company within the specified deadline.

For a named individual to have the legal right to vote on an investor's behalf, the investor must also issue a corporate letter of representation specifying that the individual can attend the meeting and vote on the investor's behalf.

Corporate letters of representation can present problems for asset servicing institutions. Consider the following example:

Example

Bank A is an asset servicing institution whose name is on the register of a company. Bank A has two clients who hold stock in that company and are designated holders in CREST.

One of these holders has requested a corporate letter of representation, as they wish to vote and/or speak at the meeting.

The problem is that the letter of representation entitles the holder to vote all the stock in Bank A's name, which may not accord with the wishes of the other client. There is no systematic solution to this problem; the asset servicing institution will have to negotiate a solution with the client concerned.

The diagram on the next page shows how the voting process works in practice. A proxy agent may be appointed by the issuing company to handle the information flow efficiently. The custodian will send a list of all beneficial owners to the proxy agent, who will then send details of the meeting directly to them rather than via their intermediaries. Announcements will also be made via the market regulatory news services. Clients will send their proxy votes to their asset servicing departments, who will send them on to the company or through a proxy agent if this has been outsourced, via the company registrar.

4.3 The Implications for Asset Servicing

The main issue for asset servicing departments in administering proxy votes on behalf of clients is the time taken to receive the instruction from the client and send it on to the company. This process has been improved by technological advances and outsource companies (see Chapter 8, Section 12) specialising in proxy voting.

Corporate Governance

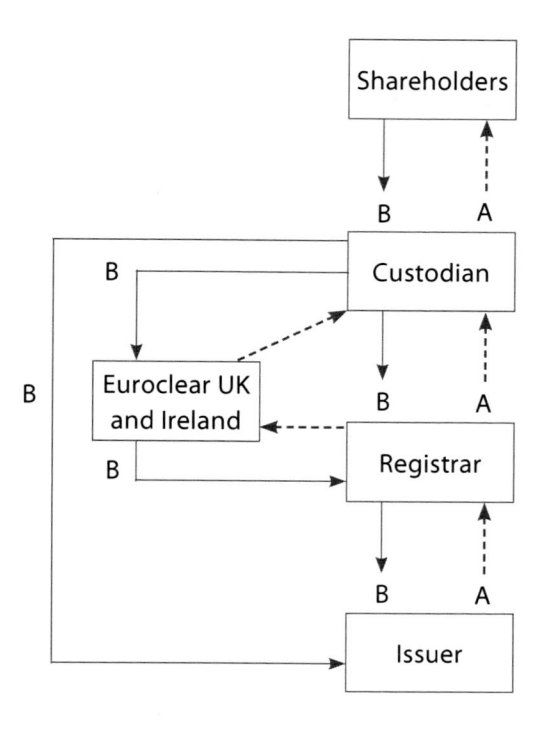

[Diagram showing information flows between Shareholders, Custodian, Euroclear UK and Ireland, Registrar, and Issuer, with arrows labelled A and B]

A = Notification information
B = Instruction information

From the client's perspective, they require certainty that their vote has been registered and that a clear audit trail exists. Most of these issues can be addressed by the introduction of electronic proxy voting. In January 2003, Euroclear UK and Ireland introduced an electronic proxy voting service for domestic securities. This service covers company meeting announcements, the appointment and giving of instructions to a proxy and meeting results.

There is an increasing demand for proxy voting internationally but local regulations do not always cover international investors. This can create issues for asset servicing departments who are contractually obliged to deliver this service.

Many asset servicing departments have outsourced this service. This has the following benefits:

- improved services
- faster turnaround times
- less risk, and
- greater ability to generate revenue.

5. International Markets

Learning Objective

5.1.1 Know the timescales for a company calling a meeting across the selected markets

5.2.2 Know the different methods of appointing a proxy in selected markets

5.1 Italy

Ordinary shareholders' meetings have to be called within four months from the closure of their fiscal year, usually on 31 December. These four months can be extended to six months if the company statutes foresee this and if the company must issue consolidated group annual statements. The peak season is around April.

Italian legislation means that the official announcement for both AGMs and EGMs must be published 15 days before the date of the meeting in the official stock exchange gazette or in the national press. The announcement must specify the time, the place and the date of the meeting along with the agenda.

Italian law stipulates that physical attendance is required at the meeting. Shareholders vote by attending the meeting, either personally or by appointing a representative. Postal votes are not allowed.

Eligible shareholders can participate in the general meeting by presenting a valid admission ticket issued by their local custodian. The beneficial owner entitled to participate and exercise the voting rights can be an individual or a company. If the beneficiary is a company, it must be represented in person.

There are no legal or corporate restrictions on foreign shareholders voting at general meetings.

There is no obligation on Italian companies to publish the results of their general meetings, but the results have to be deposited/registered with the Registro delle Imprese, the Italian register of companies. Results of listed companies' general meetings are published in the official bulletin of the Italian stock exchange during the days following the general meeting.

5.2 US

Listed companies are obliged to hold annual general meetings, which are open to all shareholders. Companies are required to announce the meeting, provide the agenda, distribute annual reports, and make the meeting results available upon request. The majority of annual meetings occur during the end of the first quarter and the beginning of the second quarter.

Foreign shareholders are not restricted from voting, and entitlements are calculated based on record date. Shareholders may attend meetings in person, mail in a proxy card to vote their shares, or appoint a proxy to vote on their behalf. There are no restrictions upon who can act as a proxy.

5.3 Japan

Voting deadlines in Japan are tight, since shareholder meetings are generally only announced two weeks in advance and are virtually all held on the same day. Voting rights can be exercised either by physical presence or by proxy. However, it is not common for local custodians to attend meetings on behalf of shareholders. This is because the fiscal year generally ends on 31 March and most companies hold their annual meetings simultaneously in late June, making it virtually impossible for custodians to attend all of the meetings.

All fully paid ordinary shares carry voting rights. Certain categories of shares, such as odd lot shares and non-voting stock, do not carry voting rights. Shareholders are entitled to vote based on the number of registered positions as of record date.

Most issuers publish the results of the meeting though they are not legally obliged. The meeting results are dispatched by mail a week after the meeting.

6. Debt Securities

Learning Objective

5.1.6   Understand the implications of consent solicitations

5.1.7   Understand the reasons for calling a bondholders meeting

In Section 2.2 of Chapter 2, we learned about the purpose of a prospectus and we also learned about some of the information that might be included in the prospectus of a debt security. However, during the life of the security, events may occur that render the details originally published in that prospectus out of date or impractical to apply. When such an event takes place, the issuer needs to contact its investors and obtain their agreement to any necessary changes. Consent solicitations and bondholders meetings are the usual ways that the issuer seeks to achieve this.

6.1 Consent Solicitations

A consent solicitation is a request by one party, usually but not exclusively the issuer or its agent, to the holders of a particular debt security asking for their consent to a material change in the description of that security that was originally published in its prospectus.

If the majority of stakeholders provide their consent before the consent expiry date, the issuer may then follow through with the proposed amendments. Bondholders who have consented to the amendments may also receive a consent payment.

Example

In July 2009, Quicksilver Resources Inc. announced a consent solicitation seeking to amend the definition of 'Designated Subsidiary' contained in the indenture governing its 1.875% Convertible Subordinated Debentures Due 2024 in order to provide Quicksilver with greater strategic and operational flexibility, including greater flexibility to grow and expand the operations of Quicksilver Gas Services Holdings LLC; Quicksilver Gas Services LLP; its general partner, Quicksilver Gas Services GP LLC; and its subsidiaries.

The terms of the consent solicitation were as follows: Quicksilver offered a consent fee of $5.00 per $1,000 principal amount of the 1.875% Convertible Subordinated Debentures Due 2024 to holders of record at the close of business on 21 July 2009 who validly provided their consent to the proposed amendment by the expiration time of 5:00 pm, New York City time on 31 July 2009.

6.2 Bondholders' Meetings

As the name implies, these are special meetings to which all investors in either a particular bond issue, or all bond issues by a common borrower are invited to express their opinions and then vote on a proposed change to details published in the relevant prospectuses. They are equivalent to the EGMs of equity investors described in Section 3.2 of this chapter.

There are a number of reasons why it might be necessary to convene such a meeting, which is called specifically for, and limited to, the bondholders of a company. The most common reason is that the company is unable to pay interest or repay principal on some or all of its debt. The usual business may include appointing a person or a committee to represent the interests of the bondholders in any discussions with the issuer or other creditors of the issuer.

The actions that the meeting might be asked to approve could involve a possible restructuring of the bonds via a debt exchange offer (see Chapter 4, Section 7) or conversion of debt to equity, or a mixture of both.

End of Chapter Questions

Think of an answer for each question and refer to the appropriate section for confirmation.

1. What business is transacted at an AGM?
   Answer reference: Section 3.1

2. What percentage of voting rights is required to convene an EGM in the UK?
   Answer reference: Section 3.2

3. What is the definition of proxy voting?
   Answer reference: Section 4

4. Why are proxy votes employed?
   Answer reference: Section 4.1

5. What document is required in order to transfer the legal right to vote from an investor to a third party?
   Answer reference: Section 4.2

6. What are the main implications of the proxy voting process for the asset servicing department?
   Answer reference: Section 4.3

7. What are the two ways in which a debt security issuer might seek its bondholders' approval for a change to details in its original prospectus?
   Answer reference: Section 6

Chapter Six
Tax

1. Introduction	131
2. Withholding Tax (WHT), Double Taxation Treaties (DTTs) and WHT Reclamation	131
3. Different Tax Regimes	139
4. European Proposals for a Financial Transaction Tax	143

This syllabus area will provide approximately 2 of the 50 examination questions

1. Introduction

Tax is an important part of asset servicing, with many organisations providing different levels of tax services which vary according to the markets and the types of clients they service.

The term and concept of taxation is familiar to us all on a personal level as we all pay income tax, road licence tax and value-added tax (VAT). This shows the variety of tax at an individual level.

For the purposes of this workbook, however, we are only concerned with certain specific aspects of taxation. This chapter will focus on explaining those aspects, and the terms you are likely to come across, with the focus on the tax treatments of the markets featured in the syllabus.

2. Withholding Tax (WHT), Double Taxation Treaties (DTTs) and WHT Reclamation

Learning Objective

6.1.3 Know the definition of withholding tax

6.1.4 Understand how withholding tax is applied based on the following: residency; product; tax regime (at source or reclaimable); beneficiary; corporate action events that are treated as dividends

6.1.9 Understand the term 'deduction at source' and its implications

2.1 Withholding Tax (WHT)

Withholding tax (WHT) is a tax that is levied by national tax authorities, aimed at income earned by non-residents on their foreign investments. It is deducted at source (see below) by the asset servicing institution in the country concerned.

The actual rate of WHT varies by country; this can be at any rate, but is usually between 0% and 35%. The tax authority levying the tax is that of the issuing company's country.

WHT is dependent upon a variety of circumstances; these include the country of residence of the client, the registration details of the sub-account and the country of issuance of the shares. For example, in Taiwan the stock dividend is made up of both retained and capital shares, and WHT is only payable on the retained portion of the dividend.

A problem occurs for investors if tax is also due on their income in their home country. If it is a UK investor, a dividend payment would also attract UK income tax, leaving the investor with a further reduced return on the original investment. Double taxation treaties (DTTs) exist between countries in order to prevent, or at least alleviate, this double taxation.

WHT is deducted at source; in other words the custody agent in the country that is levying the tax will receive the payments gross. Then it has to deduct WHT from any payments that it is making to overseas investors, and account for the deduction to both the investors and the tax authorities.

2.2 Double Taxation Agreements (DTAs)

Learning Objective

6.1.1 Know the definition of a double taxation treaty

6.1.2 Understand the use of double taxation treaties and why they are created

Double taxation agreements (DTAs), or double taxation treaties (DTTs), are bilateral agreements between two countries. They are negotiated and ratified at ministerial level and exist in order to encourage and maintain an international consensus on cross-border economic activity, and to promote international trade and investment.

The bilateral agreements are designed to:

- protect against the risk of double taxation if the same income is taxable in two countries
- provide certainty of treatment for cross-border trading activity
- prevent tax discrimination against UK business interests abroad
- protect the UK government's taxing rights and protect against attempts to avoid or evade UK tax liability, and
- improve the exchange of information between the taxation authorities of states.

There are more than 1,300 DTTs worldwide and the UK has the largest network of treaties, covering over 100 countries. A list of these countries as at December 2016 is shown below. This list is continually updated; the up-to-date list, which also shows brief details of the scope of each treaty, is maintained by HM Revenue & Customs (HMRC) at www.hmrc.gov.uk/taxtreaties/dtdigest.pdf.

Each agreement is unique, although there is a standard model produced by the Organisation for Economic Co-operation and Development (OECD) that is used as a template for most agreements.

Under the terms of a typical DTA, the rate of tax incurred by a foreign investor will be equal to the standard rate of WHT levied from non-residents, minus the agreed tax credit (see Section 2.3) between the countries.

No reclaim of UK tax credits is possible for non-UK residents as the UK no longer withholds tax on domestic dividends, either notional or actual.

Countries Covered by the UK's Network of DTTs

Albania	Denmark	Ivory Coast	Montserrat	South Africa
Algeria	Egypt	Jamaica	Morocco	Spain
Antigua and Barbuda	Estonia	Japan	Myanmar	Sri Lanka
Argentina	Ethiopia	Jersey	Namibia	St Kitts and Nevis
Armenia	Falkland Islands	Jordan	Netherlands, The	Sudan
Australia	Faroe Islands	Kazakhstan	New Zealand	Swaziland
Austria	Fiji	Kenya	Nigeria	Sweden
Azerbaijan	Finland	Kiribati	Norway	Switzerland
Bahrain	France	Korea	Oman	Taiwan
Bangladesh	Gambia	Kosovo	Pakistan	Tajikistan
Barbados	Georgia	Rep. of Kuwait	Panama	Thailand
Belarus	Germany	Latvia	Papua New Guinea	Trinidad and Tobago
Belgium	Ghana	Lesotho	Philippines	Tunisia
Belize	Greece	Libya	Poland	Turkey
Bolivia	Grenada	Lichtenstein	Portugal	Turkmenistan
Bosnia & Herzegovina	Guernsey	Lithuania	Qatar	Tuvalu
Botswana	Guyana	Luxembourg	Romania	Uganda
British Virgin Islands	Hong Kong	Macedonia (FYR)	Russia	Ukraine
Brunei	Hungary	Malawi	Saudi Arabia	Uruguay
Bulgaria	Iceland	Malaysia	Senegal	USA
Canada	India	Malta	Serbia	Uzbekistan
Chile	Indonesia	Mauritius	Sierra Leone	Venezuela
China	Ireland	Mexico	Singapore	Vietnam
Croatia	Isle of Man	Moldova	Slovak Republic	Zambia
Cyprus	Israel	Mongolia	Slovenia	Zimbabwe
Czech Republic	Italy	Montenegro	Solomon Islands	

2.3 Tax Reclamation

Learning Objective

6.1.8 Know the life cycle of a tax reclaim

6.1.12 Understand the need to provide proof of residency to the fiscal authorities for the purpose of reclaiming tax and obtaining relief at source

2.3.1 The Tax Reclaim Process

The reclaim differs both in the process and the time taken by the local authority to validate the reclaim. As a guide, the main steps in the reclaim process may be as follows:

1. The issuing company instructs its paying agent to pay a dividend.
2. The paying agent pays the WHT due to the local tax authority.
3. The client or its custodian receives tax relief in one of two ways:
   a. either by receiving a tax credit against UK tax, meaning that the investor can use the WHT already paid as a credit against their UK tax liability, or
   b. by a tax reclaim from the overseas tax authority.

The Custodian Tax Reclaim Process

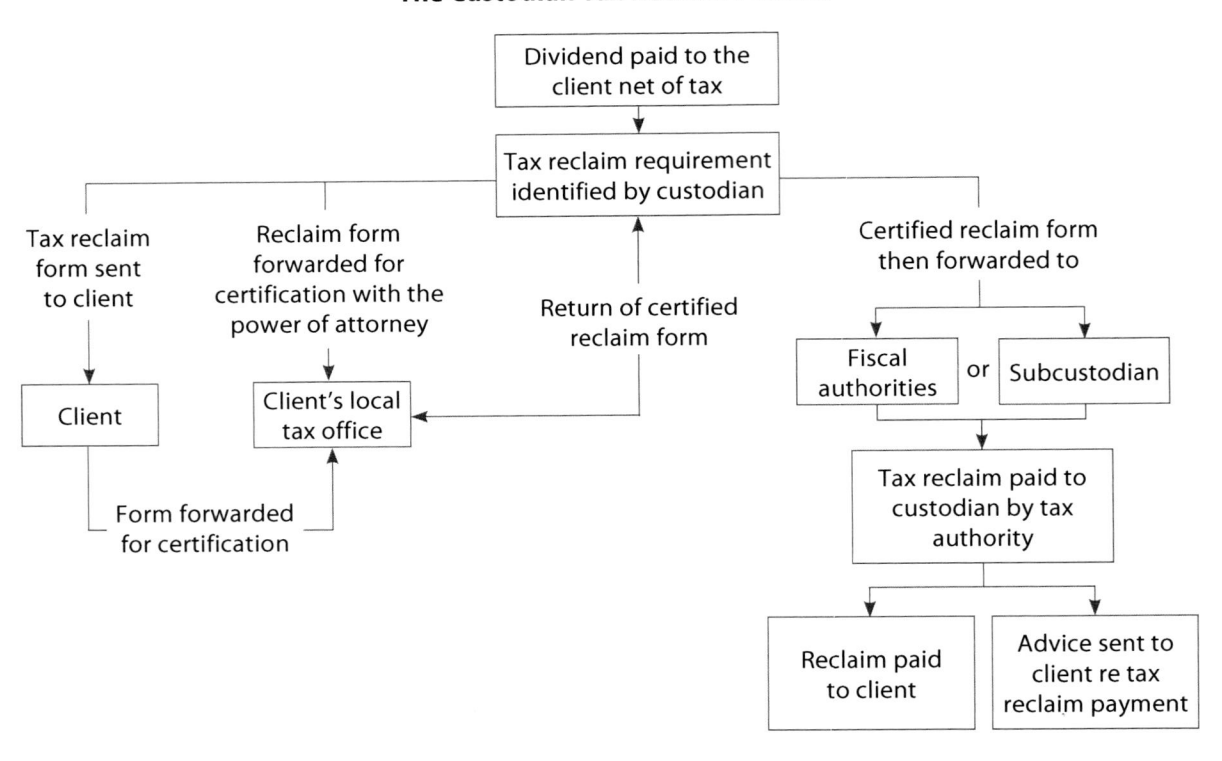

```
                        Dividend paid to the
                         client net of tax
                                │
                                ▼
                        Tax reclaim requirement
                        identified by custodian

   Tax reclaim      Reclaim form                          Certified reclaim form
   form sent        forwarded for                         then forwarded to
   to client        certification with the   Return of certified
                    power of attorney        reclaim form
        │                   │                                    │
        ▼                   ▼                           ┌────────┴────────┐
      Client          Client's local                  Fiscal    or   Subcustodian
                      tax office                    authorities
        │                   ▲                                 │
        │   Form forwarded  │                                 ▼
        └── for certification┘                        Tax reclaim paid to
                                                      custodian by tax
                                                          authority
                                                              │
                                                   ┌──────────┴──────────┐
                                                   ▼                     ▼
                                              Reclaim paid        Advice sent to
                                               to client         client re tax
                                                                reclaim payment
```

To perform the tax reclaim process on behalf of a client, the asset servicing group must be in possession of the relevant tax documents. The following information and documentation is required:

- certificate of residence from the client's local tax office
- power of attorney from its client
- the completion of a tax questionnaire; this provides details such as the client's tax identification number, place of incorporation and registered address
- copies of US Qualified Intermediary (QI) tax documents (if trading US securities); these ensure that the client is operating in accordance with US tax law, and
- market-specific tax documents: in certain markets, the client is required to complete tax documentation in order to receive income payment at source at the treaty-eligible rate.

This information must be requested and received in a timely manner in order to allow completion of the relevant tax forms within the correct time limit. Most markets operate a statute of limitations (the time in which you have to file a tax reclaim for any excess WHT) on filing the reclaims.

The time it takes to obtain a tax reclaim varies quite significantly between jurisdictions, and is also affected by instrument type. The Netherlands usually settles claims in two to three months, while, at the other extreme, some Italian claims take years to settle.

2.4 US Tax Legislation that Affects Asset Servicing Firms Operating Outside the US

Learning Objective

6.1.10 Understand the role of a Qualified Intermediary

6.1.11 Know the implications of the US Foreign Account Tax Compliance Act (FATCA)

Two pieces of US legislation, the Qualified Intermediary (QI) regime of 2001 and the **Foreign Account Tax Compliance Act (FATCA)** of 2010, may have significant operational impact on asset servicing firms which operate outside the US.

The primary difference between the QI regime and FATCA is that QI is focused on obtaining personal tax information of non-US resident holders about US securities, whereas FATCA aims to identify revenue due to the Internal Revenue Service (IRS), the US tax authority, on foreign investments held by US residents.

2.4.1 The QI Regime

The IRS, the US tax authority, established a QI Program in 2001 in an attempt to encourage foreign investment into the US and to simplify procedures for tax collection and tax reporting. Foreign institutions granted QI status have a commitment to report to the IRS a list of their non-US clients with investment interests in US securities. Subsequently, QIs will withhold taxes due on US securities held in these investors' accounts and will advance to the IRS these tax obligations owed.

QIs and Asset Servicing

An asset servicing department is responsible for reclaiming WHT on behalf of its client.

This can be a complex, manual and burdensome process owing to the following issues:

- There is no standard global approach to tax reclamation. Each country sets its own timescales for claims and repayment; for Italy it has been known to take over ten years to obtain a refund, and in some cases settlement of a reclamation has never been achieved.
- Calculation of the amount of tax that can be reclaimed is complex, with different tax rates in different countries and different investment instruments having various levels of tax levied on them.
- As international investment continues to grow, more reclaims are becoming viable. The process of checking and collating the documentation is manually intensive and expensive to administer.

Despite these issues, efficient WHT reclamation is increasingly important because the amount that can be reclaimed represents a significant source of additional revenue for clients.

2.4.2 FATCA

Introduction and Timetable

FATCA was enacted in March 2010 and came into force in January 2013. It is an important development in US efforts to combat tax evasion by US persons holding investments in offshore accounts.

FATCA requires certain US taxpayers holding financial assets outside the US to report certain information about financial accounts held by US taxpayers (as well as foreign entities in which US taxpayers hold a substantial ownership interest) to the IRS.

FATCA also affects some non-US financial institutions, known as foreign financial institutions (FFIs), such as UK securities and investment companies. The original IRS rules stated that FFIs would need to register with the IRS between 1 January and 30 June 2013 and sign an agreement with the IRS by 1 July 2013 to ensure that they avoid a 30% WHT on income generated by US investments after 1 January 2014.

The UK-US Agreement

The UK (along with France, Germany, Italy, Spain and many other countries) took part in joint discussions with the US government to explore an intergovernmental approach to FATCA, supporting the overall aim of combating tax evasion, while reducing risks and burdens on financial institutions. An intergovernmental agreement was signed in September 2012 which provides a mechanism for UK financial institutions to comply with their obligations without breaching the data protection laws. Under this agreement, financial institutions pass information to HMRC who will then automatically exchange this information with the IRS.

Because of the very complex due diligence requirement of FATCA, many financial firms in the UK are not accepting US citizens or residents as clients.

Implementation of the Act

Existing Accounts

FFIs will be required to investigate all existing accounts to determine whether the owner of the account is a US resident, a US citizen, or a US-registered company. Accounts of less than $50,000 for an individual and $250,000 for an entity can be treated as non-US accounts, but all other client information must undergo a search for indications of US status. The aim of the electronic search is to find US data without initially having to personally contact the client. Where the search results indicate that the account owner is of interest to the US authorities, the FFI needs to check whether all the appropriate IRS documents are on file for that customer. An FFI can rely on Know Your Customer (KYC) documents that it has already collected, providing that these contain the required level of detail and are in the format demanded. Client relationships for which there is not yet sufficient documentation available need to be further scrutinised and requests made for documents from the account holders.

There are special due diligence arrangements for accounts of more than $1,000,000 that are more onerous and anticipate that a relationship manager could know the status of their account holders, irrespective of the documentation held. Their knowledge of the account must be taken into consideration as part of the review.

If an FFI does not receive the requested documentation from a customer, then the customer is considered a recalcitrant account holder, which ordinarily would result in the application of a 30% FATCA WHT and reporting to the IRS; however, UK FFIs will report to HMRC. For clients with pre-existing accounts with valid US tax documentation already in place, FATCA documentation was not required until 30 June 2016.

New Accounts

When a new account is opened (1 July 2014 for individuals' accounts and 1 January 2015 for entity accounts, such as companies and charities), FFIs must obtain and examine documentary evidence establishing US or non-US status of individual account holders. For new individual accounts that are identified as held by US persons, the FFI will obtain Form W-9 from the individual holders of the accounts. All the client onboarding information collected in connection with a new individual financial account will be examined to identify the possibility of potential US status.

Accounts need to be scrutinised when the following arises:

- documentation suggesting that account holders are US residents or US citizens
- a US address associated with an account holder of the account (whether a residence address or a correspondence address)
- a US place of birth for an account holder of the account, or
- any other details of potential US status, including a 'care of' address, holding address, or PO box
- a power of attorney or signatory authority granted to a person with a US address
- standing instructions to transfer funds to an account maintained in the US or directions received from a US address, or
- a US telephone number.

Withholding and Reporting

In general, a withholding agent (a US or foreign person that has control, receipt, custody, disposal, or payment of any item of income of a foreign person that is subject to withholding) is required to withhold 30% on a withholdable payment made to an FFI, unless the FFI meets the requirements we have already covered. In addition, an FFI must withhold 30% on any payment it makes to a recalcitrant account holder, as well as any payment it makes to another FFI, unless that FFI meets certain requirements. However, none of these procedures for withholdings will apply to UK FFIs that are subject to the agreement between the US and UK.

Under the terms of the intergovernmental agreement, UK FFIs need to report the following information about their US accounts to HMRC:

- the name, address, and taxpayer identification number (TIN) of each account holder which is a specified US person, and, in the case of any account holder which is a US-owned foreign entity, the name, address, and TIN of each substantial US owner of such entity
- the account number
- the account balance or value at year end.
- gross dividends, interest and other income paid or credited to the account (timing will be determined in the FFI agreement).

Reporting of gross proceeds is included in the 2016 reporting.

An FFI reporting to the HMRC will be required to submit its FATCA reporting prior to 31 May following the reporting year, with HMRC onward reporting to the IRS by September of the same year.

2.4.3 Common Reporting Standard (CRS)

The Common Reporting Standard (CRS), formally referred to as the Standard for Automatic Exchange of Financial Account Information, is an information standard for the Automatic Exchange of Information (AEoI), developed in the context of the OECD. The legal basis for exchange of data is the Convention on Mutual Administrative Assistance in Tax Matters and the idea is based on the US FATCA implementation agreements.

On 6 May 2014, 47 countries tentatively agreed on a CRS: an agreement to share information on residents' assets and incomes automatically in conformation with the Standard. Until now, the parties to most treaties which are in place for sharing information have shared information upon request, which has not proved effective in preventing tax evasion. The new system is supposed to transfer all the relevant information automatically and systematically. This agreement is informally referred to as GATCA (the Global Account Tax Compliance Act), but the CRS is not just an extension of FATCA. The CRS has a much more ambitious scope, and modelling the standard on the FATCA rules has created problems for implementing it in Europe, complains one legal expert. A private sector advocacy group that represents financial services and law firms went even further in predicting a showdown between the two regimes.

CRS Reporting

The European Union adopted the CRS on 1 January 2016 by applying specific amendments on the directive for administrative cooperation in the field of taxation. First reporting will be executed in 2017.

Information to be Exchanged

Each country will annually automatically exchange with the other country the below information in the case of Jurisdiction A with respect to each Jurisdiction B Reportable Account, and in the case of Jurisdiction B with respect to each Jurisdiction A Reportable Account:

- the name, address, TIN and date and place of birth of each reportable person
- the account number
- the name and identifying number of the Reporting Financial Institution
- the account balance or value as of the end of the relevant calendar or, if the account was closed during such year or period, the closure of the account.

Reportable Accounts

OECD does not specify what is reportable – it allows the participating countries to determine what accounts are reportable. 'Reportable Account' means a Jurisdiction A Reportable Account or a Jurisdiction B Reportable Account, as the context requires, providing it has been identified as such pursuant to due diligence procedures, consistent with the Annex, in place in Jurisdiction A or Jurisdiction B. This means that either jurisdiction may negotiate and determine its own Reportable Accounts in its agreement. For example, the US, with its citizenship-based taxation, has established in its FATCA intergovernmental agreements that accounts held by US citizens and US persons for tax purposes in the other country's jurisdiction are required to be reported via FATCA.

3. Different Tax Regimes

Learning Objective

6.1.5 Know the following tax regimes: reclaim procedures; relief at source; combination of reclaim procedures and relief at source; no relief

6.1.6 Understand the advantages and disadvantages of the following tax regimes: reclaim procedures; relief at source

3.1 US

WHT on Dividends and Interest

Dividends – generally, dividend payments to non-resident investors are subject to WHT at 30%.

Interest – US source interest and original issue discount (OID) received by non-residents are subject to 30% WHT.

There are categories of interest received by non-residents which are not subject to US withholding tax. These include interest on bonds issued by a state or political subdivision, such as government or municipal bonds.

Institutions that are tax-exempt in their own countries may be granted tax exemption by the US IRS.

DTTs

The general rule is that the issuer, its paying agent or the US custodian is duty-bound to withhold the tax at the statutory rate for recipients domiciled for tax purposes in non-treaty countries at the appropriate treaty rate for recipients where there is a DTA.

In order for a non-resident investor to receive favourable treatment under a tax treaty, the investor must prove entitlement to treaty benefits. Depending on the client, this generally requires the investor to file IRS Forms W–8 BENE, W–8 BEN, W–8 EXP or W–8 ECI or W–8IMY.

Tax Relief at Source

Tax relief at source may be possible within the US.

Tax Reclaim Procedures

In the event that a foreign investor has suffered an excess of tax, the investor may request a refund of any WHT by filing a US Non-Resident Alien Income Tax Return (form 1040 NR), or an Annual Tax Return of a Foreign Corporation (form 1120 F) with the IRS. The forms must be filed after the year end and before the statute of limitations for filing, which is currently within three years of the tax year.

3.2 Japan

WHT on Dividends and Interest

Dividends – a standard WHT rate of 7% was introduced on 1 April 2003. However, in 2011 the Cabinet Office announced a temporary increase of WHT on interest and dividend income to pay for the reconstruction required as a result of the 2011 earthquake. Under this proposal the rates increased by 2.1% in January 2013, and were then doubled from January 2014. This double rate, together with its temporary increase, will last for 25 years. Therefore, the rate for 2013 was 7.147% and for the years 2014 through 2037 the rate will be 15.315%; in 2038 the rate will fall to 15%.

Interest – it is usual for interest payments to entities residing in countries that did not enter into a tax treaty with Japan to be taxed at a rate of 15.315%. Entities residing in countries that have a tax treaty with Japan are taxed as per the treaty, which is usually at 10% or 15%.

Currently, the following entities may apply for WHT exemption:

1. Non-resident individuals and corporations residing outside Japan.
2. UK occupational pension funds.
3. US/UK tax-exempt pension funds such as US and UK local government pension schemes established for local government employees with a trust structure.
4. US corporate pension funds with a trust structure.
5. Foreign investment trusts, which must be publicly marketed and offered only to investors outside Japan.

In general, exemption can be applied as long as the beneficial owner can be identified and assets are not held in an omnibus account structure.

DTTs

Issuers withhold taxes on dividend or interest income at the statutory rates or at the reduced treaty rates.

Tax Relief at Source

Tax relief at source is available in the Japanese market. With the introduction of the Tax Reform Act on 1 April 2003, the provisions of DTTs to reduce the dividend WHT rate from 20% to 15% are not applicable.

On 30 March 2004, the governments of the US and Japan ratified an income tax treaty which came into force on 1 July 2004. This means that tax relief at source is available for US-resident investors who meet the stipulated conditions by submitting the necessary tax documents. In addition, relief at source is also available to relevant UK, French and Australian pension funds.

For an investor who receives Japanese source interest payments to be taxed at the reduced rates, the recipient must prove that they are entitled to the treaty benefits. The recipient's local custodian must submit an application form for income tax convention on their behalf to the local tax office through the issuing company or registrar.

Tax Reclaim Procedures

Tax reclaims are not usually required, as taxes (except on Treasury bills) are withheld at source. WHT can be refunded by filing the necessary documents through the local agent to the local tax office. Reclaims can take six months to be processed.

Tax regulation which took effect in April 2001 stipulated that all foreign financial intermediaries operating outside Japan must obtain foreign indirect participant (FIP) status and that the last intermediary in the chain immediately preceding the final investor who has a direct contractual relationship with a non-resident investor has to become a qualified foreign intermediary (QFI). The QFI status is required to authorise the foreign financial intermediary to act as a tax representative on behalf of non-resident investors who are holding Japanese Government Bonds (JGBs) in book entry form.

3.3 Italy

Learning Objective

6.1.7 Understand the reclaim procedures with respect to a UK resident having suffered the maximum withholding tax rate on income generated on investments in Italy

3.3.1 WHT on Dividends and Interest on Bonds

Dividends paid to non-resident investors by Italian-listed companies on ordinary and preference shares are subject to a WHT. The tax is withheld by the local custodians, who act as WHT agents (*sostituti d'imposta*).

The rates of WHT which apply to different types of investment after 1 January 2017 are shown in the following table:

Dividends

Dividends received by European Union (EU) parents qualifying for the EU Parent–Subsidiary Directive	Dividends received by Swiss parents qualifying for the EU/Switzerland agreement	Dividends received by EU and European Economic Area (EEA) shareholders qualifying for the Italian domestic reduced rate	Dividends received by others
Nil	Nil	1.2%	26% (see notes)

Note 1: a refund of up to 11/26 of the Italian tax suffered may be available if the recipient is not an Italian resident, to the extent tax is paid in the recipient's country of residence.
Note 2: a reduced rate might be available under an applicable treaty.

Interest

- Interest on government bonds and other bonds issued by other public bodies –12.5% (see notes).
- Interest on qualifying publicly traded bonds or bonds issued by 'large issuers' – 26% (see notes).

Note 1: an exemption might be sought by 'whitelisted' recipients (ie, a recipient that is resident in a country with an adequate exchange of information regime).
Note 2: a reduced rate/exemption might be available under an applicable treaty.

Saving shares (*azione di risparmio*) can only be issued by companies whose ordinary shares are listed on the stock exchange. Holders of saving shares enjoy preferential treatment with respect to profit-sharing. These shares must pay a dividend of at least 5% of their par value.

The tax withheld at source is paid once a month by the Italian custodian to the Italian tax authorities (by the 15th day of the month following the payment date of the dividend).

Tax Relief at Source – Dividends

Non-resident investors may obtain a reduced WHT rate at source under certain eligibility conditions and upon presentation of specific documentation.

- **Eligibility conditions** – in order to be eligible for the reduced tax rate, the investor must be non-resident in Italy and also be of a country which has an adequate exchange of information agreed with Italy. The reduced WHT rate is determined as laid down in the DTT concluded between the investor's country of residence and Italy.
- **Documentation requirements** – the non-resident investor has to submit to the Italian custodian acting as withholding agent a declaration certifying the beneficial ownership of the dividends, along with a certificate of residency issued by the tax authority of the investor's country of residence. These documents must be received and accepted by the investor's local custodians before the first dividend payment date and must be renewed annually.

Tax Reclaim Procedures – Dividends

If a reduced rate is not applied at source at the time the dividend is paid, refund claims have to be initiated. Since 1 January 2001, the deadline to submit tax reclaims to the fiscal authorities was extended to 48 months from the date when the net dividend was credited. The procedure for claiming tax refunds is fairly long. The average time for an investor to recuperate excess tax paid is estimated at ten years, but could be longer.

Tax Relief at Source – Interest on Bonds

Non-residents from countries that have a DTT with Italy, and supranational organisations recognised by Italian law, are not subject to Italian WHT on interest payments on public debt securities.

Eligible investors are considered exempt providing that the appropriate document is acknowledged and considered as valid by the Italian intermediaries.

Italian banks, along with Clearstream and Euroclear Bank acting as intermediaries, are responsible for calculating and collecting the WHT on a trade-by-trade basis. This is done through a single general tax account maintained by each intermediary. Once a month, the net balance of the general tax account is paid on to the Italian fiscal authorities. A single general tax account is used for payment of both WHT on dividends and interest. In addition, once a month, local intermediaries have to report all government bonds movements for non-taxed accounts to the Italian tax authorities.

Tax Reclaim Procedures – Interest on Bonds

Beneficial owners may reclaim excess tax withheld at source through the standard reclaim procedure. The standard procedure is only applicable to Italian government bonds rather than all Italian bonds. From January 2001, the deadline to submit tax reclaims was extended from 18 to 48 months from the date of payment. A refund can take ten years or more.

3.3.2 Italian Tax Reform

The Italian government is progressively reforming its tax system to reduce the tax burden to simplify administration and to harmonise it with the other European tax systems.

3.4 Relief at Source versus Reclaim Procedures

Owing to the specific nature of taxation, and the fact that treatments vary as to structure and location, it is not possible to generalise as to the benefits or disadvantages of relief at source against the standard reclaim procedure. It is, however, fair to say that from an asset servicing point of view relief at source has the following advantages: income is paid gross, therefore there are usually no time delays in receiving tax relief; and it is more efficient than suffering and then reclaiming WHTs.

From a custodian's point of view, the cost of operating a tax reclaim service is usually higher. From an operational risk point of view, if the custodian incurs a problem with the reclaim, they will usually have to advance monies due to the client incurring potential interest losses on the advanced funds until fund settlement of the reclaim is achieved.

Standard reclaims are less efficient, involving more forms and a longer-drawn-out process. They involve lower fees for the client but incur less risk for the custodian.

4. European Proposals for a Financial Transaction Tax (FTT)

Learning Objective

6.1.13 Know the principles of the European financial transaction tax

4.1 Background

The EU financial transaction tax (FTT) is a proposal made by the European Commission (EC) to introduce an FTT within some of the EU's member states. This was intended to come into force on 1 January 2014, but was later postponed until 1 January 2016. This latter date has subsequently been passed without the proposal coming into force and without a replacement date, thus far, being established. Discussions on the implementation of proposals between interested EU member states were ongoing at the end of 2016.

The introduction of such a tax would normally have to be agreed unanimously by all EU member states, but it became apparent during discussions among member states that such unanimity was not achievable in practice. Therefore, in October 2012, the EC proposed that the use of **enhanced cooperation** should be permitted to implement the tax in the states that wished to participate. This framework proposal, supported by 11 EU member states, was approved in the European Parliament in December 2012, and by the Council of the European Union in January 2013.

The 11 member states that originally agreed to implement the tax were Austria, Belgium, Estonia, France, Germany, Greece, Italy, Portugal, Slovakia, Slovenia and Spain. This has now been reduced to ten member states, as Estonia withdrew from negotiations in late 2015.

4.2 Scope and Rates of Tax

The tax would impact financial transactions between financial institutions charging 0.1% against the exchange of shares and bonds, and 0.01% across derivative contracts, if just one of the financial institutions resides in one of these ten states.

However, under the EU's enhanced cooperation rules, all EU member states would be required to collect the tax. This means, for example, that if a UK institution conducted a trade in the UK with a Belgian bank, it would be required to collect the tax on Belgium's behalf.

4.3 Legal Challenge by the UK

In April 2013, the UK launched a legal challenge of the decision authorising the use of enhanced cooperation to implement the FTT with the European Court of Justice. In April 2014, the European Court of Justice dismissed this action, but did not rule out the possibility the UK could challenge the legality of the FTT itself if it is eventually approved. The UK has threatened a new challenge if and when the FTT is approved.

Due to the current uncertainties, it is not yet possible to provide any practical information as to how the implementation of this tax will affect policies, systems and procedures.

End of Chapter Questions

Think of an answer for each question and refer to the appropriate section for confirmation.

1. What is WHT?
   Answer reference: Section 2.1

2. What does a DTA try to prevent?
   Answer reference: Section 2.2

3. What is referred to when discussing the time in which you have to file a tax reclaim for any excess withholding tax on filing the reclaims?
   Answer reference: Section 2.3.1

4. What are the different purposes of the QI regime and FATCA?
   Answer reference: Sections 2.4.1 and 2.4.2

5. Under the FATCA legislation, what information are UK-based FFIs required to report about their US-resident account holders, and to whom do they report it?
   Answer reference: Section 2.4.2

6. What are the Common Reporting Standards (CRS) formally referred to as?
   Answer reference: Section 2.5.3

7. What is the standard withholding tax rate for dividends in:
   A. the US?
   B. Japan?
   C. Italy?
   Answer reference: Sections 3.1, 3.2 and 3.3.1

8. Which types of investor may apply for exemption from Japanese withholding tax exemption?
   Answer reference: Section 3.2

9. What are the two main advantages of tax relief at source as opposed to the standard reclaim procedure?
   Answer reference: Section 3.4

10. What is the proposed rate of the European Financial Transactions Tax on a qualifying trade in an equity option?
    Answer reference: Section 4.2

Chapter Seven
Participants

1. Introduction   **149**
2. Participants   **149**

This syllabus area will provide approximately 3 of the 50 examination questions

1. Introduction

Asset servicing involves processing events in which there are a number of bodies and organisations who actively participate in the process. Their participation and significance depends on the servicing event and process undertaken. This process flows from the issuing or affected company on one side, through the local market and subcustodians, on to the investor or shareholder on the other.

The list of participants which follows is not designed to be exhaustive. For example, the regulatory body of the market would be a participant, if only indirectly. The list does, however, reflect the main players in an asset servicing event.

2. Participants

2.1 Issuer

Learning Objective

7.1.1 Know the role played by the issuer

The issuer is a company or government entity that issues securities through the market (via an initial public offer or IPO), or via a private placement, in order to raise capital. The entity receives a capital benefit as a result of the issue. The intended use for the capital will be described in full in the prospectus attendant upon the issue.

When raising funds, the issuer will require specialist advice in order to:

- choose the most appropriate security, eg, shares, bonds, debentures
- manage the mechanics of arranging the security, and
- manage the selling of the security into the **primary market**.

For this reason, it will appoint an investment bank as its lead manager.

2.2 Custodian

Learning Objective

7.1.2 Know the role played by the custodian/subcustodian

A custodian is a financial institution that provides securities settlement, safekeeping and asset servicing for its clients, possibly on a global scale. It charges a fee for this service. This fee may be calculated on the basis of the amount of assets held under custody and/or the number of transactions processed.

Custodians also offer a wide range of related services, apart from the fundamental ones, which take advantage of their expertise and high-volume-processing technology. The services can be categorised as core and value-added.

Some clients appoint a single custodian to provide these services for all countries. Such a custodian is then known as a global custodian. However, the firm that is acting as global custodian may not have offices in all the countries where its clients hold assets. If that is the case, the global custodian will appoint another firm to act for it in those countries. This local firm is known as the subcustodian.

2.2.1 Core Services

Core services are those that are considered to be standard across the industry and are provided by all custodians. They are closely related to the basic processes of managing clients' securities, and include:

- safekeeping
- settlement
- cross-border transaction processing
- asset servicing, and
- cash management.

2.2.2 Value-Added Services

Value-added services is a general term for services other than the core services; these provide an enhancement to the client's portfolio. This enhancement can be in the form of additional revenue, reduced costs, or additional information that provides the client with a competitive advantage. These services include:

- securities lending
- investment accounting
- reporting
- class actions
- proxy voting
- performance evaluation, and
- fund accounting and other operational processes.

Increasingly, these value-added services are becoming part of a custodian's core services as they develop their offerings in light of the increased interest of fund managers in outsourcing elements of their operations. See Chapter 8, Section 12 for more information on outsourcing.

2.3 Transfer Agent/Registrar

Learning Objective

7.1.3 Know the role played by the transfer agent/registrar

The registrar is the company appointed by an issuing company to maintain the records of legal ownership of securities. The term used in the US and Canada for this function is transfer agent.

The responsibilities of the registrar include:

- initial registration and distribution of newly issued securities
- monitoring the quantity of shares or bonds in circulation to ensure they are correct, and
- security registration; this includes the duty of certifying that the security is genuine.

In the UK, the registrar can be a separately run subsidiary of a commercial bank, or an independent company specialising in the role.

2.4 Underwriter

Learning Objective

7.1.17 Know the role of the underwriter

Underwriters of a share issue agree, for a fee, to buy any portion of the issue not taken up in the market at the issue price. The underwriters then sell the shares they have bought when market conditions seem opportune to them, and may make a gain or a loss on this sale. The underwriters agree to buy the shares if no one else will, and the company's investment bank will probably underwrite some of the issue itself.

If investors have a very negative view of why a rights issue is being made and what it says for the future of the company, the share price can fall substantially. This was seen in 2008 with HBOS and RBS, when the price of shares on the open market fell below the discounted rights issue price. The rights issues were flops and the underwriters ended up having to take up all unsubscribed new shares.

If no premium was attained during the sale of new ordinary shares sold by the underwriters, no lapsed rights proceeds will be distributed and nil-paid shares will be removed from clients' accounts with no associated value.

2.5 Lead Manager

Learning Objective

7.1.4 Know the role played by the lead manager

The lead manager is the principal investment house in a syndicate handling a new issue of securities, and is appointed by the issuing company. The lead manager is said to 'run the book' on behalf of the issuer, hence this firm may also be known as the bookrunner.

The lead manager's responsibility is the coordination of the activities of the syndicate in **placing** the issue in the primary market. These activities include the distribution and documentation of the issue to:

- select suitable co-managers, in consultation with the issuer
- determine the terms of the issue, in consultation with the issuer
- select the underwriters
- select the exchange
- select the selling group (see below), and
- ensure the securities are placed; this is done in liaison with the appointed registrar, who would manage the physical registration and issuance to security holders.

The selling group, in this context, is those financial institutions who are involved in selling or marketing a new issue of debt or equity but not necessarily participating in the underwriting consortium.

2.6 Trustee

Learning Objective

7.1.5 Know the role played by the trustee

A trustee is a person appointed to administer a trust.

The trustee is the holder of legal title to the investments that make up the trust and will act in a fiduciary capacity to its clients. This means that the trustee has delegated authority for performance of the fund and must ensure that the investments are properly safeguarded. The trustee must also ensure the trust acts in an ethical and responsible manner.

Apart from the trustee, a trust involves:

- the person creating the trust (known as the settlor), and
- the beneficiary or the person receiving the proceeds from the trust.

In order to ensure that the integrity of the trust is safeguarded, regulations will generally state that:

- the trustee must keep accounting records of the funds held, invested and distributed
- client assets and non-client assets must be segregated (see Chapter 8, Section 9)
- the trustee must comply with the wishes of the settlor
- the trustee cannot take advantage of their position for profit to the detriment of the beneficiary
- the trustee can only invest in classes of instruments defined by local regulations.

2.7 Tender Agent

Learning Objective

7.1.6 Know the role played by the tender agent

The process of tendering securities is the auctioning of a security to the highest bidder. Prospective buyers will submit a formal bid to buy a certain amount of securities at a certain price. The tender process is initiated when the issuing company announces the tender and sets a cut-off date for the receipt of bids.

Once the cut-off date has passed, the issuer will allocate securities first to bidders offering the most desirable terms, then to the next desirable and so on until all securities have been allocated.

The tender agent is the agent bank that manages this tender process on behalf of the issuer.

2.8 Receiving Agent

Learning Objective

7.1.7 Know the role played by the receiving agent

A receiving agent is appointed by an issuer to handle payments and stock movement in respect of certain corporate events. For example, with a rights issue, the receiving agent will handle the return of nil-paid rights and the application of monies in return for fully paid rights. The receiving agent processes instructions from registered shareholders and the asset servicing departments of custodians. It does this either directly or via a third party, such as a securities trading organisation or **clearing agent**. In the UK, the receiving agent is often the same as the registrar.

The receiving agent must comply with local client protection regulations and must have a suitable credit rating.

2.9 Calculation/Paying Agent

Learning Objective

7.1.8 Know the role played by the calculation agent

7.1.9 Know the role played by the paying agent

The **calculation/paying agent** collects monies for disbursement from the issuer; these include dividend payments and proceeds from tender offers. The paying agent advises clearing agents of the monies due, and instructs them to make the appropriate payment to the holders of securities.

The calculation/paying agent acts under the control and authority of the issuer and executes instructions on its behalf in return for a fee.

Because the calculation/paying agent holds assets on behalf of its client, it must comply with local regulations in ensuring appropriate protection for client assets, including compliance with regulatory rules relating to client segregation and reporting in a timely and accurate manner.

The client must have confidence that the calculation/paying agent is creditworthy and, for this reason, it will usually have a minimum 'A' credit rating.

2.10 Central Securities Depositories (CSDs)

Learning Objective

7.1.10 Know the role played by the central securities depositories

A central securities depository (CSD) is an entity holding all the securities for a particular market. This centralises the securities of a particular market, making settlement easier.

In mature markets, the dominant method of holding will be in dematerialised or non-physical form. This has the following benefits:

- **Settlement of transactions via book entry accounting** – this allows the electronic transfer of securities between seller and buyer.
- **Netting of transactions** – this is when trading partners agree to offset their obligations to settle individual trades. By doing so, they reduce a large number of individual settlements to a single delivery. It is on this netted position that the two trading partners settle their outstanding obligations to transfer cash or securities. Rather than having to settle securities and cash on a trade-by-trade (gross) basis with each of the counterparties that it conducts business with during the trading day, the **central counterparty (CCP)** will net down each participant's respective sales and purchases to a single transfer of securities and a single transfer of cash each day.
- **Operating a delivery versus payment (DvP) settlement environment**.

These three benefits reduce the **settlement risk** inherent in the market at the same time as improving safekeeping and making collateral management more efficient.

In less mature markets, paper securities (often bearer securities) still exist and can be transferred between seller and buyer (within the CSD). This creates inefficiencies in the transfer and settlement process because of the need to physically move and/or reregister the security. The risk of loss and theft also increases. This also slows down settlement.

Each market will have a CSD. The CSDs of the UK, US, Italy and Japan are:

- UK – Euroclear UK and Ireland (EUI)
- US – the Depository Trust Company (DTC), part of the Depository Trust & Clearing Corporation (DTCC)
- Italy – Monte Titoli
- Japan – JASDEC.

As well as CSDs, which are nationally based, there are two international central securities depositories (ICSDs). These are Euroclear Bank and Clearstream. They were originally set up to hold and clear eurobonds on behalf of institutional investors. They also provide custody services.

As the business world becomes increasingly global, there is pressure upon national CSDs to merge to offer a single settlement and clearing platform – for example, Euroclear acquired UK-based CREST and the CSDs of France, Belgium, Sweden, Finland and the Netherlands. When CREST was acquired by Euroclear, it changed the company name to Euroclear UK and Ireland (EUI), but the name of the system that EUI uses is still called CREST.

2.11 Central Counterparties (CCPs)

Learning Objective

7.1.11 Know the role played by the central counterparties

The use of a CCP is a practice employed by a number of exchanges to reduce credit risk. The CCP sits between the buyer and seller of a security and acts as a guarantor of contracts. The CCP assumes the credit risk, thereby limiting the exposure of its members by protecting them from the impact of default.

The clearing house of an exchange may act as the central counterparty, rather than two exchange members being involved in a direct counterparty-to-counterparty contract, whereby each party assumes the other's risk. The clearing house acts as the intermediary counterparty to each. If a member defaults, the clearing house will guarantee the performance of the contract to the other member.

2.11.1 Position-Monitoring and Margin

Because the CCP thus takes on the **credit risk** for all trades, its primary concern is the management of risk. To do this, CCPs have very stringent membership requirements and continuously review the creditworthiness of existing members. On the London International Financial Futures and Options Exchange (LIFFE), where the risk exposure of open positions rises and falls over time, position-monitoring and margining are employed to manage the ongoing risk of default.

- **Position-monitoring** – this is the daily analysis of an individual member's exposure risk in relation to their ability to cover their margin liabilities and delivery obligations.
- **Margining** – this is the means of receiving collateral on open positions to insure against the risk of default. Two types of margin calls are made by the CCP:
  - **initial margin** – the call when a position is first opened, and
  - **variation margin** – the call paid or received at the end of each day, reflecting the daily profit or loss on the open position.

2.12 Conversion Agent

Learning Objective

7.1.12 Know the role played by the conversion agent

As explained in Chapter 4, Section 3, a **conversion event** occurs either at the end of the life of the convertible security or at the behest of the stock holder, or when the characteristics of a financial instrument are changed. The conversion process is managed by a conversion agent, on behalf of the issuer. The conversion agent will receive the conversion notices from the client and will instruct the depositary accordingly. The conversion agent is also known as the exchange agent.

2.13 Stock Lenders and Borrowers

Learning Objective

7.1.13 Know the role played by stock lenders and borrowers

Many kinds of market participants lend or borrow securities.

Reasons for Borrowing Securities

- Market makers and other sell-side firms often run short positions, ie, they have sold more stock than they have bought. They will therefore borrow stock in order to settle their sales on the correct **value date**.
- Any buy-side or sell-side firm may have a situation where securities that they have bought cannot be delivered for some reason. If they have sold the stock to another party, then they, of course, will be unable to deliver what they have not received. They therefore borrow stock to cover for delivery failures.

- Hedge funds often sell stock short because they expect the price of the security concerned to fall in the future, when they will buy it back at the lower price. They too will borrow stock in order to settle these short sales on the correct value date.
- Hedge funds also use stock borrowing as part of strategies to influence the management of the company concerned, particularly in matters relating to mergers and acquisitions. If a hedge fund borrows stock, then it can vote the borrowed stock at company meetings.
- To take advantage of arbitrage opportunities around a corporate action. For example, the lender may be looking to lapse entitlements in a rights issue, whereas a borrower may see an opportunity to make a profit by subscribing and immediately selling the resulting shares.

Reasons for Lending Securities

- By way of example, traditional fund managers do not sell short; they are sometimes referred to as 'long-only' fund managers in this context. They are prepared to lend stock because of the fee they receive.

2.14 Multilateral Trading Facilities (MTFs)

Learning Objective

7.1.14 Know the role played by multilateral trading facilities

A multilateral trading facility (MTF) brings together multiple parties (eg, retail investors or other investment firms) that are interested in buying and selling financial instruments, and enables them to do so. Such facilities include crossing networks or matching engines that are operated by an investment firm or a market operator. Instruments may include shares, bonds and derivatives. Other forms of MTF include in-house systems controlled by approved market operators or larger investment banks. BATS and Chi-X are examples of MTFs.

Traders will usually submit orders electronically, whereby a matching software engine is used to pair buyers with sellers.

2.15 Trade Associations, Infrastructure and Industry-led Working Groups

Learning Objective

7.1.15 Know the roles of trade associations, infrastructure and industry-led working groups

Firms in the financial services industry join together in a number of groups to share expertise about concerns they have in common. The purpose of such groupings include:

- lobbying government departments and regulators about concerns
- making rules and recommendations about best practice and the use of common standards in their industry segment, and conducting surveys about the extent to which these standards and recommendations are applied

- reacting to specific common events and new legislation, and providing advice and guidance about how to implement change.

Some of the most active trade associations include the following:

- The **Association of Global Custodians** – established in 1996, the Association of Global Custodians is a group of 11 financial institutions that provide securities safekeeping services and asset servicing functions worldwide to primarily institutional cross-border investors. As a non-partisan advocacy organisation, the association represents members' common interests on regulatory and market structure matters through comment letters, white papers and interaction with legislative and regulatory authorities and financial industry organisations. The member banks are competitors, and the association does not involve itself in member commercial activities or take positions concerning how members should conduct their custody and related businesses.
- The **Investment Association (IA)** – the IA represents the UK investment management industry. Its members manage over £5 trillion of assets on behalf of UK and overseas clients. Many of its policy positions are set out in the responses sent to consultations by the government, regulators, the European Commission (EC) and others. It maintains links with parliamentarians in both Westminster and the European Parliament, and has contributed regularly to the deliberations of parliamentary select committees. It publishes and commissions research into various aspects of the industry.
- The **International Securities Lending Association (ISLA)** – ISLA is a trade association established in 1989 to represent the common interests of participants in the securities lending industry. ISLA works closely with European regulators and, in the UK, has representation on the Securities Lending and Repo Committee – a committee of market practitioners chaired by the Bank of England. The Association has contributed to a number of major market initiatives, including the development of the UK Securities Borrowing and Lending Code of Guidance and the industry-standard lending agreement – the Global Master Securities Lending Agreement (GMSLA).
- The **Association for Financial Markets in Europe (AFME)** – AFME is the voice of Europe's wholesale financial markets. It represents the leading global and European banks and other significant capital market players. It focuses on a wide range of market, business and prudential issues and offers a pan-European perspective, bringing to bear deep policy and technical expertise and constructive influence on European and global policymakers. Focusing on the creation of a single integrated post-trading process for securities transactions in Europe, the Post-Trade Division seeks to achieve harmonisation, standardisation and consolidation through best practice and regulation. Providing clearing, settlement and custody solutions to reduce costs and risks of market participants, the Division's work covers the operational, legal, tax, and regulatory aspects of post-trading.

2.16 TARGET2-Securities (T2S)

Learning Objective

7.1.16 Know principles of T2S and its participants

TARGET2-Securities (T2S) is the European securities settlement engine which aims to offer centralised delivery-versus-payment (DvP) settlement in central bank funds across all European securities markets. It is important to note that T2S is not a CSD, but a platform which will enable CSDs to increase their competitiveness.

Timeline of T2S

After market consultations and a decision by the Governing Council of the European Central Bank (ECB), the project was launched in 2008. Testing by CSDs commenced in October 2014 and the platform launched operations in June 2015.

The development and operation of T2S was assigned to four central banks of the Eurosystem – those of France, Germany, Italy and Spain. Technical details of the project are available at the ECB T2S project website (ecb.europa.eu/paym/t2s/html/index.en.html).

The implementation timetable is as follows:

Wave 1 – 22 June 2015–31 August 2015 – five CSDs

- Monte Titoli S.p.A. (Italy)
- Bank of Greece Securities Settlement System (BOGS)
- Depozitarul Central S.A. (Romania)
- SIX SIS Ltd. (Switzerland)
- Malta Stock Exchange.

Wave 2 – 29 March 2016 – three CSDs

- National Bank of Belgium Securities Settlement System (NBB-SSS)
- Euroclear (France, Netherlands, Belgium)
- Interbolsa (Portugal).

Wave 3 – 12 September 2016 – five CSDs

- Euroclear France
- Euroclear Belgium
- Euroclear Nederland
- VP Lux (Luxembourg)
- VP Securities A/S (Denmark).

Wave 4 – 6 February 2017 – six CSDs

- Clearstream Banking AG (Germany).
- Oesterreichische Kontrollbank Aktiengesellschaft (Austria)
- Központi Elszámolóház és Értéktár Zrt. – KELER (Hungary)
- LuxCSD S.A. (Luxembourg)
- Centrálny depozitár cenných papierov SR, a. s. (Slovakia)
- KDD - Centralna klirinško depotna družba, d.d. (Slovenia).

Wave 5 (Final Wave) – 18 September 2017 – five CSDs

- Iberclear – BME Group (Spain)
- Euroclear Finland Oy
- AS Eesti Väärtpaberikeskus (Estonia)
- Lietuvos centrinis vertybinių popierių depozitoriumas (Lithuania)
- Latvijas Centrālais depozitārijs (Latvia).

Source: www.ecb.int/paym/t2s/about/press/html/index.en.html

Objectives of T2S

The fundamental objective of the T2S project is to integrate and harmonise the highly fragmented securities settlement infrastructure in Europe. It aims to reduce the costs of cross-border securities settlement significantly (prior to T2S, transactions across T2S countries could be up to ten times more costly than domestic transactions) and to increase competition and choice among providers of post-trading services in Europe.

The European settlement infrastructure prior to the launch of T2S is shown in the following diagram:

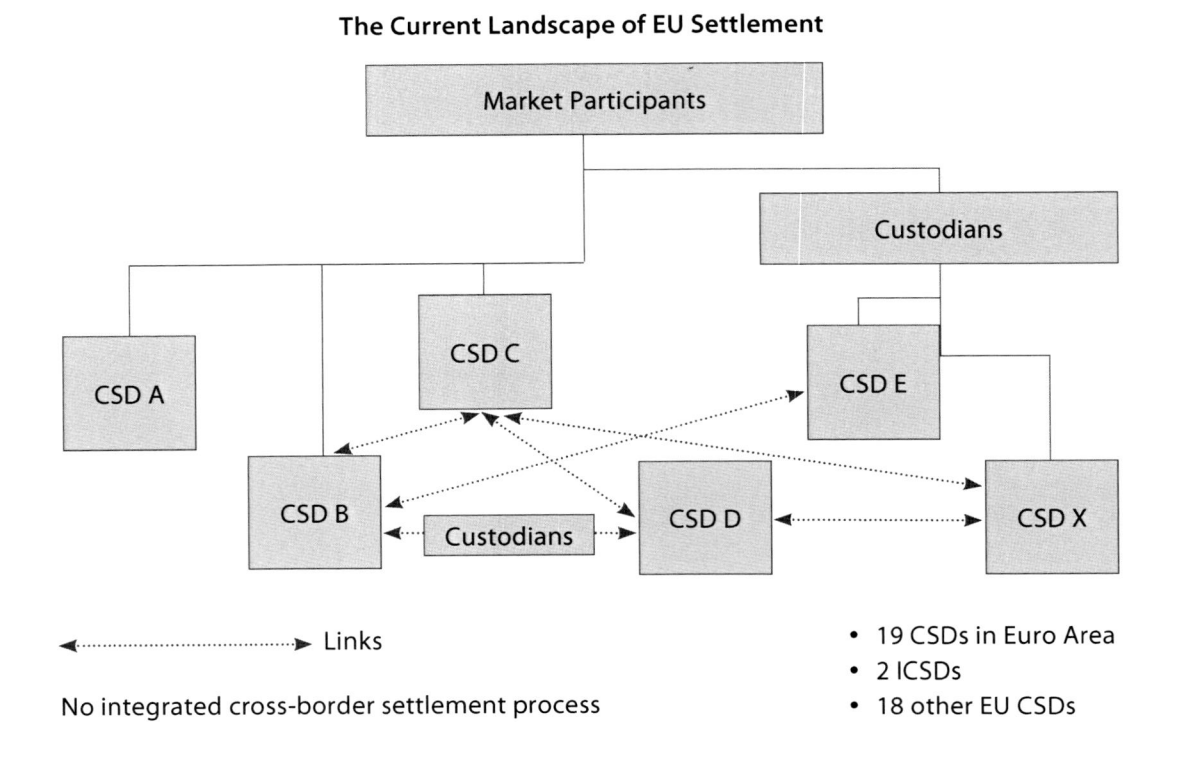

The Current Landscape of EU Settlement

[Diagram: Market Participants connect to Custodians, CSD A, CSD B, CSD C; Custodians connect to CSD E, CSD X; dotted-line Links connect CSDs B, C, D, E, X and Custodians]

◀·······▶ Links

No integrated cross-border settlement process

- 19 CSDs in Euro Area
- 2 ICSDs
- 18 other EU CSDs

Prior to the T2S launch, each CSD would settle according to its own technical set-up and respective national legal requirements; as a result, interaction between CSDs became inefficient and costly. Post-T2S, the situation can be represented as:

The Future Landscape with T2S

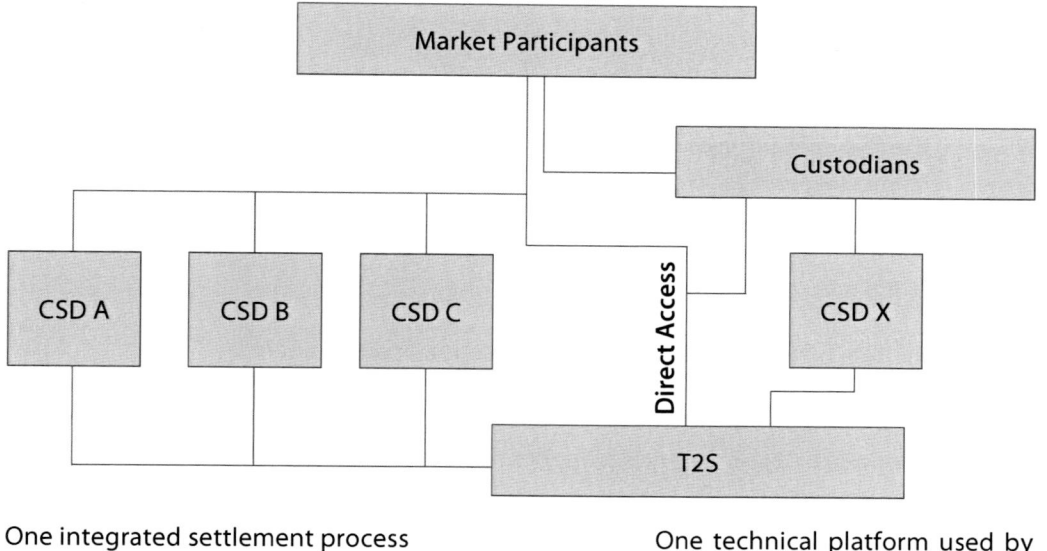

```
                    Market Participants
                    ┌──────────┬──────────┐
                    │          │          │
                    │          │     Custodians
                    │          │     ┌─────────┐
    ┌──────┐   ┌──────┐   ┌──────┐   │  ┌──────┐
    │CSD A │   │CSD B │   │CSD C │   │  │CSD X │
    └──────┘   └──────┘   └──────┘ Direct └──────┘
        │         │          │    Access     │
        │         │          │     ┌─────────┘
        └─────────┴──────────┴─────┤
                                   T2S
```

One integrated settlement process   One technical platform used by
(domestic and cross-border)   CSDs for securities settlement

T2S will provide all participating CSDs with a single platform for security settlement in Europe, with interaction between CSDs occurring on a harmonised basis. Essentially, the platform provides a definitive step towards a single market for financial services, with industry bodies engaged in determining further opportunities that exist in the harmonisation of processing standards for pre- and post-settlement/ corporate action activities.

End of Chapter Questions

Think of an answer for each question and refer to the appropriate section for confirmation.

1. What are the five core services of a custodian?
   Answer reference: Section 2.2.1

2. What are the main responsibilities of a registrar?
   Answer reference: Section 2.3

3. What is the usual minimum credit rating required for a paying agent?
   Answer reference: Section 2.9

4. What is the role of a CSD and why is it important?
   Answer reference: Section 2.10

5. What is the CSD in Japan?
   Answer reference: Section 2.10

6. How does a CCP manage its credit risk?
   Answer reference: Section 2.11.1

7. Give two reasons for borrowing stock and one for lending stock.
   Answer reference: Section 2.13

8. What is the purpose of T2S?
   Answer reference: Section 2.16

Chapter Eight
Legal and Compliance

1.	Introduction	165
2.	Client Assets Rules	166
3.	Ownership/Residency Restrictions	167
4.	Markets in Financial Instruments Directive (MiFID)	168
5.	Global Agreements	172
6.	1933 Securities Act (As Amended)	173
7.	Qualified Institutional Buyers (QIBs)	174
8.	Sophisticated Investor Letters (SILs)	175
9.	Client Money Rules	175
10.	Price-Sensitive Information	176
11.	Foreign Ownership Restrictions	176
12.	Outsourcing	177
13.	Sanctions	177
14.	Different Market Regulators	178

This syllabus area will provide approximately 3 of the 50 examination questions

1. Introduction

This chapter introduces and defines some of the regulations and rules governing investment business that are pertinent to asset servicing. It starts by looking at the Client Assets Rules as set out by the UK regulator, then goes on to examine **foreign ownership restrictions** and highlights some legal agreements that govern repos and stock lending. Other jurisdictions have similar regulators and similar rules.

Prior to 1 April 2013 the UK regulator was the Financial Services Authority (FSA), but the Financial Services Act 2012 created three new bodies to replace the FSA. This was as a reaction to the financial crises of 2008. These new bodies are as follows:

Financial Policy Committee (FPC)

This Financial Policy Committee (FPC), established in the Bank of England (BoE), has responsibility for 'macro-prudential' regulation, or regulation of the stability and resilience of the financial system as a whole. Its role is:

> Contributing to the Bank's objective to protect and enhance financial stability, through identifying and taking action to remove or reduce systemic risks, with a view to protecting and enhancing the resilience of the UK financial system.

Prudential Regulation Authority (PRA)

The Prudential Regulation Authority (PRA), a department of the Bank of England, is responsible for prudential regulation of financial firms that manage significant risks on their balance sheets – in other words, it is responsible for the regulation and supervision of 'significant' individual firms including all deposit-taking institutions, insurers and other prudentially significant firms.

The PRA has a primary objective of enhancing financial stability by promoting the safety and soundness of PRA-authorised firms in a way which minimises the disruption caused by any firms that do fail. In fulfilling its objective, it takes a view on the likelihood of failure of a firm.

This process is subject to continuous assessment, with more focused supervisory action on those firms deemed most at risk of failure.

Financial Conduct Authority (FCA)

The Financial Conduct Authority (FCA) is responsible for conduct issues across the entire spectrum of financial services; it is also responsible for market supervision. In addition, it is responsible for the prudential regulation of approximately 25,000 smaller firms that are not regulated by the PRA.

The FCA looks to achieve the right outcomes for consumers and market participants. It has three operational objectives:

1. Ensuring that markets operate with integrity.
2. Promoting effective competition.
3. Requiring firms to put the well-being of their customers at the heart of how they run their business.

2. Client Assets Rules

The FCA publishes the Conduct of Business Rulebook, setting out the rules governing the way firms carry out investment business. It also sets out rules for the administration of client assets. This is the Client Assets Sourcebook (CASS).

2.1 Mandates – Client Assets Rules (CASS 8)

The mandate rules apply to those firms that control, rather than hold, clients' assets or are allowed to create liabilities in the name of a client. The rules ensure that firms establish and maintain records and internal controls and risk policies to prevent the misuse of the authority granted by the client.

Section 8 of the Client Assets Rules deals with mandates. There are various circumstances in which a client may grant a firm control over its assets. When it does so, it is said to grant the firm a mandate. Examples include:

- permission to use securities held for discretionary stock lending purposes
- access to a bank account, for example when a direct debit is set up to fund a monthly purchase of shares
- permission to retain credit card details so that they do not have to be resent for all future transactions
- standing instructions to always make the same election on, for example, dividend options and dividend reinvestment plans (DRIPs).

A firm that holds authorities of the sort referred to in CASS 8 must establish and maintain adequate records and internal controls, proving its duty of care and due diligence in respect of its use of the mandates, which must include:

- an up-to-date list of the authorities and any conditions placed by the client or the firm's management on the use of them
- a record of all transactions entered into using the authority and internal controls to ensure that they are within the scope of authority of the person and the firm entering into the transaction
- the details of the procedures and authorities for the giving and receiving of instructions under the authority
- if the firm holds a passbook or similar documents belonging to the client – internal controls for the safeguarding, which must encompass loss, unauthorised destruction, theft, fraud or misuse, of any passbook or similar document belonging to the client held by the firm.

3. Ownership/Residency Restrictions

Learning Objective

8.1.1 Understand how tax domicile restrictions may impact investors when participating in a corporate action

8.1.2 Understand the difference between residency and tax domicile with regard to eligibility to receive a benefit or participate in an event

Some restrictions may be placed on what kinds of securities an investor may hold (and therefore what options they may choose when an event creates a new security) depending on their tax domicile.

Domicile is defined as 'a person's legal home'. An investment fund, issuing company or corporate investor is a 'person' in this sense.

Domicile is not the same as residence. For example, an employee who was transferred by their employer from the US to the UK would be resident in the UK, and domiciled in the US. An investment company might be incorporated (and therefore domiciled) in the Cayman Islands but managed from London or New York. A person may have more than one residence but only one domicile.

The legal domicile of a person is important, since it, rather than the actual residence, often controls the jurisdiction of the taxing authorities.

The types of restrictions that may be placed on an investor because of their tax domicile include, but are not limited to, the following examples:

1. A company may offer shares to its employees at a discounted price. The terms of the offer satisfy the tax authorities of the country in which the company is domiciled, but do not satisfy the tax authorities of some of the countries in which some of its employees are domiciled. In such a case, those employees are not able to take up the offer.
2. The corporate action of a company domiciled in Country A creates a type of security which Country B either does not permit its citizens to own at all, or which places an onerous tax burden on them. If this happens, then any shareholders in Country B need to take a cash alternative, or, if no such alternative is provided, to sell the resultant holding at the earliest possible opportunity.

As well as restrictions that are based on tax domicile, other restrictions may be placed on investors which limit their participation in a corporate action. Institutional investors can be barred from taking up issues of new shares in cases when the issue is aimed at the private investor market only. Non-residents may not be able to participate in an issue of new shares because of a country's foreign ownership restrictions. Foreign ownership restrictions are examined in more detail in Section 11.

4. Markets in Financial Instruments Directive (MiFID)

Learning Objective

8.1.10 Understand the concept, purpose and reporting requirements of MiFID and the high-level goal of MiFID II

4.1 Introduction

The Markets in Financial Instruments Directive (MiFID) was enacted in 2004 and came into force on 1 November 2007, replacing the previous Investment Services Directive that was introduced in 1993. The legislation is detailed, prescriptive and wide-ranging – MiFID's physical presence is twice the size of any of its predecessors.

MiFID applies to all firms in the European Economic Area (EEA) (the 27 European Union (EU) states plus Iceland, Norway and Liechtenstein) and is concerned primarily with:

- authorisation of investment firms
- classification of clients
- conflicts of interest
- handling of client money and client assets
- handling of client orders, including pre-trade and post-trade transparency plus best execution.

4.2 Authorisation of Investment Firms and 'Passporting'

A firm that has its head office in one EEA state and branches in others will be regulated for prudential purposes by the national regulator of the state in which its head office is located. As a result, a UK firm with a branch in France would have its capital adequacy monitored by the appropriate UK regulator, and not by the French regulator. However, the French regulator would still have a responsibility to regulate the French branch's business conduct as far as clients in France are concerned.

In this case the UK regulator is said to have issued a passport to the firm. The passport enables the firm to carry on those activities that are regulated in the UK in any other EEA country.

4.3 Classification of Clients

MiFID requires that each trading party be classified as one of the following:

1. **Eligible counterparty** – eg, another regulated bank or stock exchange member firm.
2. **Professional client** – eg, a pension fund.
3. **Retail client** – eg, a private individual.

These classifications have increasing levels of investor protection (eligible counterparties given the least, and retail the most). Clear procedures must be in place to classify clients and assess their suitability for each type of investment product, the appropriateness of any investment advice given and the suitability of any transaction suggested to them.

4.4 Conflicts of Interest

MiFID recognises that conflicts of interest may occur when an investment firm may, for example, be acting for:

- both investors in and issuers of the same security at the same time
- more than one investor that has an interest in a particular security
- investors that have an interest in a particular security at the same time that the firm itself has an interest in the same security.

MiFID requires firms to have a conflicts management policy that requires them to:

1. take steps to prevent conflicts of interest giving rise to the material risk of damaging clients' interest
2. identify, proactively, business areas where conflicts are likely to arise
3. document each potential conflict and describe how its effect should be mitigated, and
4. disclose this policy to clients on request.

4.5 Handling of Client Money and Client Assets

MiFID rules include a general requirement to make adequate arrangements to safeguard clients' money and client assets such as securities that the firm may hold on their behalf. There are specific rules about:

- record-keeping
- segregation, and
- reconciliation.

4.6 Handling of Client Orders and Trade Execution

This is by far the most complex area of MiFID. It imposes different rules on different types of industry participant. However, in the main these rules apply to investment exchanges and broker-dealers rather than custodians, and only one of them is dealt with in this workbook. This is the requirement to obtain best execution when executing an order to buy or sell securities or derivatives.

Broadly speaking, best execution places an obligation on the firm executing the order to get the lowest available price for its customer when the customer is buying, and the highest available price when the customer is selling. Other execution factors to be taken into account are costs, speed, likelihood of execution and settlement, size, nature or any other consideration relevant to the execution of an order. The relative importance of each factor will depend on the following criteria and characteristics:

- the client, and how it is categorised
- the client order
- the financial instruments involved, and
- the execution venues to which that order could be directed, and the direct and/or implicit execution costs of each venue.

Article 21 of the MiFID regulations requires firms that execute orders on behalf of clients to:

1. establish an execution policy, which must contain information on the venues used to execute client orders. Those venues must allow it to consistently obtain the best possible result for execution for their clients
2. disclose the policy to clients and obtain their consent to that policy
3. monitor the effectiveness of arrangements in order to identify and correct any deficiencies and review the appropriateness of the venues in its execution policy at least yearly, and
4. upon client request, be ready to demonstrate that the client's order has been executed in line with its execution policy.

Any asset servicing institution that offers a trade execution service must comply with Article 21 of MiFID.

4.7 Client Agreements

MiFID requires investment firms that provide services other than investment advice to provide a basic written agreement with their retail clients, setting out the essential rights and obligations of the firm and the client. There is no MiFID obligation to provide client agreements to professional clients or when no investment advice is being given.

Client agreements need to be in place before providing services.

The content includes:

- information about the firm and its services
- instruments and strategies
- execution venues (best execution)
- costs and associated charges
- order handling
- client money and assets, and
- conflicts of interest.

4.8 MiFID Reporting Requirements

Investment exchanges must publish the details of all trades executed in their systems. The exact detail of what information is to be published is left to the regulator of the country concerned. Additionally, investment firms must publish details of trades in relevant instruments executed in the over-the-counter (OTC) markets.

Publication must be close to real time, and in any event within three minutes of trade execution. Exceptions are made for trades taking place outside a venue's normal trading hours, when publication must be carried out prior to the start of the next trading day.

4.9 MiFID II

Subsequent to the European Commission's (EC's) December 2010 consultation to reform the Markets in Financial Instruments Directive (MiFID), the Commission published its legislative proposals, which took the form of a revised Directive (MiFID II) and a new Regulation (MiFIR), on 20 October 2011.

In general terms, these proposals represent a comprehensive and profound set of reforms which will lead to a reshaping of the financial markets, the products and services that banks provide and the relationship between banks and their customers.

Although the directive is driven by European regulators, it will have a wider impact, as capital markets are increasingly global. When non-European firms transact with European customers, MiFID II will apply.

4.9.1 Timing

The European Parliament endorsed MiFID II and MiFIR on 15 April 2014, and the Council of the European Union adopted the legislation on 13 May 2014. The MiFID II legislation was published on 12 June 2014. Both MiFID II and MiFIR entered into force on 2 July 2014, and are required to be transposed into national law by 3 July 2017. They must apply within member states by 3 January 2018.

4.9.2 Purpose

MiFID II will significantly change the way the majority of OTC products are priced, traded and reported.

The objectives MiFID II seeks to achieve are as follows:

- increased transparency of markets, eg, around trading costs
- more structured marketplaces
- lower-cost market data
- improved best execution
- orderly trading behaviour within markets
- more explicit costs (as regards trading and investing).

4.9.3 Impact on Participant Businesses

Depending on the scope and nature, participant businesses may be required to:

- report trades to the local regulator
- trade certain derivatives on regulated trading venues
- publish quotes and post-trade information for trading activity across most asset classes
- perform more extensive testing of trading algorithms
- produce annual reports to assess the quality of executions on the trading venues most frequently utilised
- make separate payments for commissions and broker research
- comply with position limits and reporting obligations on commodity derivatives.

5. Global Agreements

To reduce the legal risk and improve the efficiency of securities lending, the industry developed global agreements to standardise the terms and conditions for lending and borrowing. These have had a major impact on improving the liquidity of the securities lending market. Two such agreements are:

- the **Global Master Securities Lending Agreement (GMSLA)**, and
- the **Global Master Repurchase Agreement (GMRA)**.

5.1 The Global Master Securities Lending Agreement (GMSLA)

Learning Objective

8.1.3 Know how the GMSLA deals with income distributions and events in respect of securities out on loan

The GMSLA is the accepted industry contractual template for securities-lending transactions. It covers situations where corporate actions take place or income payments are made while the stock is out on loan. The template contains the following conditions:

- Income payments such as interest, dividends or other distributions received by the borrower are to be repaid to the lender.
- When income is paid to the borrower in the form of securities, the securities are aggregated into the loan and delivered to the lender at the end of the loan period.
- Rights relating to corporate action events such as conversions, subdivisions, consolidations and takeovers may be exercised by the lender. The lender can instruct the borrower to take up the rights within a mutually agreed time frame, to sell them, or to take up a proportion of them. Delivery of the resulting security will take place at the end of the loan period.
- The borrower has no obligation to arrange for voting rights to be exercised by the lender.

5.2 The Global Master Repurchase Agreement (GMRA)

Learning Objective

8.1.4 Know how the TBMA/ISMA master agreement deals with income distributions and stock events in respect of bonds out on repo

Similar to the GMSLA, the GMRA is the accepted industry contractual template, developed during the 1990s, covering repos and buy/sellback transactions. It was developed by The Bond Market Association (TBMA) and the International Securities Market Association (ISMA), which has since become known as the International Capital Market Association (ICMA). They drafted a market standard legal agreement with a view to compliance with English law.

It deals with corporate actions as follows:

- Income payments that are received by the repo buyer must be credited to the seller on the same day.
- Income payments credited to the repo seller must be made gross of tax unless otherwise agreed.

6. 1933 Securities Act (as Amended)

Learning Objective

8.1.5 Understand the two basic objectives of the 1933 Securities Act (as amended): information concerning securities offered for public sale; avoiding deception in the sale of securities

In the US, the **1933 Securities Act (as amended)** was enacted in the wake of the Great Depression (when a large number of small private investors lost everything they owned), to protect the public, who were not **sophisticated investors**, from the issuance and distribution of fraudulent securities. It is also called the Full Disclosure Act (and also known as the Truth in Securities law by the Securities and Exchange Commission (SEC)) and requires issuers to register a detailed and truthful statement with the SEC, describing any new offering. The requirements for disclosure include:

- the price of the public offering
- details of the issuer, the name, type of business, capitalisation, funded debt, details of directors, history of previous issues, major shareholders and relevant financial statements
- details of the underwriters, the names and addresses, copies of the contracts and agreements
- jurisdiction, and
- a formal assessment of the legality of the issue.

If the issuer fails to provide the necessary information, the purchaser can litigate to recover any subsequent losses.

Exemptions to the Act include the following bodies:

- local or national government
- banks (but not bank holding companies)
- trustee companies, and
- any securities, such as **commercial paper (CP)** and bankers' acceptances that have a maturity of less than 270 days.

7. Qualified Institutional Buyers (QIBs)

Learning Objective

8.1.7 Know the definition of US qualified institutional buyers (QIBs)

SEC Rule 144a was established in April 1990 to address the specific requirements of participating in private placements.

As mentioned in Chapter 2, Section 2.2, private placements are a means of issuing securities to specific investors rather than to the general public. Because they are not listed in the normal manner, there is not the same level of disclosure or registration as listed securities.

Private placements are allowable only if purchasers are qualified institutional buyers (QIBs). QIBs are defined as sophisticated investors who invest, on behalf of themselves, their client and other QIBs, at least $100 million worth of securities. In addition, if the investing institution is a bank, it must have a minimum net worth of $25 million.

Securities sold under a private placement are a form of restricted security in that, once the transaction has been completed, the purchaser may not resell to the general public for a minimum period of time, usually one year. This is known as the holding period and it begins when the securities are bought and paid for fully.

The purchaser of securities sold under a private placement must certify to the issuer that the purchase is for investment purposes only and that there is no intention to immediately re-offer the securities publicly. This forms part of the contract between both parties.

Even after the one-year holding period expires, the number of shares that may be sold into the public market is still carefully controlled. During any three-month period this amount cannot exceed either:

- 1% of the outstanding shares of the same class being sold, or
- 1% of the average reported weekly trading volume during the four weeks preceding the filing of a notice of the sale on form 144.

Because of these restrictions, the affected security is not as liquid as a listed security even of the same company, and therefore may have a lower market value.

8. Sophisticated Investor Letters (SILs)

Learning Objective

8.1.6 Know the definition of sophisticated investor letters (SILs) and when they can be used

In the UK, under the **Financial Services and Markets Act 2000 (FSMA)**, a person in the course of business is prohibited from communicating an invitation or inducement to engage in investment activity unless the person is authorised or the communication has been approved by an authorised person. The scope of the provision is wide and includes various forms of communication, including electronic media, solicited and unsolicited calls and letters, newsletters and prospectuses.

There are a few exceptions, one of which is a communication to a certified sophisticated investor. A sophisticated investor is one in possession of a **sophisticated investor letter (SIL)** that has been produced and signed by an authorised person. This letter states that the investor is sufficiently knowledgeable to understand the risks associated with the stated type of investment, for example, a derivative or security. The letter is deemed to be current if it has been produced within the three years preceding the communication.

9. Client Money Rules

Learning Objective

8.1.8 Understand the impact of Client Money Rules on asset servicing functions

Client money is money belonging to clients which an investment business is holding on behalf of the client. It could either be free money (ie, cash that is not needed to settle particular transactions) or settlement money and, in either case, it must be kept in a bank account separate from the firm's own money.

Financial institutions are legally bound by the regulatory rules to segregate all client money on a daily basis. These requirements create a statutory trust under which a firm must keep all client money separate from its own and which ring-fences this client money from the claims of the firm's creditors should it fail.

This protection is currently provided by the FCA Client Money Rules, which stipulate that all client money must be identified and adequate capital segregated on a daily basis. The regulator takes a serious view of failures to segregate and reconcile client assets (such as securities held in a safekeeping account) and client money. For example, in 2012, an **investment management company** was fined £9.5 million by the FSA (the predecessor regulator to the FCA) for failing to make sure that £1.3 billion in client assets were properly ring-fenced for more than three years.

The US investment group placed client money in short-term money-market deposits without making sure that the receiving banks knew they were holding assets that belonged to customers rather than the firm itself.

The regulations regarding reconciliation of client money and client assets are covered in Chapter 9.

10. Price-Sensitive Information

Learning Objective

8.1.9 Understand the impact of price-sensitive information

Price-sensitive information is information about a company's trading or other affairs which would, if generally known, be expected to have an influence on its share price; this could be an influence to increase or decrease the share price.

For example, an asset servicing institution, or one of its employees, might find out in advance of the formal announcement that a particular company is about to receive a takeover approach from another company. If an individual were to use that information to trade in the company's shares in the stock market they could be found guilty of the serious criminal offence of insider dealing.

The UK regulatory rules say that all price-sensitive information must be made available to the market as soon as practicable in an attempt to ensure that all investors get the same news on a company's trading at the same time.

11. Foreign Ownership Restrictions

Learning Objective

8.1.11 Know the implications of foreign ownership limits

Some countries impose limits on the percentage of share capital that may be owned by foreign investors in companies in particular industries. Such limits are usually applied to industries that are deemed to be critical to developing and maintaining the country's infrastructure, such as airlines, airports and telecoms. Examples include the US, which restricts foreign ownership of airline stocks to 49%, and India, which places a 26% limit on foreign ownership of insurance companies.

The practical consequence of these restrictions for asset servicing institutions is that sometimes a purchase of stock by one of their clients means that the foreign ownership limit is breached. If the breach is very large then the client needs to be advised, and may have no alternative other than to sell some of its holding. However, if the breach is small and the stock concerned is widely traded, then subsequent sales by other foreign holders in the next few days may regularise the situation, so the client could be advised to 'wait and see' for a short period. In the meantime, the holding cannot be registered in the client's name, and the client may not be entitled to receive dividends or other benefits or to vote. The stock can only be registered in **street name**, ie, the name of a broker who is a resident of the country concerned.

If an asset servicer has advised its client to 'wait and see' then it needs to have processes in place to continually monitor the level of foreign ownership of the stock concerned, and register it correctly at the earliest possible opportunity.

12. Outsourcing

Owing to the increasing use of outsourcing services by asset servicing companies, there are guidelines produced by the UK regulator to govern situations where fund managers have elements of their activities, including asset servicing, undertaken by an internal or external party. This is called outsourcing.

The guidelines cover the different stages of an outsource arrangement, for example:

- **Selection of an outsource provider** – undertake due diligence to identify how the outsource will affect the fund manager's overall risk profile.
- **Implementation** – build a set of appropriate key performance indicators (KPIs) which will be used to monitor the effectiveness and control of the outsource provider.
- **Maintenance** – the outsource provider should provide access to information, records, premises and data as necessary for the fund manager to monitor the service provided.
- **Termination** – the contract between the fund manager and the outsource provider should have rights for either party to terminate the contract under certain circumstances.

This policy came into force on 31 December 2004.

13. Sanctions

Learning Objective

8.1.12 Understand the concept of sanctions

Sanctions (and embargoes) are political trade restrictions put in place against target countries with the aim of maintaining or restoring international peace and security.

An example of a recent high-profile sanction being introduced was that against Russia (restrictive measures in view of Russia's actions in destabilising the situation in Ukraine), whereby a first set of sanctions was imposed on 31 July 2014 by the EU, essentially in line with those also set by the US government.

The level of sanctions can be specific and unique to each scenario, they can apply to both goods and services (such as banking), and can be against individuals or sovereign states.

Due to the nature of asset servicing, there must be specific checks in place within the sequence of process. Procedures and protocols should be developed, subsequent to interpretation of specific sanctions, to determine whether any underlying clients or assets are subject to sanctions upon which a corporate action event has been announced. Subsequent action is likely to be specific and will require engagement with business compliance and control officers to ensure appropriate action is taken.

14. Different Market Regulators

14.1 Italy

Regulatory Legislation

There are several Acts of Parliament that provide the legal framework for the Italian securities market. The main Acts are:

- the Legislative Decree of 24 February 1998, which is the consolidated law on financial instruments and financial intermediaries (TUF).
- the Bank of Italy Regulations of 8 September 2000 concerning the management of settlement services for transactions of non-derivative financial instruments.

Regulatory Organisations

The authorities primarily responsible for regulating and supervising the Italian securities market are the Bank of Italy and the Commissione Nazionale per le Società e la Borsa (CONSOB).

The Italian central bank, the Bank of Italy, is in charge of the following tasks:

- Supervision of banks, brokers, investment firms and funds. The Bank of Italy's responsibilities in this field extend to risk limitation and the stability of intermediaries, whereas the market regulator (CONSOB) is responsible for supervising compliance with the rules for transparency and proper conduct.
- Together with CONSOB, supervision of MTS Italy, which is the electronic market for the trading of debt securities.
- Cooperation with the Italian Antitrust Authority (AGCM) to promote and protect competition on the credit sector and prevent mergers and acquisitions from creating a dominant position in the market.
- Combating money laundering together with the Italian Foreign Exchange Office (UIC).

CONSOB was established in 1974 and reports to the Ministry of Treasury. CONSOB is the supervisory body overseeing the stock exchange; its remit includes monitoring market operating practices and regulating the activities of brokers. CONSOB is the authority for ensuring transparency and correct behaviour by securities markets participants, and the disclosure of complete and accurate information to the investing public by listed companies. Evidence suggesting acts of insider trading, manipulation or rigging must be reported to CONSOB, which is the body responsible for investigating potential market violations; CONSOB has the legal power to enforce regulations.

Legal and Compliance

The AGCM is the competition authority. It has powers to control and report to parliament and the government on areas such as agreements restricting freedom of competition, abuse of dominant position and mergers or acquisitions.

14.2 Japan

Regulatory Legislation

There are several Acts of Parliament that provide the legal framework for the Japanese securities market. The main Acts are as follows:

- Securities Exchange Act 1948.
- First Commercial Code 1890.
- Law Concerning Central Securities Depository and Book-Entry Transfer (the CSD Law) 1984.
- Law Concerning Book-Entry Transfer of Corporate Debt Securities (2001).

Regulatory Organisations

The major organisations responsible for the market regulations and developments in Japan are the Ministry of Finance, the Bank of Japan, the Financial Supervisory Agency and the Securities and Exchange Surveillance Commission:

- **Ministry of Finance** – the Ministry of Finance works closely with the Financial Supervisory Agency to plan and establish the policies relating to the bankruptcies of financial institutions and financial risk management.
- **Bank of Japan** – as the central bank, the Bank of Japan, together with the Ministry of Finance, is jointly responsible for supervising banks and regulating the money and foreign exchange markets.
- **Financial Supervisory Agency** – the Financial Supervisory Agency was established in June 1998 as an independent entity of the prime minister's office. The FSA took over the supervisory and inspections functions of the financial services industry.
- **Securities and Exchange Surveillance Commission** – the Ministry of Finance introduced the Securities and Exchange Surveillance Commission on 20 July 1992 to ensure the smooth and regular operation of the stock exchanges and the fairness of securities and financial futures trading.

14.3 US

Regulatory Legislation

The main focus of securities regulations is on the market for common stocks. Both federal and state laws regulate securities. The first of the laws to be ratified was the Federal Securities Act of 1933 (as amended), which regulates the public offering and sale of securities in interstate commerce. The 1933 Act prohibits the offer or sale of a security not registered with the SEC. It requires the disclosure of information to the prospective security's purchaser. The objective of these requirements is to enable purchasers to make fully informed and reasoned decisions based on reliable information.

Issuers of securities registered under the Securities Exchange 1934 Act must file various reports with the SEC to provide the public with adequate information. The 1934 Act also regulates proxy solicitation and requires certain information to be given to a corporation's shareholders as a prerequisite to soliciting votes. It permits the SEC to create rules and regulations to protect the investing public by prohibiting manipulative or deceptive devices via mail or other means of interstate commerce.

Regulatory Organisations

The major organisations responsible for the market regulations and developments in the United States are the SEC, the Commodity Futures Trading Commission, the National Association of Securities Dealers (NASD) and the Federal Reserve System.

The SEC, which was created by the Securities Exchange Act of 1934, is the principal regulator and supervisory body with responsibility over all securities issuance and trading, securities firms, investment companies, including mutual funds, investment advisers and all self-regulatory organisations (SROs), including the NASD, the NYSE, NASDAQ and all of the regional exchanges.

The NASD, which operates within SEC oversight, is the largest SRO in the US, with a membership that includes virtually every broker/dealer in the nation that is involved in a securities business with the public. Through its subsidiaries, the NASD develops rules and regulations, conducts regulatory reviews of members' business activities, and designs and operates marketplace services and facilities. The NASD helps to establish and coordinate the policy agendas of its subsidiaries and oversees their effectiveness.

End of Chapter Questions

Think of an answer for each question and refer to the appropriate section for confirmation.

1. What firms do the mandate rules apply to?
   Answer reference: Section 2.1

2. Which type of client receives the lowest level of protection under MiFID?
   Answer reference: Section 4.3

3. What does best execution mean?
   Answer reference: Section 4.6

4. What are the main purposes of MiFID II?
   Answer reference: Section 4.9.2

5. Why has the financial services industry developed global lending agreements?
   Answer reference: Section 5

6. What does GMSLA stand for?
   Answer reference: Section 5.1

7. What are the main actions covered by the GMRA?
   Answer reference: Section 5.2

8. Which US Act seeks to protect the public from the fraudulent issue and distribution of securities?
   Answer reference: Section 6

9. What are the requirements for disclosure under the Act?
   Answer reference: Section 6

10. What are the rules around the resale of restricted securities?
    Answer reference: Section 7

11. What does SIL stand for and what is its purpose?
    Answer reference: Section 8

12. What does price-sensitive information mean, and what do the UK regulatory rules say about it?
    Answer reference: Section 10

13. What are the names of the main regulators in the US?
    Answer reference: Section 14.3

Chapter Nine
Risks and Controls

1. Risk	185
2. Credit Risk and Market Risk	185
3. Operational Risk	187
4. Reconciliation and Segregation of Duties	190

This syllabus area will provide approximately 2 of the 50 examination questions

1. Risk

One of the major issues facing any institution such as a custodian that is employed by a client to service a portfolio of assets is to allow for the transference of risk. How the asset servicer then manages this risk is absolutely key to the success of the whole operation. This issue has become more prevalent in recent years and a far greater focus has been placed on the mitigation and management of risk. Virtually all institutions and all custodians have risk management departments and control functions whose sole role is to negate and limit the exposure the company may have to risk.

A greater appreciation within the financial services industry of the effects of risk has been brought about by many factors:

- **Greater and more efficient regulation by the market regulators** – examples such as the Sarbanes-Oxley Act (SOX), the New Capital Accord from Basel and the Basel Sound Practices for the Management and Supervision of Operational Risk have led to a greater focus on the mitigation of risk.
- **Major corporate scandals and major loss-making events** – some extremely high-profile financial scandals dating back to the mid-1980s such as the Maxwell case, Barings in the 1990s and more recent events such as Enron, AIG and Lehman Brothers.
- **Increased competition in the marketplace** – asset servicing has seen the growth of much greater competition in recent years. This has squeezed income streams. This reduction in income and profit has seen a greater focus on the elimination of risk.

There are many risks associated with asset servicing. The three common categories of financial risk are:

- **credit** – the risk of loss caused by the failure of a counterparty to pay its obligations.
- **market** – the risk of loss of earnings or capital arising from changes in the value of financial instruments and exchange rates.
- **operational** – the risk of direct or indirect loss (which can be a loss of reputation) resulting from inadequate or failed internal processes, people and systems or from external events.

It is this third risk which this chapter will look at in detail, after some background information on credit and **market risk**.

2. Credit Risk and Market Risk

2.1 Credit Risk

Credit risk is most simply defined as the potential that a counterparty will fail to meet its obligations in relation to agreed terms.

Securities firms need to manage the credit risk inherent in their entire portfolio, as well as the risk inherent in individual credits or transactions. For most banks, loans are the largest and most obvious source of credit risk. However, other sources of credit risk extend throughout the activities of a bank, including in the banking book and trading book, and both on and off the balance sheet. There is credit risk in various business lines other than lending, including trade financing, foreign exchange transactions, financial futures and options, and settling transactions.

The term 'credit risk' may embrace a range of risk elements:

- **Issuer risk** – the risk that an issuer may default on its obligations. In the case of a debt instrument, for example, this will be the risk that the issuer fails to meet interest payments and to redeem principal on the instrument on redemption date.
- **Counterparty risk** – the risk that an institution defaults on obligations outstanding to a trade counterparty prior to trade settlement.
- **Settlement risk** – occurs when there is a non-simultaneous exchange of value (eg, cash and securities).

2.2 Market Risk

Market risk is the risk of loss of earnings or capital arising as a result of movements in market prices, including interest rates, exchange rates and equity values.

Financial institutions have always faced the risk of losses on- and off-balance sheet arising from undesirable market movements. However, the sharp increase of proprietary trading in many banks has heightened the need among regulators to ensure that these institutions have the management systems to control, and the capital to absorb, the risks posed by market-related exposures.

That said, the primary focus in the 1988 Basel Accord was on credit risk, and market risk only gained a high profile when the Basel Committee on Banking Supervision published a policy document on the supervisory treatment of market risk in April 1993. This proposed that firms should set aside capital to cover the price risks inherent in their trading activities. This document put forward a standardised measurement framework to calculate market risk for interest rates, equities and currencies.

Market risk can become an issue in securities operations in several ways:

- If a settlement is delayed or a trade fails, there is the possibility that the value of the instrument will fall during this period until settlement has been finally achieved.
- If the custodian misses a corporate action (eg, a rights issue), it may be required to compensate the investor for lost entitlements. If the price of the securities moves against the custodian before this exposure is closed down, this can result in major financial losses for the custodian concerned.
- If a trade confirmation remains unmatched and it is discovered, for example, that both parties have reported a sale, instead of one a sale and the other a purchase, one may have to reverse the transaction in the market and incur a loss because the market price has changed.
- Late or failed transactions, or a missed rights issue, in illiquid markets can be difficult to rectify as additional stock may not be available to borrow or buy.

3. Operational Risk

3.1 The Causes of Operational Risk

Operational risk is defined by the Basel Committee on Banking Supervision as *'the risk of loss resulting from inadequate or failed internal processes, people and systems, or from external events'*.

All types of operational risk can be traced back to:

- processes that are involved in executing the business
- people or staff employed by the institution
- technology that is developed to support the processes and the people
- the environment within which the people, processes and technology operate. The environment has both internal influences and external influences, such as economics, law, tax policy, a change of government, the labour market, the pace of change, war and natural disasters.

3.1.1 Process Causes

Processes are activities designed to perform certain functions such as the disbursement of dividends or interest payments to clients. They are designed to be efficient and to prevent errors. If there are flaws in the process, then mistakes are made and losses result.

Some common generic examples of process issues that create operational risk are:

- lack of effective procedures and/or procedural documentation
- lack of capacity – that is, the ability of a firm to cope with business demand
- volume sensitivity – this means that staff workload increases in proportion to increasing volumes; it becomes an issue if there is a high degree of manual processes, such as in withholding tax (WHT) reclamation, and
- lack of effective controls.

3.1.2 People Causes

In the financial services industry, people are often thought of as an organisation's greatest asset. This is reflected by the high proportion of a firm's costs being attributed to staff compensation. However, the operational risks due to people-related issues are difficult to assess. This is partly because of the difficulty in measuring their effects. As the visibility of the human factor has improved, it has become even more apparent how damaging losses due to people issues can be.

In asset servicing, some of the common human causes of operational risk include:

- human error, an example being trade inputting or checking client instructions
- staff acting in an unauthorised manner or with a lack of supervision
- lack of integrity and honesty, which could lead to fraud
- lack of customer care
- lack of skills and/or insufficient training
- poor communication
- concentration of expertise, and
- in peak times, tiredness.

3.1.3 Technology Causes

All firms use technology in order to improve the effectiveness and efficiency of their processes, especially repetitive tasks. Its use is accepted as improving controls and reducing cost and, in the age of e-commerce, its importance to asset servicing is greater than ever before. However, it is also a cause of operational risk. Some technology causes are:

- lack of system availability due to operational failure, inadequate security or power failure
- lack of system integrity – if systems do not automatically pass information between themselves, there is a need for manual re-keying between systems, and inter-system reconciliations are required to ensure the integrity of data
- inadequate testing of systems in their development stage leading to later production problems; and
- lack of flexibility if a new issue or an amendment to previous issues arises.

More and more often we are seeing corporate actions, more so in emerging markets, which do not follow a logical or formulaic sequence, thus preventing automation in any way.

3.1.4 Environmental Causes

The three causes of process, people and technology are inherent in the internal structure of an organisation. The environmental causes have an impact by exacerbating the risks that already exist in these areas, and the other causes of risk cannot be adequately understood without taking these environmental issues into account. Some examples of environmental causes are:

- changes in the regulatory or tax environment
- the accelerating increase in trade volumes as a result of increased market activity, resulting in greater pressure on staff, their processes and technology, and
- the increasing pace of change. The management of change is a major area that is becoming an ever-greater issue for financial institutions as the environment in which they operate becomes more and more complex.

3.2 Key Risks in Asset Servicing

Learning Objective

9.1.1 Know the key risks of corporate action processing

Provided below are examples of asset servicing risks and their implications:

- **Providing/receiving inaccurate information** – if asset servicing institutions provide incorrect or inadequate information to fund managers then the fund managers will not be best placed to make a sound decision. Through basing a decision on the information provided, they may choose unwisely and lose value on their investments. The asset servicing team may be required to compensate the fund manager to rectify the position if incorrect information has altered its decision and negatively impacted it. If, on the other hand, asset servicing receives incorrect information from a fund manager in terms of a decision taken, this is the fund manager's responsibility and, as such, corrective action would be taken as a relationship issue and on a reasonable endeavours basis.

- **Providing/receiving incomplete information** – as per the above, asset servicing/custodians would be responsible for any costs/losses incurred. However, if full information is not available because of market conditions, the asset service department would not be held liable or responsible.
- **Failing to provide any information** – as a result, the fund manager may not be aware of the event and will be unable to take a decision.
- **Applying incorrect instructions** – the asset servicing department would be duty-bound to rectify the situation to reflect the fund manager's decision for the event. As a consequence, it may incur unlimited losses/costs depending on market conditions. Any profit made by the team may be passed on to the client, although, depending on the status of the fund, some clients may decline due to undue enrichment rules.
- **Failing to apply instructions** – again, asset servicing would be forced to make the client good to reflect the fund manager's decision for the event. As a consequence, it may incur unlimited losses/costs depending on market conditions.
- **Missed deadlines** – if the fund manager is responsible for missing the deadline by not submitting the instruction, this is not an asset servicing risk. The fund manager may miss the internally set deadline and will then be advised that the response will be dealt with on a 'reasonable endeavours' basis. Alternatively, the fund manager may miss the custodian deadline and, if applicable, the default action will be applied. If asset servicing misses the custodian deadline it then becomes responsible for reimbursing the fund manager with any losses incurred, and these are unlimited and dependent on market conditions.
- **Updates of entitlement** – the correct and timely updating of in-house systems to reflect client positions is vitally important, both for trading and fund accounting. Erroneous trades posted onto a system can lead to missed entitlement. For example, if the trade capture section within a custodian had neglected to input a transaction on the in-house custody system, this could have severe implications for the asset servicing team, who would not be able to reconcile the position to the market. A situation could develop whereby a protection might be required with a market counterparty. This will be subject to a deadline if it is a voluntary corporate action. If this deadline is missed and results in a monetary loss the custodian may have to make the client good.

3.3 Implications of Misleading Information

Learning Objective

9.1.2 Understand the risks arising from misleading information

Asset servicing departments are only as good as the information received from their subcustodians. If this is inaccurate, the fund manager may be provided with incorrect information and thereby make a decision that is not fully informed. In such an event, the custodian may be required to make good any claims made by the fund manager.

- **Poor or wrong investment decision** – if a fund manager makes a poor investment decision, the fund may suffer a loss. Only if it can be determined that a manager has acted against the fund mandate (for weighting/exposure, etc) will the client be compensated.
- **Missing deadlines** – if misleading information is passed on, this could lead to missing a deadline. The entity who passed on the information would then be held liable. As most asset servicing voluntary events have a strict deadline, this would again lead to the custodian making the client's position good. An example of this would be a missed deadline relating to a rights issue. As the issue would be backed by an **underwriting**, once the deadline for acceptance has been reached then no

further call monies can be accepted. In this scenario the custodian may be required to buy shares in the open market and credit them to their client's account, debiting the client for what the original call money would have been. If there was a premium on these shares in relation to the call price, then this would lead to a monetary loss.
- **Providing inaccurate terms, valuations and pricing** – this could lead a fund manager to make a decision it would not otherwise make. For example, the fund manager may choose to lapse instead of take up rights. Asset servicing may be required to rectify this, post-event, by buying in or selling stock and suffering any associated loss.
- **Pricing is vitally important to unit trust managers** – one of the major risks they face relating to the incorrect pricing of a unit trust would be reputational risk. Regulatory requirements are very strict in relation to the rules on pricing and therefore the guilty company may receive a fine and bad press; this can severely affect reputation.

4. Reconciliation and Segregation of Duties

Learning Objective

9.1.3 Understand the importance of reconciliation and segregation of duties

4.1 Reconciliation of Clients' Securities

All firms have regulatory obligations under the FCA's Client Asset (CASS) rules. This set of rules was radically revised following the publication of the FCA's Policy statement PS14/9 in June 2014. As the revised rules, for many firms, required procedural and/or software changes, they were implemented in three stages. The target date for the third and final stage was 1 June 2015. The rules described and analysed in this section are the rules that were operative from that date.

CASS 6.6.8 through to 6.6.58 is a very large group of rules that deal specifically with reconciliations of customer assets. These rules include:

- permissible reconciliation methods
- frequency of reconciliation
- separation of duties
- problem resolution
- reporting problems to the regulator.

Permissible Reconciliation Methods

Rules 6.6.10 through to 6.6.32 define, in very great detail, the following reconciliation methods:

- An **Internal Custody Record Check** – a check as to whether the firm's records and accounts of the safe custody assets held by the firm (including, for example, those deposited with third parties) correspond with the firm's obligations to its clients. This means that if the firm's records show that it is holding 1,000 units of a particular asset for each of ten clients, then it must hold 10,000 units in total. These assets may be held by the firm's custodian, or they may be held physically by the firm, or there might be some combination of the two.

- A **Physical Asset Reconciliation** – the name the regulator gives to the process of reconciling any assets that are held physically. The rules permit two possible methods of performing this reconciliation:
    - the **Total Count Method**, whereby all the customer assets held by the firm are counted and reconciled on the same day, and
    - the **Rolling Stock Method**, whereby one group of assets is counted and reconciled on one day, and other groups are counted and reconciled on other days.
- An **External Custody Reconciliation** – the process of agreeing the firm's records of custody assets with the records of its custodians.

Frequency of Reconciliations

Rule 6.6.44 requires firms to decide how often to perform these reconciliations. It does not prescribe a 'one size fits all' rule. The rule requires firms to decide for themselves how often to carry out these checks but, when making the decision: they must take into account the:

1. frequency, number and value of transactions which the firm undertakes in respect of clients' safe custody assets
2. risks to which clients' safe custody assets are exposed, such as the nature, volume and complexity of the firm's business, and where and with whom safe custody assets are held.

Rule 6.6.45 requires that firms keep a written record of the decision process that they used to choose a particular reconciliation frequency, and Rule 6.6.46 orders them to review such decisions regularly in the light of changing business activities, processes or volumes.

Separation of Duties

Rule 6.6.47 requires firms, whenever possible, to ensure that checks and reconciliations are carried out by a person who is independent of the production or maintenance of the records to be checked and/or reconciled.

Problem Resolution

CASS 6.6.49 and CASS 6.6.50 require firms to promptly investigate discrepancies and Rule 6.6.54 requires them to make good any shortfall from their own resources if the discrepancies cannot be resolved in any other way.

Reporting Problems to the Regulator

CASS 6.6.57 requires a firm to notify the Financial Conduct Authority (FCA), in writing and without delay, if it discovers:

1. its internal records and accounts of the safe custody assets held by the firm for clients are materially out of date or materially inaccurate or invalid
2. it will be unable, or materially fail, to take the steps required under CASS 6.6.54 for the treatment of shortfalls, or
3. it will be unable, or materially fail, to conduct an internal custody record check in compliance with CASS 6.6.11 to CASS 6.6.19 , or
4. it will be unable, or materially fail, to conduct a physical asset reconciliation in compliance with CASS 6.6.2 to CASS 6.6.30, or
5. it will be unable, or materially fail, to conduct an external custody reconciliation in compliance with CASS 6.6.34 to CASS 6.6.37.

Client Money Reconciliations

The rules concerning the reconciliation of client money are covered by Section 7.15 of the Client Money Rules.

- CASS 7.15.12 requires firms to carry out a client money reconciliation. This is a reconciliation of its internal records and accounts of the amount of client money that the firm holds for each client with its internal records and accounts of the client money the firm should hold in client bank accounts or has placed in client transaction accounts.
- CASS 7.15.13 stipulates that when carrying out an internal client money reconciliation, a firm must use the values contained in its internal records and ledgers (for example, its cash book or other internal accounting records) rather than the values contained in the records it has obtained from banks and other third parties with whom it has placed client money (for example, bank statements).
- CASS 7.15.14 stipulates that an internal client money reconciliation should be one of the steps a firm takes to arrange adequate protection for clients' assets when the firm is responsible for them.
- CASS 7.15.27 and 7.15.28 deal with reconciliation frequencies, and CASS 7.15.29 through to 7.15.32 deal with what actions firms must take when discrepancies are revealed. These rules are broadly the same as CASS 6.6.49 through to 6.6.54 which were explained in the previous section of this workbook.
- CASS 7.15.33 requires firms to notify the FCA 'in writing without delay' if it discovers:
    1. its internal records and accounts of the client money held by the firm for clients are materially out of date, or materially inaccurate or invalid, or
    2. it will be unable or materially fail to take the steps required under CASS 7.15.29 through to 7.15.32 for the treatment of shortfalls.

End of Chapter Questions

Think of an answer for each question and refer to the appropriate section for confirmation.

1. What is the definition of credit risk?
   Answer reference: Sections 1 and 2.1

2. What is the definition of market risk?
   Answer reference: Sections 1 and 2.2

3. What are the four main causes of operational risk?
   Answer reference: Section 3.1

4. List three of the key risks in asset servicing and explain the consequences to the client and to the asset servicing company.
   Answer reference: Sections 3.2 and 3.3

5. What must a regulated firm do if it finds that its internal records and accounts of the safe custody assets held by the firm for clients are materially out of date?
   Answer reference: Section 4.1

Glossary and Abbreviations

Glossary and Abbreviations

1933 Securities Act (as amended)

The US Act designed to protect the public from the issuance and distribution of fraudulent securities, also called the Full Disclosure Act. It requires issuers to register a detailed and truthful statement with the SEC describing any new offering.

Acceptance Date

The date specified by company registrars/agents by which client instructions need to be lodged.

Accrual

A method of accounting in which each item of income or expense is entered as it is earned or incurred, regardless of when actual payments are received or made.

Accrued Interest

The amount of interest that has been earned on a bond but not yet paid to the bondholder (because payment is made only on set dates).

Administrator

The person assigned by the courts who takes over executive responsibility of a company in liquidation in order to ensure that creditors are protected.

Agent Deadline

A deadline set by an agent by which time it must receive responses to voluntary corporate actions in order that it can collate them and meet the Market Deadline.

Allotment Letter

Document sent out by the company's registrars to shareholders on the register at *Record Date* of a rights issue, showing entitlement and cash amount due on call date.

American Depositary Receipt (ADR)

Depositary receipts are instruments which simplify the international buying, selling and holding of securities. Depositary receipts represent equities but may also represent preferred shares, convertibles and debt, with or without warrants. All depositary receipts are based upon the same principle: they create a substitute instrument for international ownership of shares in a company when use of the original instrument (share certificate) would entail inconvenience, delay, added expense and unnecessary risk. Originally designed for overseas companies to gain US listings where access to the local market was difficult for US clients. Less important now due to global relocation of major US trading houses.

Annual General Meeting (AGM)

Meeting held annually to discuss and vote on the three mandatory resolutions, and those recommended by a company's board.

Arbitrage

The simultaneous purchase and sale of substantially identical assets in order to profit from a price difference between the two assets.

Asset-Backed Securities (ABSs)

Bonds that entitle the holder to the cash flows of a specified pool of company assets. These assets are usually loans made by the originating institution. The most common form of ABS results from repackaging mortgages (also called, more specifically, mortgage-backed securities). Other types are backed by obligations such as car loans, student loans and credit card receivables.

Asset Stripping

When a firm mounts a takeover on a target firm with the intent of breaking it up and selling its assets for profit, rather than running it as a going concern.

Association for Financial Markets in Europe (AFME)

AFME is the voice of Europe's wholesale financial markets, representing the leading global and European banks and other significant capital market players. It focuses on a wide range of market, business and prudential issues and offers a pan-European perspective, bringing to bear deep policy and technical expertise and constructive influence on European and global policymakers.

At-the-Money
A warrant or other derivative that will return neither a profit nor loss if it is exercised.

Authorised Share Capital
The maximum amount of share capital that a company can issue without the need to change the memorandum.

Auto-Depository Compensation
A depository automatically reclaims a corporate-actions-related benefit on behalf of the party holding stock if for any reason (eg, late booking or failed trade) the benefit was not paid to the correct party.

Bearer Security
A type of security where physical possession of the certificate is proof of ownership.

Beneficial Owner
The ultimate entity that exercises controls over, and receives the entitlements from, a particular asset. In the modern context this entity is seldom the name registered on the company register. A fund manager may well hold private client assets. There is normally a chain of custodianship of the asset. A global custodian will hold these in turn as part of the fund manager's holdings. In the case of overseas holdings a subcustodian to the order of the global custodian may in turn hold these. The registered holder on the books of the company will be the subcustodian, but the beneficial owner will still be the private client. Ultimate ownership must be tracked back through the books of several custodians and a fund manager.

Board Lot
Standard tradeable unit of shares in the market.

Bond
Fundamentally a bond is an acknowledgement in paper or book entry form of a loan made to a company that is redeemable under conditions specified at the time that the loan was made. Most bonds (but not all) will pay income at any agreed rate at specified periods. Most bonds specify the final date when the capital sum lent to the company must be repaid. Some bonds allow the holding to be converted into shares or other instruments issued by the company.

Bonus Issue
An issue of fully paid new shares from a company's reserve, free of payment, to the existing shareholders in proportion to the existing holdings at a specified date (the Record Date). The object of such an issue may be to make the market in the shares more 'liquid' by increasing the number in circulation. Companies do not always issue the same type of shares for a bonus.

Bullet Redemption
The redemption of a bond by a single lump sum payment.

Calculation Agent
The agent bank responsible for telling the paying agent how much is being paid on an issue based on its terms and conditions.

Call Date
The date specified by a company for which the payment of new shares is required.

Call Option (on a bond)
A clause in a bond's issue giving the issuer the right to ask for early redemption.

Call Payment
The cash a shareholder sends to a receiving agent as payment for additional shares in a rights issue.

Glossary and Abbreviations

Call Provision

A special feature of a bond giving the issuer the right to redeem the security before maturity.

Call Warrant

A warrant that gives the holder the right to buy the underlying share.

Capital Gains Tax (CGT)

A tax on the increase in the value of an asset ie, the difference between its sale and purchase price.

Capital Growth

The increase in the value of a financial instrument which is realised when the instrument is sold.

Capital Repayments

A payment made by a company to its shareholders to repay some of its issued share capital.

Central Counterparty (CCP)

An entity that sits between the buyer and seller of an exchange-traded security and acts a guarantor of contracts. By this means, the exchange assumes the credit risk, thereby limiting the exposure of its members by protecting them from the impact of default.

Central Securities Depository (CSD)

An institution that holds all the securities for a particular market. By doing so, it centralises the securities of a particular market, making settlement easier.

Certificates of Deposit (CDs)

Certificates of deposit (CDs) are unsecured, short-term, interest-bearing instruments. A CD represents a sum on a fixed-term deposit with a bank or building society.

Class Action

Globally, but mainly in the United States, minority shareholders who are not satisfied with the actions taken by a company and take the view that this may have materially affected the share price in the market. This results in a class action for compensation. Other purchasers of the stock over the same period are invited to join the action.

Clean Price

The price of a bond excluding *Accrued Interest*.

Clearing

The process whereby the two parties to a trade assume responsibility for it.

Clearing Agent

An agent that manages the process of clearing on its clients' behalf. This includes matching the settlement details of seller and buyer.

Commercial Paper (CP)

Unsecured, short-term bearer security. It is usually issued by a company in the same way that a bank issues a CD, except that it is not usually interest-bearing (ie, priced at a discount to the face value).

Commodity Price Risk

This is the risk of an adverse movement in the price of a commodity.

Common Stock

The US term for Ordinary Shares.

Consideration

The entity paid or received for a trade.

Consolidation

When a company consolidates its existing share capital into fewer shares of a higher par value. This change will alter (decrease) the number of shares authorised within the company and will therefore affect the market price per share. Also known as a Reverse Split.

Conversion Agent

The agent bank appointed by the bond issuer to manage the mechanics of a conversion.

Conversion Event

An event when the characteristics of a financial instrument are changed.

Convertibility

A special feature of a bond giving the holder the right to exchange the bond for a set number of shares at a stated price.

Convertible Preference Shares

Preference shares that can be converted to ordinary shares at any point, giving the investor some flexibility over the instrument's income stream.

Corporate Action

Any activity instigated by a company which may affect its capital shares and/or cash.

Counterparty

One party of a trade legally bound to make good delivery or a good payment.

Counterparty Risk

The risk that a counterparty will default on its obligations.

Coupon

The periodic interest rate declared on a bond or bearer security. Owing to the bearer nature, these are paid usually by sending a removable part of the certificate (the coupon) to the registrar.

Credit Rating

A measure of the quality of a bond and a reflection of the creditworthiness of the issuer, determined by external rating agencies such as Moody's and Standard & Poor's.

Credit Risk

The risk of loss caused by the failure of a counterparty to pay its obligations.

Cum-dividend

Term used to indicate that shares are being transferred with (cum) the right to receive the dividend.

Cumulative Preference Share

A type of preference share which carries the right to receive any fixed dividend not paid by the issuer in the previous year.

Custodian

Organisation which holds clients' assets in safe custody, ensures that they are not released without proper authorisation and ensures the timely and accurate collection of dividends and other benefits.

DACE (Deadlines and Corporate Event) Notices

Notification of corporate actions, produced by Euroclear and distributed electronically to their members.

Data/Information Vendors

Companies which provide securities-related information to the investment management community for a fee.

Debenture

A type of bond that in the US is unsecured and in the UK is secured on specified assets of the company.

Default

Failure of a debtor to pay interest or to repay principal when payment is due.

Glossary and Abbreviations

Defence

During a takeover, the target company may not wish to be taken over. It may, therefore, adopt a strategy called defence to prevent the takeover going through.

Deferred Shares

A class of share where the holder is only entitled to a dividend if ordinary shareholders have been paid a specified minimum dividend. Deferred shares carry negligible rights. They do not usually carry voting rights or entitle the holder to any dividends or a return of capital on a winding-up except in very limited circumstances.

Dematerialised

Securities where certificates or documents of title have been eliminated and replaced by book entry records.

Demerger

An issue of shares free of payment to existing shareholders, similar to a *Bonus Issue*, but entitlements received are shares to be quoted separately from the parent company. The action turns the subsidiary into an independent company, which has its own shares and listing on the market. It effectively demerges the subsidiary from its parent.

Depositary Receipt (DR)

Negotiable certificates that represent a fraction or multiple of a number of foreign shares. They allow investors to invest in foreign securities using their local exchange.

Depository

A centralised body which typically enables members to hold book entry accounts for dematerialised securities, settles transactions between members on a delivery-versus-payment basis, and provides basic custody services. May also hold certificated securities in secure storage.

Derivative

An instrument whose value is derived from an underlying instrument such as a share or the price of a commodity, rather than having intrinsic value. Examples are options, swaps and warrants.

Dirty Price

The price of a bond including accrued interest.

Dissenting Shareholders

Shareholders in a company which has met the criteria of being taken over, who for their own reasons do not wish to receive the takeover consideration and, thereby, remain nominally shareholders of the old company. Dissent is not allowed in all markets worldwide.

Dividend

Allocation, in the form of cash, of a portion of company profits to a shareholder on a pro rata basis. Dividends may also be paid in the equivalent amount of shares (stock dividend).

Dividend Reinvestment Plan (DRIP)/Bonus Share Plan (BSP)

When a company offers its shareholders the option to enrol in a dividend reinvestment or bonus share plan. Once enrolled in the plan, it is like a standing instruction until cancelled. Certain companies also give investors the option to enrol in the plan at time of purchase.

Double Taxation Agreement (DTA)

A bilateral agreement between two states that exists in order to encourage and maintain an international consensus on cross-border economic activity and to promote international trade. From an investor's perspective, it contains clauses that prevent double taxation if the same income is taxable in two states. Also called a Double Taxation Treaty (DTT).

Drawings

Drawings and partial redemptions are similar. The company makes repayment at various stages of the life of the security, usually with reduction in the nominal value. The holdings are placed in a pool and the bonds to be redeemed are selected by lottery.

Dutch Auction

Similar to a tender except that the company offers to purchase its common shares at an amount between two prices to be determined by the company. Shareholders are invited to tender their shares at a price they are prepared to accept.

Enhanced Cooperation

Enhanced cooperation is a European Union principle which allows those countries of the Union that wish to continue to work more closely together to do so, while respecting the legal framework of the Union. The member states concerned can thus move forward at different speeds and/or towards different goals.

Escrow

An account held by the registrar in CREST which is a pool of all the accepted shares in relation to a takeover. Once in escrow, these shares are not normally tradeable.

Eurobond

Bonds issued outside the country of the borrower, denominated in a currency which is generally not that of the issuer's country. Settlement takes place through the international clearing system (Euroclear and Clearstream). This market is regulated by ICMA (formally known as ISMA).

Ex-Date

A cut-off date designated to identify trades which are entitled to the issue. Purchases up to this date will qualify as will any sales traded after this specific date.

Ex-Dividend

Term used to indicate that shares are being transferred without (ex) the right to receive the next dividend.

Expiry Date

The last day for which an offer can be accepted.

Extraordinary General Meeting (EGM)

A meeting of shareholders called at any time for a special purpose.

Financial Conduct Authority (FCA)

The Financial Conduct Authority replaced the Financial Services Authority as the body responsible for regulating conduct in retail and wholesale markets, supervising the trading infrastructure that supports those markets and for the prudential regulation of firms not prudentially regulated by the Prudential Regulation Authority (PRA).

Financial Services and Markets Act 2000 (FSMA 2000)

FSMA 2000 which came into force on 1 December 2001 replaced and consolidated a variety of previous legislation surrounding the financial services industry in the UK.

Financial Transaction Tax (FTT)

A proposal made by the European Commission to introduce a financial transaction tax (FTT) within some of the member states of the European Union. This was intended to come into force on 1 January 2014, but was later postponed to 1 January 2016. This latter date has subsequently been passed without the proposal coming into force and without a replacement date, thus far, being established.

Floating-Rate Note (FRN)

A type of bond issued by a company when the interest paid is determined by a marketplace such as LIBOR.

Foreign Accounts Tax Compliance Act (FATCA)

FATCA is a development by the US tax authorities in their efforts to combat tax evasion by US persons holding investments in offshore accounts. It was enacted in March 2010 and came into force in January 2013.

Foreign Ownership Restrictions

Limits and restrictions of various kinds imposed by countries on individuals, firms and financial institutions in order to control ownership of shares, thereby protecting the national interest and/or to protect investors.

Free of Payment

a. The movement of assets for which there is no associated (cash) countervalue.
b. The movement of assets, which is not dependent on the simultaneous payment of the cash countervalue.

Fully Paid Rights

Once a call payment has been made during a rights issue, the shareholder then holds fully paid rights rather than nil-paid rights.

Global Agreements

Standard legal documents covering securities lending designed to standardise terms and conditions for lending and borrowing in order to reduce the legal risk and improve the efficiency of the practice.

Global Depositary Receipts (GDRs)

Non-US depositary receipts that usually settle through international central securities depositaries. Also known as International Depositary Receipts.

Global Master Repurchase Agreement (GMRA)

The accepted industry contractual template for performing repo and buy/sell back transactions.

Global Master Securities Lending Agreement (GMSLA)

The accepted industry contractual template for performing stock lending transactions.

Government Bonds

Long-term, interest-bearing securities. They are issued by governments to finance fiscal deficits or capital spending.

In-the-Money

A warrant or other derivative that will return a positive value if it is exercised. It may not make a profit, as it will depend on the price paid for the derivative.

Initial Margin

A means employed by an exchange of receiving collateral when a position is first opened. Initial margin is collected at the start of each day's trading.

Initial Public Offering (IPO)

The initial sale of a company's shares to the public. This will involve publishing a prospectus which sets out the details of the company to be floated, setting an offer price for the shares and receiving applications.

Interest Rate Convention

A method of calculating the interest payable on interest-bearing bonds.

International Depositary Receipts (IDRs)

Non-US depositary receipts that usually settle through international central securities depositories. Also known as Global Depositary Receipts (GDRs).

Investment Management Company

An institution that provides its clients with a full range of investment management and custody services.

ISO 15022

A message standard introduced in 2002 which, as one of its benefits, was designed to allow for better automation of corporate action messages.

ISO 20022

A more comprehensive message standard developed in 2005 which is based on the use of a standard data dictionary and XML message rules.

Issued Share Capital

The total value of share capital that has been issued by the company. Note that this may be different to the Authorised Share Capital.

Issuer

A company or government entity that chooses to raise money in the capital markets through the issue of securities.

Issuer Risk

The risk of default when one institution holds debt securities issued by another institution.

Lapsed Rights Proceeds

Lapsed rights proceeds are sometimes paid on allotments for which the call has not been paid.

Lazy Money

The value lost when a warrant that is in-the-money is not exercised prior to expiry date.

Lead Manager

The principal investment house in a syndicate handling a new issue of securities. It will be appointed by the issuing company. The lead manager is said to 'run the book' on behalf of the issuer.

Liquidation

A company goes into liquidation when the business objectives can no longer be applied owing to factors such as debt default by the company. The company assets are realised and creditors and holders of capital paid out according to their priority, if adequate funds are available. Also the reduction of the number of units in issue in an authorised unit trust.

Long Coupon

The amount paid on the second coupon date of a bond that is equivalent to something more than the whole coupon. This results from a bond being issued between two coupon dates.

Mandatory Conversion

Compulsory conversion of stock or shares into another class of stock or shares.

Mandatory Corporate Action

A corporate action that does not require a decision on the part of the investor.

Margin

Collateral on open positions to insure against the risk of default.

Market Deadline

A deadline set by the firm whose shares are subject of the voluntary corporate action. All responses must be received at the firm or its agent by this date and time for the response to be acted upon.

Market Risk

The risk of loss of earnings or capital arising from changes in the value of financial instruments.

Maturity

The period of time to redemption of a bond.

Merger

When two or more companies combine capital and operate their business as one company.

Multilateral Trading Facility (MTF)

A facility that brings together multiple parties (eg, retail investors or other investment firms) that are interested in buying and selling financial instruments, and enables them to do so.

Netting

Settlement of cash or securities by summing up credits and debits and delivering or claiming the resulting amount in one movement. Netting can be bilateral, multilateral or continuous net settlement.

New Issue

Also called a placement or initial public offering (IPO). Issue of new shares to the general public as part of the process of obtaining a stock market listing or the creation of a new company.

Nil-Paid Security

An entitlement to buy additional shares in a company at a discount to market price, given as part of a rights issue. The security is nil-paid as the shareholder does not need to transfer any cash to receive it.

Non-Cumulative Preference Shares

If the company fails to pay a preference dividend the entitlement to the dividend is simply lost. There is no accumulation.

Non-Renounceable

Ownership cannot be transferred to another beneficiary and entitlements are not tradeable.

Non-Voting Shares

These shares usually have all the rights of ordinary shares but do not confer any voting rights. However, some class 'A' shares do not entitle holders to vote in any circumstances.

Odd Lot

A quantity of shares which is less than the normal trading unit, not an exact multiple of a board lot. Will often be traded at a disadvantageous price to a board lot.

Open Offer

Right to apply for new shares by existing shareholders in proportion to their existing holding.

Operational Risk

The risk of direct or indirect loss resulting from inadequate or failed internal processes, people and systems or from external events.

Orderly Default

A process whereby a debtor state or company that is financially distressed renegotiates the terms of its debt issues with creditors.

Ordinary Shares

Shares in a company which are entitled to the balance of profits and assets after all prior charges. Also known as equity shares or common stock.

Out-of-the-Money

A warrant or other derivative that will return a negative value if it is exercised.

Par Value

Equal to the nominal or face value of a security.

Pari Passu

Ranking in all respects equal to existing shares.

Partial Redemption

Similar to redemption, the difference being repayment is made by the company at various stages of the life of the security, usually without reduction in the nominal value. The holding will remain the same but the value per unit will fall until the final payment at maturity.

Paying Agent

The agent bank collects monies for disbursement from the issuer, advises clearing agents of the monies due and makes the appropriate payment to the clearing agent.

Payment Date

During the dividend cycle, the date at which the dividend is paid to the party who held the shares on record date.

Placing

A public offer to purchase stock at a set price. When there is a floating of a company on the stock exchange or an issue of new stock, certain institutions may underwrite or agree to a placement of the issue.

Poison Pill

A strategy that is employed by a company that is the subject of a takeover bid or merger approach that is designed to increase the likelihood of negative results over positive ones for the company that has made the takeover approach.

Poison Pill Rights

A selective rights issue which allows additional shares to be issued to some shareholders. Used to deter aggressive takeovers by diluting the shareholding of the bidding company.

Position Monitoring

The daily analysis of an individual exchange member's exposure risk in relation to their ability to cover their margin liabilities and delivery obligations.

Predator

A company which is attempting to take over another company (the target company).

Pre-emption Rights

When a company proposes to issue new shares, existing shareholders may have the right to be offered a pro rata part of the new shares before they are offered to a new shareholder. The rights are contained either in the Articles of Association or imposed by Section 89 of the Companies Act 1985.

Preference Shares

Preference shares normally rank in priority for dividend and, in a winding-up or other repayment of capital, for return of paid up capital together with any arrears of dividend but do not participate in any further distribution of assets. Preference shareholders are usually only entitled to vote at a general meeting of the company where rights are directly involved if their dividend is in arrears.

Primary Market

The capital marketplace where a bond, equity or loan is initially issued.

Private Placement

The sale of bonds to a hand-picked group of institutional investors (ie, not into the public marketplace). As a result the sale is not governed by the same regulations as a normal issue and the bonds are restricted.

Proxy Voting

Voting on company issues by a representative (the proxy) of the shareholder. Note all UK companies must hold an annual general meeting every 15 months and a minimum of 21 days' notice of the AGM must be given to shareholders. Only 14 days' notice need be given of an extraordinary general meeting unless a special resolution is being proposed.

Proxy Voting Agent or Voting Service Provider

A specialist firm which performs some or all of the corporate governance functions on behalf of investors.

Prudential Regulation Authority (PRA)

The Prudential Regulatory Authority (PRA), a subsidiary of the Bank of England, is responsible for the prudential regulation of financial firms, including banks, investment banks, building societies and insurance companies.

Put Option (on a bond)

A clause in a bond's issue giving the bondholder the right to ask for early redemption.

Put Warrant

A warrant that gives the holder the right to sell the underlying share.

Qualified Institutional Buyer (QIB)

A sophisticated investor who invests (on behalf of themselves or other QIBs) at least $100 million worth of securities.

Reasonable Endeavours

The term used when a custodian or broker receives an instruction that it cannot guarantee to execute because of deadline, local market practices, or factors beyond the custodian's or broker's control.

Receiving Agent

The agent bank that receives corporate action payments from the clearing agent on behalf of its client.

Record Date

The date that determines the eligibility of a shareholder to receive the current declared dividend.

Redemption/Repayments

Redemption and repayments are basically similar operations whereby either loan stock is repaid or redeemable securities are redeemed on a specific date. These securities have a limited lifespan at the end of which stock is usually redeemed at par.

Register

The records detailing, for example, owners and transfers..

Registrar

A company charged with the responsibility of keeping a record of the owners of corporations' securities and preventing the issue of more than the authorised amount.

Repatriation

The specific act of bringing capital sent to a foreign location or income earned from that investment back into the investor's home country.

Repo (Repurchase Agreement)

An arrangement whereby one party (the repo seller) sells a security to another party (the repo buyer) and simultaneously agrees to repurchase the same security at a subsequent date at an agreed price.

Restrictions

A special feature of a bond whereby unregistered bonds are acquired from the issuer in private sales (called a *Private Placement*). As a result, they have restricted transferability for a certain period of time.

Reverse Repo

The same arrangement as a repo viewed from the security buyer's perspective, ie, the arrangement is set up in order to borrow securities using cash as collateral.

Rights Issue

Offering of ordinary shares to investors who currently hold shares which entitle them to buy subsequent issues at a discount from the offering price.

Sanctions (and embargoes)

Political trade restrictions put in place against target countries with the aim of maintaining or restoring international peace and security.

Scrip Dividend

This is a choice of payment of a dividend in shares rather than cash.

SEC Rule 144a

An amendment to the 1933 Securities Act (as amended), issued in April 1990 to address the specific requirements of participating in private placements by non-US domiciled entities in the US market.

Secondary Market

The capital marketplace where a financial instrument is traded once it has been issued.

Security Identification Number

This is a unique security reference number and must conform with an internationally recognised standard such as the International Securities Identification Number (ISIN) code or Committee on Uniform Securities Identification Procedures (CUSIP) number.

Settlement Risk

The risk that occurs when there is a non-simultaneous exchange of value and one party defaults.

Short Coupon

The amount paid on the first coupon date of a bond that is equivalent to something less than the whole coupon. This results from a bond being issued between two coupon dates.

Sophisticated Investor

Certain issues carry restrictions, whereby US shareholders are not eligible to participate in issues, as entitlements received are not registered under the United States Social Security Act of 1933 (as amended). This restriction can at times be waived upon production of a Sophisticated Investor Letter (SIL) which exempts the company from any legal responsibilities for the ownership of these shares.

Sophisticated Investor Letter (SIL)

A letter that certifies to the issuer that a purchase made under a private placement is for investment purposes only and that there is no intention to immediately re-offer the securities publicly.

Special Purpose Vehicle (SPV)

A company set up by an institution that has a very high credit rating and is used to issue structured financial instruments.

Stamp Duty

A UK tax levied on the transfer of chargeable securities in physical form.

Stamp Duty Reserve Tax (SDRT)

A UK tax levied as the transfer of chargeable securities in dematerialised form.

Stock Borrowing

A method by which market makers are able to borrow securities in order to make up a shortage in those securities and in exchange for a fee.

Stock Dividend

A dividend paid in stock rather than cash in proportion to their original holding as at a specified date.

Stock Lending

Authorised institutions lend their assets and, when permitted, those of their clients to market makers through a network of intermediaries in exchange for a fee.

Stock Situation Notice (SSN)

A notice issued by the London Stock Exchange to advise of the details of an event and dates.

Straight-Through Processing (STP)

Process whereby an instruction or information received is processed without manual intervention.

Street Name

A brokerage account where the customer's securities and assets are held under the name of the brokerage firm, rather than the name of the individual who purchased the securities or assets. Although the name on the certificate is not that of the individual, they are still listed as the real and beneficial owner and would usually have the rights associated with the security. However, the beneficial owner may not have these rights if the reason that the stock is registered in street name is because of a breach of a foreign ownership limit.

Strike Price

For a warrant or option, the predetermined price at which the holder can buy the underlying share.

Stripping

The action of removing the coupons from a normal bond and selling them separately with a face value and maturity equal to each interest payment. Both the coupons and the original bond become zero coupon bonds.

Glossary and Abbreviations

Subdivision

When a company multiplies its existing shares into new shares of a lower par value. This occurs when the number of outstanding shares is changed as a result of a vote approved by shareholders and authorised by the company's board of directors. There is no change in the market value of the company, hence the total value of all shares prior to the split must equal the total value of all shares after the subdivision. A subdivision is also known as a split, stock split, split-up or forward split.

SWIFT

Society for Worldwide Interbank Financial Telecommunications. It runs a secure electronic communications network between banks. It has introduced the MT56 series of messages under ISO 15022 that are a standardised way of sending corporate action notifications.

Takeover

A voluntary event when a bidding company attempts to acquire a controlling interest (50% plus one share) in a target company.

Target2-Securities (T2S)

A European securities settlement engine which aims to offer centralised delivery-versus-payment (DvP) settlement in central bank funds across all European securities markets.

Tender Agent

The agent bank that manages the tender process on behalf of the issuer.

Tender Offer

An offer to purchase outstanding shares of a security at a specified price. The company can make the offer itself, or through a subsidiary of the company or another company.

Trade Date

The date a trade was dealt.

Treasury Bills

Short-term domestic bonds issued by governments to raise short-term finance. They are generally non-interest-bearing, issued at a discount with a term of 13, 26 or 52 weeks.

Trustee

A person who administers a trust. The trustee will be the holder of legal title to the investments that make up the trust and will act in a fiduciary capacity to its clients.

Underwriter

A company, usually an investment bank, that supports a new issue of shares by agreeing, for a fee, to purchase any shares from the company which are not taken up by existing shareholders or the marketplace.

Underwriting

An agreement to take up any residual shares left over from an offer for a commission.

Value-Added Services

Related to custody, value-added services is a general term for services over and above the core services that in some way provide an enhancement to the client's portfolio.

Value Date

A date attached to a particular entry of funds posted to a bank account. Intended to reflect the date on which such funds are deemed to cease to be available to the bank in the case of a debit entry, or to become available to the bank in the case of a credit entry.

Variation Margin

A means employed by an exchange of receiving collateral on an open position that is paid or received at the end of each day, reflecting the daily profit or loss on the open position.

Voluntary Redemption

Option given by the company to redeem stock for cash before fixed maturity date.

Warrant

A security attached to a company's debt or equity issue or, in certain cases, on a stand-alone basis. Each warrant unit allows the holder to purchase a predetermined number of shares of the company's common stock at a predetermined price within a certain time frame (usually less than 15 years).

Warrant/Options Exercise

Periodically, holders of warrants (or, in the case of Australia, options) have the right/option to subscribe for ordinary shares in the company at a set price per share. This option usually occurs on a six-monthly or annual basis with a stipulated lifespan. Warrant issued by the company. Option issued by a broker.

Withholding Tax (WHT)

A tax levied by local tax authorities on the income earned by non-residents on their foreign investments.

XML

A flexible way to create common information formats and share both the format and the data on the worldwide web, intranets, and elsewhere. XML is a formal recommendation from the World Wide Web Consortium (W3C) similar to the language of today's web pages, the Hypertext Markup Language (HTML).

Yield

A bond's yield is its return on capital, expressed as a percentage.

Zero Coupon Bond (ZCB)

A bond which matures at a premium to the offer price but does not pay a coupon in its lifetime.

Glossary and Abbreviations

ABS	Asset-Backed Security		**DVP**	Delivery versus Payment
ADP	Automatic Data Processing		**EEA**	European Economic Area
ADR	American Depositary Receipt		**EGM**	Extraordinary General Meeting
AFME	Association for Financial Markets in Europe		**EUI**	Euroclear UK and Ireland
AGM	Annual General Meeting		**FATCA**	Foreign Account Tax Compliance Act
AIM	Alternative Investment Market		**FCA**	Financial Conduct Authority
BIS	Bank for International Settlements		**FIP**	Foreign Indirect Participant
CASS	Client Asset Sourcebook		**FPC**	Financial Policy Committee
CCP	Central Counterparty		**FRN**	Floating-Rate Note
CDI	CREST Depositary Interest		**FSMA**	Financial Services and Markets Act (2000)
CFD	Contracts for Difference		**FTT**	Financial Transaction Tax
CGT	Capital Gains Tax		**FX**	Foreign Exchange
CP	Commercial Paper		**GATCA**	Global Account Tax Compliance Act
CRS	Common Reporting Standard		**GCA**	Global Corporate Actions
CSD	Central Securities Depository		**GDR**	Global Depositary Receipt
CUSIP	Committee on Uniform Securities Identification Procedures		**GMRA**	Global Master Repurchase Agreement
DACE	(Euroclear) Deadlines and Corporate Events		**GMSLA**	Global Master Securities Lending Agreement
DR	Depositary Receipt		**HMRC**	Her Majesty's Revenue & Customs (the UK tax authority)
DRIP	Dividend Reinvestment Plan		**IA**	Investment Association
DTA	Double Taxation Agreement		**ICMA**	International Capital Market Association (formally known as the International Securities Market Association)
DTC	Depository Trust Company			
DTCC	Depository Trust & Clearing Corporation		**ICSD**	International Central Securities Depository
DTT	Double Taxation Treaty		**IDR**	International Depositary Receipts

IPO	Initial Public Offering	**P&L**	Profit and Loss
IRS	Internal Revenue Service	**PRA**	Prudential Regulatory Authority
ISIN	International Security Identification Number	**QFI**	Qualified Foreign Intermediary
		QI	Qualified Intermediary
ISMA	International Securities Market Association	**QIB**	Qualified Institutional Buyer
ISLA	International Securities Lending Association	**RFD**	Ranking For Dividend
		SDRT	Stamp Duty Reserve Tax
JASDEC	Japan Securities Depository Center	**SEC**	Securities and Exchange Commission
JGB	Japan Government Bond	**SEDOL**	Stock Exchange Daily Official Listing
KPI	Key Performance Indicator	**SGM**	Special General Meeting
KYC	Know Your Customer	**SIL**	Sophisticated Investor Letter
LIBOR	London Interbank Offered Rate	**SOI**	Securities of Interest
LSE	London Stock Exchange	**SOX**	The Sarbanes-Oxley Act
MiFID	Markets in Financial Instruments Directive	**SPV**	Special Purpose Vehicle
MiFIR	Markets in Financial Instruments Regulation	**SSN**	Stock Situation Notices
		STP	Straight-Through Processing
MOD	Manufactured Overseas Dividend	**SWIFT**	Society For Worldwide Interbank Financial Telecommunications
MT	Message Type		
MTF	Multilateral Trading Facility	**T2S**	TARGET2-Securities
NAV	Net Asset Value	**TBMA**	The Bond Market Association
NYSE	New York Stock Exchange	**TIN**	Taxpayer Identification Number
OECD	Organisation for Economic Co-operation and Development	**VSP**	Voting Service Provider
		WHT	Withholding Tax
OID	Original Issue Discount	**YTM**	Yield to Maturity
OSLA	Overseas Stock Lending Agreement	**ZCB**	Zero Coupon Bond
OTC	Over-the-Counter		

Multiple Choice Questions

Multiple Choice Questions

The following questions have been compiled to reflect as closely as possible the standard you will experience in your examination. Please note, however, that they are not actual CISI examination questions.

1. In the UK, shareholder meetings must be announced a minimum of how many days before the meeting?

    A. 14
    B. 21
    C. 28
    D. 42

2. When two companies issue bonds otherwise on the same basis, a difference in the coupon offered will typically reflect a difference in:

    A. corporate structure
    B. credit risk
    C. international representations
    D. recent profitability

3. A nil-paid security will normally involve what type of corporate action?

    A. Rights issue
    B. Open offer
    C. Scheme of arrangement
    D. Consolidation

4. What type of event is an open offer?

    A. Voluntary
    B. Optional
    C. Mandatory with options
    D. Mandatory

5. Which of the following is used to determine who receives the dividend on a share?

    A. Payment date
    B. Ex-date
    C. Record date
    D. Announcement date

6. Which of the following methods of bond redemption can be considered as elective corporate actions?

    A. Bullet
    B. Put option
    C. Call option
    D. Drawing by lottery

7. What is the entitlement on a bonus issue if the client is holding 100 shares in a bonus with a ratio of 50 for every 1, assuming the ex-date is the 15th of the month and the client sold 10 on the 15th and purchased 50 on the 14th?

    A. 4,000
    B. 5,000
    C. 7,000
    D. 7,500

8. Deferred shareholders will only receive a dividend if:

    A. exceptional profits are declared
    B. ordinary shareholders have been paid a specific minimum
    C. the issuer goes into liquidation
    D. the shares are held until the maturity date

9. By definition, a corporate action will affect a company's share:

    A. capital
    B. dividend
    C. price
    D. ownership

10. Under the GMSLA, how are the rights relating to conversions dealt with while a security is on loan?

    A. The borrower can exercise the right to convert
    B. The lender can exercise the right to convert
    C. The right to convert automatically lapses
    D. The borrower and lender must agree jointly to convert

11. Why would an investor wish to convert securities traded under Regulation S to those traded under Rule 144a?

    A. They wish to create an ADR
    B. They wish to deal in the securities in Japan
    C. They wish to take advantage of an early redemption date
    D. They wish to trade in the US without SEC registration

12. An investor buys 100 call warrants for a premium of £0.40 each and a strike price of £1.00. What will the share price have to reach for the investor to make a profit of £50?

    A. £51.00
    B. £1.90
    C. £1.40
    D. £0.90

13. Which one of the following statements regarding poison pill rights is true?

    A. They are common in the UK
    B. They are illegal in the US
    C. They are meant to deter aggressive takeovers
    D. They are usually in the form of low-cost convertible bonds

14. When a share is traded as a special-ex transaction, this signifies that the:

    A. buyer will be entitled to any dividend
    B. buyer is prohibited from trading again until after the ex-date
    C. seller will be entitled to any dividend
    D. seller is prohibited from trading again before the ex-date

15. What is a stock situation notice?

    A. A market notification published by a listed company about its own shares
    B. An investment bank analyst's view of the potential performance of a share
    C. A market notification published by the London Stock Exchange
    D. Euroclear's view of the potential performance of a bond

16. Which of the following is eligible to appoint a proxy?

    A. Proxy agent
    B. Shareholder
    C. Nominee company
    D. Issuing company

17. An investor holds 5,000 shares in a company priced at £8.50 per share. The company subsequently makes a 1-for-5 share rights issue at £6.50. Nil-paid rights on the share issue will therefore be worth:

    A. £1.67
    B. £2.00
    C. £6.50
    D. £8.17

18. Dividends on US shares are usually paid:

    A. three-monthly
    B. four-monthly
    C. six-monthly
    D. annually

19. Lazy money is an expression usually used in relation to which type of corporate action?

    A. Warrants
    B. Rights
    C. Open offers
    D. Takeovers

20. A zero coupon bond will usually pay interest:

    A. annually
    B. bi-annually
    C. monthly
    D. never

21. Which of the following will assist a company that might require funds for research and development?

    A. Rights
    B. Scrip
    C. Consolidation
    D. Bonus

22. On which of the following dates will stock movement normally take place?

    A. Record date
    B. Effective date
    C. Ex-date
    D. Expiry date

23. Following a liquidation there are sufficient funds to pay preference shareholders. Consequently, they will receive the:

    A. pre-liquidation market price
    B. nominal value
    C. equitable value decided by the liquidator
    D. unpaid net dividends only

24. Shares that were issued with a restriction are now deemed to be ranking *pari passu*. Which one of the following is therefore true?

    A. The share price has been reduced
    B. They attract a reduced level of dividend
    C. They are now treated like the company's existing non-restricted shares
    D. The company must now offer additional shares of the same value

Multiple Choice Questions

25. Investors who hold depositary receipts will receive dividends:

    A. in their own currency
    B. in the currency of the issuer
    C. only if the security has been issued on a sponsored basis
    D. only if they are eligible for rights issues

26. MT568 – Corporate Action Narrative – will be used specifically when:

    A. cash is to be credited to client accounts only
    B. cash has been debited from client accounts only
    C. there is a change in status of a corporate action event
    D. complex instructions or details need to be provided

27. A lead manager is primarily responsible for:

    A. safekeeping of the securities issued and asset servicing
    B. handling security purchase payments and stock movement
    C. taking on the credit risk in new security transactions
    D. overseeing syndicate activities in the issue of new securities

28. When a corporate letter of representation is issued, the investor concerned:

    A. is legally obliged to attend the company meeting in person
    B. has nominated a specific person to attend the company meeting and register a vote
    C. has expressed an intention to vote by post by a specified date
    D. has given the company authority to vote on their behalf

29. Which of the following is a recognised asset servicing risk when there is failure to inform the customer of the existence of a forthcoming event?

    A. The fund manager may miss the opportunity to take part in a particular event
    B. The asset servicer will have breached the client money rules
    C. The fund manager will have to rely on other information sources
    D. The asset servicing department may be unable to reconcile the position to the market

30. A warrant has been exercised 'at-the-money'. This means that the market price:

    A. equalled the strike price
    B. was lower than the strike price
    C. was higher than the strike price
    D. was lower following the exercise

31. One of the main reasons for a 'redenomination' of shares is:

    A. low profits
    B. excessive trading activity
    C. high inflation levels
    D. SDRT changes

32. The purpose of FATCA is to:
    A. obtain personal tax information on non-US-resident holders of US securities
    B. obtain personal tax information on UK-resident holders of US securities
    C. identify revenue earned on foreign investments held by US residents
    D. identify revenue earned on foreign investments held by UK residents

33. A significant difference between scrip dividends and dividend reinvestment schemes is that:
    A. scrip dividends require compulsory share purchase
    B. scrip dividends require payment of broker's commission
    C. dividend reinvestment plans primarily benefit major shareholders
    D. dividend reinvestment plans are offered without a reference price

34. The primary role of a central counterparty is to:
    A. guarantee the performance of contracts to trade in securities
    B. administer securities settlement and provide asset servicing
    C. hold all securities within a particular market centrally
    D. ensure securities are properly safeguarded

35. When a company offers to buy shares by the Dutch auction method, rather than by tender, the difference in process means that:
    A. shareholders must sell at the price specified by the company
    B. at least 50% of the holding must be sold
    C. minimum and maximum purchase prices are offered
    D. the purchase price will be below current market price

36. What is the main difference between the clean price and the dirty price of a bond?
    A. The dirty price includes accrued interest
    B. The dirty price is net of taxation
    C. The clean price includes broker fees
    D. The clean price is for companies with high credit ratings

37. Withholding tax is:
    A. levied by national tax authorities on investment income earned by non-residents on their foreign investments in that country
    B. levied by the UK on investment income earned by UK nationals
    C. only levied when there is a double taxation agreement in place
    D. only levied when the investor is a higher rate taxpayer

38. Compulsory liquidation of securities generally occurs when:

   A. payment of interest has been deferred for 21 days
   B. the company's board of directors passes a resolution to proceed
   C. the company's creditors take action to obtain payment
   D. extension terms of 60 days or more are required

39. In order to be classed as a US qualified institutional buyer, what MINIMUM value of securities must the QIB invest?

   A. $25m
   B. $100m
   C. $250m
   D. $500m

40. Shareholders have been offered pre-emption rights. This means that:

   A. taking up the option will dilute the value of their holdings
   B. their holdings will be transferred to another company following a takeover
   C. the value of the new rights offered will be sufficient to compensate for the reduction in share price
   D. the number of shares held following the issue will be at least three times the number originally held

41. To convert a UK share to an ADR the investor needs to send which two instructions to its custodian?

   A. The first instruction is to deliver the UK share free of payment to the UK depository account of the American bank and the second is to receive the ADR free of payment into the depository account
   B. The first instruction is to receive the UK share free of payment to the UK depository account of the American bank and the second is to deliver the ADR free of payment into the depository account
   C. The first instruction is to deliver the UK share against payment in GBP to the UK depository account of the American bank and the second is to receive the ADR against payment in USD into the depository account
   D. The first instruction is to receive the UK share against payment in GBP to the UK depository account of the American bank and the second is to deliver the ADR against payment in USD into the depository account

42. The takeover process for a company in the UK has reached day 39. This is the last day on which the:

   A. target company announcement can be made
   B. predator company can revise its offer
   C. shareholders can withdraw acceptance of the offer
   D. shareholders of the target company can respond

43. What is the purpose of a dividend access plan?

    A. To enable investors to take advantage of the dividend tax credit paid by a UK company
    B. To enable UK investors to take advantage of the dividend tax credit paid by a UK company
    C. To enable investors to receive dividends at a time of their choosing
    D. To enable UK investors to receive dividends tax-free

44. 'B' share bonus issues are attractive to UK investors because:

    A. there is no tax to pay at the time of the bonus issue
    B. there is no tax to pay at the time of the bonus issue and no tax to pay when the resulting securities are sold
    C. there is no tax to pay at the time of the bonus issue, although when the shares are sold there may be a liability to capital gains tax
    D. they are free of tax

45. A bondholders meeting is:

    A. an annual event corresponding to an annual general meeting of shareholders
    B. an event designed for the issuer to keep the bondholders abreast of current developments
    C. a meeting that is called if and when there is the need for bondholders to agree to the restructuring of a bond issue
    D. a meeting that is called only if 10% of the bondholders request it

46. In order to set up an open market share buyback scheme the issuer has to:

    A. obtain approval in principle at an AGM or EGM
    B. advertise the fact to each investor
    C. offer a price higher than that of the market to interested investors
    D. advertise the fact to each investor and offer a price higher than that of the market to interested investors

47. If two counterparties have a number of claims against each other for the same corporate action they:

    A. must settle each and every claim individually
    B. may make a net settlement of the total value of the claims
    C. must take into account any netting that the exchange/clearing house has already carried out
    D. should take the matter up with the clearing house concerned

48. A shareholder is entitled to lapsed rights proceeds when they:

    A. have not taken up some or all of their rights, and the new shares have been sold by the underwriters
    B. have not taken up any of their rights
    C. have not taken up some or all of their rights, and the new shares have been sold by the underwriters at a profit
    D. have sold some or all of their rights

49. An agreement whereby two parties agree to exchange a set of cash flows is a:

    A. repo
    B. buy/sellback
    C. swap
    D. warrant

50. Which of the following investors is liable to pay an amount equal to the dividend due on dividend record date?

    A. A holder of a long position in the equity concerned
    B. A lender of the equity concerned
    C. A holder of a long position in a CFD based on the equity concerned
    D. A borrower of the equity concerned

Answers to Multiple Choice Questions

1.   B   Chapter 5, Section 3

In the UK, shareholder meetings must be announced at least 21 days prior to the meeting.

2.   B   Chapter 3, Section 3.1

The difference in coupon usually represents the extra credit risk, ie, the risk of the issuer defaulting on its payments.

3.   A   Chapter 4, Section 2.4

Rights are issued as a nil-paid security.

4.   A   Chapter 4, Section 2.4.4

An open offer, being a share offer, is deemed a voluntary event.

5.   C   Chapter 2, Section 3.1

The registrar uses stock ownership on the record date to determine who to pay a dividend or other benefit to (although this might not necessarily be paid to the entitled person, as derived by the ex-date).

6.   B   Chapter 3, Section 3.2.2

A put option gives the holder the right to request an early redemption. It is a voluntary event rather than a mandatory event.

7.   D   Chapter 2, Section 3

The purchaser only receives the benefit for trades before the ex-date. Hence the entitlement is: (100 +50) x 50 = 7,500.

8.   B   Chapter 1, Section 2.1.3

Deferred shareholders only receive dividends if ordinary shareholders receive a specific minimum level of dividend.

9.   A   Chapter 1, Section 2.4

A corporate action can be defined as any issue which affects a company's share capital or materially affects its share capital.

10.   B   Chapter 8, Section 5.1

Under the GMSLA, when a security is on loan, any rights relating to corporate action events such as conversions, subdivisions, consolidations and takeovers may be exercised by the lender.

Multiple Choice Questions

11.　　D　　　　Chapter 4, Section 3

In the US, securities must be registered with the SEC except under Rule 144a, which allows qualified institutional buyers (QIBs) to trade privately placed securities without restrictions; and Regulation S, which clarifies offers and sales of securities outside the US that are exempt from SEC registration requirements.

12.　　B　　　　Chapter 4, Section 4.1

Premium already paid for 100 warrants = (100 x £0.40)	=	£40.00
Amount to be paid when warrants exercised	=	£100.00
Profit required	=	£50.00
Total	=	£190.00 (equivalent to £1.90 per share)

13.　　C　　　　Chapter 4, Section 9.3

Poison pill is a strategy used by corporations in the US to discourage a hostile takeover.

14.　　C　　　　Chapter 2, Section 3.1

A special-ex transaction is a trade before the ex-date when the buyer will not be entitled to the benefit.

15.　　C　　　　Chapter 2, Section 2.3.1

Stock situation notices are produced by an analytical team at the LSE.

16.　　B　　　　Chapter 5, Section 4

A shareholder has the legal power to appoint a person to act for them in 'proxy'.

17.　　A　　　　Chapter 4, Section 2.3

Total value of investor's shares prior to the corporate event: 5,000 x 8.50 = £42,500.

After taking up the issue, the investor will have 6,000 shares in total.

Adjusted price per share: (£42,500 + (1,000 x 6.50)) ÷ 6,000 = 8.17.

Nil-paid rights will be worth = 8.17 – 6.50 = £1.67 per share.

18.　　A　　　　Chapter 3, Section 6.3

In the US, dividends are commonly declared quarterly.

19.　　A　　　　Chapter 4, Section 4.1

The payment on a lapsed warrant is referred to as lazy money.

20.　　D　　　　Chapter 1, Section 3.1

Zero coupon bonds do not pay a coupon (interest); they are normally sold at a discount.

21.   A   Chapter 4, Section 2.1

The shareholder exercises rights by buying new shares which provides funds to the company.

22.   B   Chapter 2, Section 5.1

Following corporate actions, movement of stock takes place on the effective date.

23.   B   Chapter 1, Section 2.1.2

Following liquidation, preference shares are repaid at their nominal value if there are sufficient funds available.

24.   C   Chapter 1, Section 2.3.1

When the restriction period applying to new shares ends, the share price of the new and existing shares moves to the same level and they are treated as equal in all respects, ranking *pari passu*.

25.   A   Chapter 1, Section 5.3

Holders of depositary receipts receive dividends in their native currency. Any foreign exchange transactions are the responsibility of the issuer.

26.   D   Chapter 2, Section 2.3.4

MT568 – Corporate Action Narrative – is used when complex instructions are needed regarding a corporate action event.

27.   D   Chapter 7, Section 2.5

The lead manager coordinates syndicate activities in placing a new securities issue in the primary market.

28.   B   Chapter 5, Section 4.2

A corporate letter of representation specifies that an individual can attend the meeting and vote on the investor's behalf.

29.   A   Chapter 9, Section 3.2

Failure of the asset servicing department to provide any information to the fund manager may mean that the fund manager misses the opportunity to take part in an event, and the fund manager may lose confidence in the asset servicing team.

30.   A   Chapter 4, Section 4.1

'At-the-money' means the market and strike prices matched exactly.

31.   C   Chapter 3, Section 5

Excessive inflation can result in the same amount of monetary units having continuously decreasing purchasing powers.

Multiple Choice Questions

32.   C   Chapter 6, Section 2.4.2

FATCA aims to identify revenue due to the US Internal Revenue Service on foreign investments held by US residents.

33.   D   Chapter 3, Sections 2.1.1 and 2.1.2

Scrip dividend options are offered with a known monetary value. Dividend reinvestment schemes do not allow the shareholder to know the value of their entitlement before making the election.

34.   A   Chapter 7, Section 2.11

The central counterparty acts as a guarantor of contracts.

35.   C   Chapter 4, Section 6

In a Dutch auction, the company offers to reimburse its ordinary shares at an amount between two prices to be determined by the company.

36.   A   Chapter 3, Section 3.1.2

The clean price excludes accrued interest, which is then included in the dirty price which is the final price paid by the buyer.

37.   A   Chapter 6, Section 2.1

Withholding tax is levied by local tax authorities on income earned by non-residents on their foreign investments.

38.   C   Chapter 3, Section 4

Voluntary liquidation is initiated by the company, but involuntary liquidation is initiated by the creditors.

39.   B   Chapter 8, Section 7

QIBs are sophisticated investors who must invest at least $100m-worth of securities for themselves, their client and other QIBs.

40.   C   Chapter 4, Section 2.2

If pre-emption rights exist, the shareholders will be offered new rights in proportion to their existing holdings, so that the original investments are not diluted.

41.   A   Chapter 4, Section 3.4

The mechanism is as follows (in this example, the conversion is from a UK share to an ADR):

1. An instruction is sent to a conversion agent who will cancel the local shares and reissue them as depositary receipts. In the case of ADRs this is usually a US bank.
2. Two instruction messages need to be sent to the custodian. One is to deliver the shares free of payment to the UK depository account of the American bank, and the second is to receive the ADRs into the depository account free of payment.

42.   A   Chapter 4, Section 5.1

Day 39 in the takeover process signifies the last date for the target company announcement.

43.   B   Chapter 3, Section 2.1.5

UK-based investors who receive dividend income from UK-domiciled companies are entitled to a 'tax credit' of (currently) 10% of the amount declared, which they may offset against their other tax liabilities. However, UK investors are not entitled to a tax credit on dividends paid by a non-resident company, and in recent years a number of large companies have changed the domicile of their parent company from the UK to another country with a more favourable corporate tax regime. A dividend access plan is one way of remedying this situation. Under such a plan, shareholders may choose whether they receive their dividends from a company resident for tax purposes in the UK, or from the company that issued the shares, which is resident for tax purposes outside the UK.

44.   C   Chapter 3, Section 2.2.2

Such bonus issues may be attractive to investors because they are an alternative to dividends, which are taxed. If there is a bonus issue there is no immediate liability to CGT when the shareholder receives the bonus shares, but there may be a capital gains tax liability when the shares are sold.

45.   C   Chapter 5, Section 6.2

The actions that the meeting might be asked to approve could involve a possible restructuring of the bonds via a debt exchange offer (see Chapter 4, Section 7) or conversion of debt to equity, or a mixture of both.

46.   A   Chapter 4, Section 6.1

Unlike a tender offer, which has a fixed timetable, an open market repurchases can span months or even years. Before the firm can take this action, it should seek shareholder approval in principle at an AGM or EGM, but once it has this approval, it has a great deal of flexibility.

47.   C   Chapter 2, Section 5.2

If two counterparties have a number of claims against each other, they may be able to net them to reduce the overall movement of cash or stock and the risk. If the claim is processed via an exchange, the exchange may do this automatically. In other cases, it is up to the two parties to agree bilaterally to net.

48.   C   Chapter 4, Section 2.4.5

The investor is only entitled to lapsed rights proceeds if the underwriter sold the new shares for a profit.

49.   C   Chapter 1, Section 4.3.2

A swap is an agreement whereby two parties agree to exchange a set of cash flows with each other.

50.   D   Chapter 1, Section 4.3.3

Borrowers of the stock (including repo, but not buy/sellback participants) must reimburse the lender for any dividends received during the period they have borrowed stock.

Syllabus Learning Map

Syllabus Learning Map

Syllabus Unit/ Element		Chapter/ Section
Element 1	**Capital Instruments and Transactions**	**Chapter 1**
1.1	**Equities** On completion, the candidate should:	
1.1.1	know the characteristics of ordinary shares in respect of: • dividend payment • voting rights • repayment rights in the event of liquidation • conversion rights	2.1
1.1.2	know the characteristics for preference shares in respect of: • dividend payment • voting rights • repayment rights in the event of liquidation • conversion rights	2.1
1.1.3	know the characteristics of deferred shares in respect of: • dividend payment • voting rights • repayment rights in the event of liquidation • conversion rights	2.1
1.1.4	know the characteristics of convertible preference shares in respect of: • dividend payment • voting rights • repayment rights in the event of liquidation • conversion rights	2.2
1.1.5	know the reasons why a company may issue convertible preference shares rather than ordinary shares: • when newly established • to benefit investors and issuers	2.2
1.1.6	know the difference between authorised and issued share capital	2.3
1.1.7	know the meaning of ranking *pari passu*	2.3.1
1.1.8	know the meaning of the following benefit distribution events: • dividends • scrip dividends • bonus issues	2.4
1.1.9	know the meaning of the following events: • subdivisions (splits) • consolidations (reverse splits) • demergers (spin-offs) • rights issues • tender offers • takeovers • mergers • scheme of arrangement	2.4

Syllabus Unit/ Element		Chapter/ Section
1.2	**Debt Instruments** On completion, the candidate should:	
1.2.1	know interest payment (fixed, floating or zero rate), frequency of payment (annual, semi-annual, quarterly, other), term (fixed, dual-dated, perpetual, other) and redemption (early, partial) for: • government bonds • Treasury bills • commercial paper • certificates of deposit • corporate bonds • asset-backed securities • floating rate notes • amortising bonds • zero coupon bonds • bearer bonds	3.1
1.2.2	know the characteristics of a convertible bond in respect of: • interest • term • basis of rights to convert	3.2
1.2.3	understand the impact on a bond price (up, down, no change and indeterminable) in respect of each of the following events: • interest distribution • removal of a restriction on transfer • conversion	3.3
1.3	**Transaction Types** On completion, the candidate should:	
1.3.1	know the characteristics, uses and the impact on asset servicing of:	4
	• repos/reverse repos	
	• triparty repos	
	• buy/sellbacks	
	• stock lending/borrowing	
	• synthetic products – contracts for difference and swaps	
1.4	**Depositary Receipts** On completion, the candidate should:	
1.4.1	know the definition of the following depositary receipts: • American depositary receipts (ADRs) • Global depositary receipts (GDRs) • CREST depositary interests (CDIs)	5.1 and 5.2

Syllabus Learning Map

Syllabus Unit/ Element		Chapter/ Section
1.4.2	understand the implications for investors holding depositary receipts and the impact with regard to the following: • income tax • withholding tax • voting rights • rights issues in regard to ADRs • bonus issues • income distributions • stock lending/borrowing	5.3
1.5	**Warrants** On completion, the candidate should:	
1.5.1	know the definition of a covered/uncovered warrant and the associated terms: • call • put • exercise • strike price	6
1.5.2	understand the main characteristics of the following warrants: • puts • calls • index-linked • auto-expiring	6

Element 2	**The Life Cycle of an Event**	Chapter 2
2.1	**Understand the Life Cycle of an Asset Servicing Event** On completion, the candidate should:	
2.1.1	understand the difference between: • voluntary events • mandatory events • mandatory events with options	1
2.1.2	know the key stages of the life cycle of an asset servicing event: • market announcement • event data collection and validation • notification • election processing • payment/settlement of entitlement • reconciliation	1
2.2	**Information Gathering and Data Scrubbing** On completion, the candidate should:	
2.2.1	understand the cycle of information-gathering from the company announcement	2

Syllabus Unit/ Element		Chapter/ Section
2.2.2	understand the purpose of a prospectus	2.2
2.2.3	know the different types of market notification: • Euroclear DACE (Deadlines and Corporate Events notice) • LSE – stock situation notices including name changes • DTC • SWIFT	2.3
2.2.4	know the role of a data vendor	2.3.5
2.2.5	know the SWIFT and other standards in relation to corporate events: • MT564/Corporate Action Notification • MT565/Corporate Action Instruction • MT566/Corporate Action Confirmation • MT567/Corporate Action Status and Processing Advice • MT568/Corporate Action Narrative • ISO15022 and ISO20022	2.3.4
2.2.6	understand the purpose of data scrubbing	2.4
2.3	**Event Entitlement** On completion, the candidate should:	
2.3.1	know the definition of: • record-date • ex-date • cum-entitlement • ex-entitlement • special-ex • special-cum • pay date	3.1
2.3.2	understand the significance of ex-date in establishing contractual entitlement to benefits	3.1
2.3.3	understand the significance of record date	3.1
2.3.4	understand the impact of late booking and cancellation of trades on an entitled position	3.2
2.3.5	be able to calculate an amended entitlement due to a late-booked or cancelled trade	3.2
2.3.6	understand the impact of a stock loan/borrow on an entitlement position	3.2
2.3.7	be able to calculate an entitlement when a position is subject to stock loan/borrow activity	3.2
2.3.8	understand the impact of special-ex/special-cum on entitled positions	3.1
2.3.9	be able to calculate an entitlement when a position is subject to special-ex/special-cum trading	3.1
2.3.10	understand the concept of the transformation process	3.3

… Syllabus Learning Map

Syllabus Unit/ Element		Chapter/ Section
2.4	**Response Gathering and Instruction** On completion, the candidate should:	
2.4.1	know the definitions of the following terms in relation to a mandatory event with options and a voluntary event: • issuer deadline • agent deadline • market deadline (for elections) • deposit date (protect deadline)	4
2.4.2	understand the concept of broker-to-broker buyer protection and protection through the CCP in relation to late/failed trading and stock loan activity	4
2.4.3	understand the implications of deadlines in relation to an event	4
2.5	**Payment, Claims and Post-Payment Reconciliation** On completion, the candidate should:	
2.5.1	understand how to validate a claim for the following transactions: • repo • buy/sellback • sell/buyback • stock loan • failed trade	5
2.5.2	understand the implication of pay/effective date in relation to an event	5
2.5.3	understand the implication of failing to settle a claim for nil-paid rights prior to the deadline for acceptance in the UK market	5
2.5.4	know the definition of auto-depository compensation	5
2.5.5	understand how the transformation process may generate claims	5
2.6	**Arbitrage** On completion, the candidate should:	
2.6.1	understand the concept of arbitrage	6
2.6.2	understand the impact on transaction processing	6
2.6.3	understand the impact on entitlement and reconciliation	6

Element 3	**Mandatory Events**	Chapter 3
3.1	**Dividends** On completion, the candidate should:	
3.1.1	understand that a dividend is paid from realised profits	2.1
3.1.2	know the frequency of dividends and the payment timetable for UK, US, Japan and Italy: • ex-dividend date • record dates • special-ex • special-cum • pay date	2.1 and 6
3.1.3	understand the impact of a dividend on the share price	2.1

235

Syllabus Unit/ Element		Chapter/ Section
3.1.4	know the distinction between scrip dividends and dividend reinvestment schemes	2.1.2 & 2.1.3
3.1.5	be able to calculate a scrip dividend entitlement given a cash dividend, a reference price for the shares and a record holding date	2.1.1
3.1.6	understand the concept of dividend access plans	2.1.5
3.2	**Bonus Issues** On completion, the candidate should:	
3.2.1	know the definition of a bonus issue	2.2
3.2.2	understand the reasons for initiating a bonus issue	2.2
3.2.3	know the difference between a bonus issue and a bonus issue with rights	2.2.1
3.2.4	understand the reasons for initiating a 'B' share bonus issue	2.2.2
3.2.5	understand the reasons for initiating a 'C' share bonus issue	2.2.2
3.3	**Subdivisions (Splits) and Consolidations (Reverse Splits)** On completion, the candidate should:	
3.3.1	understand the reasons why a company may subdivide or consolidate its shares	2.3
3.3.2	know the difference between a subdivision and a bonus issue	2.3.1
3.3.3	understand the impact of subdivisions and consolidations on the share price	2.3
3.3.4	be able to calculate the impact of subdivisions and consolidations on the share price	2.3
3.3.5	understand why a redenomination will occur and how it is achieved	5
3.4	**Demergers (Spin-Offs)** On completion, the candidate should:	
3.4.1	understand the reasons for initiating a demerger	2.5
3.4.2	be able to calculate the effect on book value of a demerger	2.5
3.5	**Capital Repayments** On completion, the candidate should:	
3.5.1	know the definition of a capital repayment	2.6
3.5.2	understand the reasons for initiating a capital repayment	2.6
3.5.3	know the following methods of achieving a capital repayment: • redeemable bonus issue • renominalisation • repayment	2.6
3.6	**Coupons** On completion, the candidate should:	
3.6.1	know the definition of a coupon	3.1
3.6.2	be able to calculate bond interest using the following methods: (30/360 – Actual/360 – Actual/365 – Actual/Actual)	3.1.1
3.6.3	know the difference between 'clean' and 'dirty' prices	3.1.2
3.6.4	understand that a bond may be stripped to meet investor requirements	3.1.4
3.6.5	know the definition of 'first long' and 'first short' coupon	3.1.5
3.6.6	understand how an early record date impacts a coupon calculation	3.1.2

Syllabus Learning Map

Syllabus Unit/ Element		Chapter/ Section
3.7	**Redemptions/Maturity** On completion, the candidate should:	
3.7.1	understand the following terms: • redemption (maturity) • partial redemption • early redemption • drawing • lottery	3.2
3.7.2	understand the options available to a convertible bondholder when a company redeems a bond	3.2
3.8	**Delayed/Defaulting Securities** On completion, the candidate should:	
3.8.1	know the definition of an issuer default on the servicing of interest and principal payments on bonds	3.3
3.8.2	know the difference between sovereign debt and corporate debt default	3.3
3.8.3	understand the reasons why an issuer may delay interest payments on bonds	3.3
3.9	**Liquidations** On completion, the candidate should:	
3.9.1	know the difference between voluntary and compulsory liquidation on equities	4.1
3.9.2	understand the stages of liquidation in the following markets: • UK • US	4.2
3.10	**Mergers** On completion, the candidate should:	
3.10.1	understand the reasons for initiating a merger	2.4
3.10.2	be able to calculate the effect on book value of a merger	2.4

Element 4	**Voluntary Events**	**Chapter 4**
4.1	**Rights Issues** On completion, the candidate should:	
4.1.1	understand the stages involved in a rights issue	2.4
4.1.2	understand the reasons for rights issues and the options available to the shareholder	2.1 and 2.2
4.1.3	understand the impact of rights issues on the share price and shareholding	2.3
4.1.4	be able to calculate a theoretical ex-rights price and a nil-paid rights price given a cum-rights price, a nil-paid rights issue ratio, and a subscription price	2.3
4.1.5	be able to calculate a split rights entitlement	2.4
4.1.6	understand the principles of oversubscription	2.4

Syllabus Unit/ Element		Chapter/ Section
4.1.7	know the difference between the distribution and the exercise ratios of rights in the UK and Italy	9.2
4.1.8	know the difference between renounceable and non-renounceable rights	2.4
4.1.9	know the meaning of open offers in the UK	2.4
4.1.10	understand the meaning of lapsed rights proceeds	2.4
4.1.11	understand the meaning of poison pill rights in the US	9.3
4.2	**Conversions** On completion, the candidate should:	
4.2.1	understand the reasons for initiating conversions	3
4.2.2	understand the methodology of the following conversions: • convertible bonds ⇔ equities • 144a ⇔ Reg S • 144a ⇔ Unrestricted (registered) line • preference ⇔ ordinary	3
4.2.3	understand the process for converting underlying local shares to ADRs/GDRs or vice versa	3
4.3	**Warrants** On completion, the candidate should:	
4.3.1	understand how to exercise warrants	4
4.3.2	be able to calculate the profit or loss as a result of the exercise of a warrant given the premium paid by the investor, the strike price and the underlying share price	4
4.3.3	know the meaning of in-the-money, at-the-money and out-of-the-money	4
4.3.4	understand the implications for investors if in-the-money warrants are not exercised on expiry	4
4.3.5	know the definition of lapsed warrants proceeds	4
4.3.6	be able to calculate the profit or loss as a result of the exercise of an uncovered warrant given the premium paid by the investor, the strike price and the underlying share price	4
4.4	**Takeovers** On completion, the candidate should:	
4.4.1	know the definition of a takeover	5
4.4.2	understand the impact of a takeover on share value and shareholding	5
4.4.3	know the process involved for 'acceptance' and 'no action' in the UK market	5.1
4.4.4	know what is meant by a Section 979 notice in relation to a UK takeover	5.1
4.4.5	know that buyer protection and bargain transformation will apply in respect of open transactions in a security subject to a takeover in the UK	5.1

Syllabus Learning Map

Syllabus Unit/ Element		Chapter/ Section
4.4.6	know the key dates in the takeover timetable in the UK: • offer details to target • posting of first defence • earliest closing date • last date for target company announcement • last date for predator to revise offer • final closing date for offer	5.1
4.4.7	understand what a dissenting shareholder is	5.1
4.5	**Tender** On completion, the candidate should:	
4.5.1	know the definition of a tender offer	6
4.5.2	know the difference between a tender offer and a Dutch auction	6
4.5.3	understand the meaning of an odd lot offer/mini tender offer	6
4.5.4	know the process involved for 'acceptance' and 'no action'	6
4.5.5	understand the concept of oversubscription	
4.5.6	understand the concept of scale-back	6
4.5.7	understand the reason for initiating an open market share buyback	6.1
4.6	**Debt Exchange** On completion, the candidate should:	
4.6.1	understand the meaning of a debt exchange offer	7
4.6.2	understand the stages of a debt exchange	7
4.6.3	know the process involved for 'acceptance' and 'no action'	7
4.6.4	understand the concept of scale-back	7
4.7	**Class Actions** On completion, the candidate should:	
4.7.1	know the definition of a class action	8

Element 5	Corporate Governance	Chapter 5
5.1	**Types and Dates of Company Meetings** On completion, the candidate should:	
5.1.1	know the timescales for a company calling a meeting across the selected markets	3 and 5
5.1.2	know the reasons for convening the annual general meeting and the extraordinary general meeting	3
5.1.3	know the rights of shareholders to request an EGM and the timescales	3
5.1.4	know the difference between 'abstaining' and 'taking no action'	3
5.1.5	know the difference between an ordinary resolution and a special resolution	3
5.1.6	understand the implications of consent solicitations	6
5.1.7	understand the reasons for calling a bondholders meeting	6
5.2	**Appointing a Proxy** On completion, the candidate should:	
5.2.1	understand who is entitled to appoint a proxy and who is eligible to be a proxy for the selected markets	4

Syllabus Unit/ Element		Chapter/ Section
5.2.2	know the different methods of appointing a proxy in selected markets	4 & 5
5.2.3	know the role played by the proxy voting agent also in relation to voting service providers (VSPs)	4.1
5.3	**Voting** On completion, the candidate should:	
5.3.1	know who is entitled to vote for stock lending and repos	2.1
5.3.2	know the meaning of a corporate letter of representation	4.2
5.3.3	know the purpose of using a proxy to vote	4.1
5.4	**Share Ownership** On completion, the candidate should:	
5.4.1	understand the purpose of Section 793 of the Companies Act 2006	2.1

Element 6	**Tax**	**Chapter 6**
6.1	**Tax** On completion, the candidate should:	
6.1.1	know the definition of a double taxation treaty	2.2
6.1.2	understand the use of double taxation treaties and why they are created	2.2
6.1.3	know the definition of withholding tax	2
6.1.4	understand how withholding tax is applied based on the following: • residency • product • tax regime (at source or reclaimable) • beneficiary • corporate action events that are treated as dividends	2
6.1.5	know the following tax regimes: • reclaim procedures • relief at source • combination of reclaim procedures and relief at source • no relief	3
6.1.6	understand the advantages and disadvantages of the following tax regimes: • reclaim procedures • relief at source	3
6.1.7	understand the reclaim procedures with respect to a UK resident having suffered the maximum withholding tax rate on income generated on investments in Italy	3.3
6.1.8	know the life cycle of a tax reclaim	2.3
6.1.9	understand the term 'deduction at source' and its implications	2
6.1.10	understand the role of a Qualified Intermediary	2.4
6.1.11	know the implications of the US Foreign Account Tax Compliance Act (FATCA)	2.4

… Syllabus Learning Map

Syllabus Unit/ Element		Chapter/ Section
6.1.12	understand the need to provide proof of residency to the fiscal authorities for the purpose of reclaiming tax and obtaining relief at source	2.3
6.1.13	know the principles of the European financial transaction tax	4

Element 7	Participants	Chapter 7
7.1	**Participants** On completion, the candidate should:	
7.1.1	know the role played by the issuer	2.1
7.1.2	know the role played by the custodian/sub-custodian	2.2
7.1.3	know the role played by the transfer agent/registrar	2.3
7.1.4	know the role played by the lead manager	2.5
7.1.5	know the role played by the trustee	2.6
7.1.6	know the role played by the tender agent	2.7
7.1.7	know the role played by the receiving agent	2.8
7.1.8	know the role played by the calculation agent	2.8
7.1.9	know the role played by the paying agent	2.9
7.1.10	know the role played by the central securities depositories	2.10
7.1.11	know the role played by the central counterparties	2.11
7.1.12	know the role played by the conversion agent	2.12
7.1.13	know the role played by stock lenders and borrowers	2.13
7.1.14	know the role played by multilateral trading facilities	2.14
7.1.15	know the roles of trade associations, infrastructure and industry-led working groups	2.15
7.1.16	know the principles of T2S and its participants	2.16
7.1.17	know the role of the underwriter	2.4

Element 8	Legal and Compliance	Chapter 8
8.1	**Legal and Compliance** On completion, the candidate should:	
8.1.1	understand how tax domicile restrictions may impact investors when participating in a corporate action	3
8.1.2	understand the difference between residency and tax domicile with regard to eligibility to receive a benefit or participate in an event	3
8.1.3	know how the GMSLA deals with income distributions and events in respect of securities out on loan	5.1
8.1.4	know how the TBMA/ISMA master agreement deals with income distributions and stock events in respect of bonds out on repo	5.2
8.1.5	understand the two basic objectives of the 1933 Securities Acts (as amended): • information concerning securities offered for public sale • avoiding deception in the sale of securities	6

Syllabus Unit/ Element		Chapter/ Section
8.1.6	know the definition of sophisticated investor letters (SILs) and when they can be used	8
8.1.7	know the definition of US qualified institutional buyers (QIBs)	7
8.1.8	understand the impact of Client Money Rules on asset servicing functions	9
8.1.9	understand the impact of price-sensitive information	10
8.1.10	understand the concept, purpose and reporting requirements of MiFID and the high-level goal of MiFID II	4
8.1.11	know the implications of foreign ownership limits	11
8.1.12	understand the concept of sanctions	13

Element 9	Risks and Controls	Chapter 9
9.1	**Types of Risk** On completion, the candidate should:	
9.1.1	know the key risks of corporate action processing	3.2
9.1.2	understand the risks arising from misleading information	3.3
9.1.3	understand the importance of reconciliation and segregation of duties	4

Examination Specification

Each examination paper is constructed from a specification that determines the weightings that will be given to each element. The specification is given below.

It is important to note that the numbers quoted may vary slightly from examination to examination as there is some flexibility to ensure that each examination has a consistent level of difficulty. However, the number of questions tested in each element should not change by more than plus or minus 2.

Element Number	Element	Questions
1	Capital Instruments and Transactions	5
2	Life Cycle of an Event	6
3	Mandatory Events	9
4	Voluntary Events	16
5	Corporate Governance	4
6	Tax	2
7	Participants	3
8	Legal and Compliance	3
9	Risk and Controls	2
Total		**50**

CISI Associate (ACSI) Membership can work for you...

Studying for a CISI qualification is hard work and we're sure you're putting in plenty of hours, but don't lose sight of your goal!

This is just the first step in your career; there is much more to achieve!

The securities and investments sector attracts ambitious and driven individuals. You're probably one yourself and that's great, but on the other hand you're almost certainly surrounded by lots of other people with similar ambitions.

So how can you stay one step ahead during these uncertain times?

Entry Criteria:
Pass in either:
- Investment Operations Certificate (IOC), IFQ, ICWIM, Capital Markets in, eg, Securities, Derivatives, Advanced Certificates; or
- one CISI Diploma/Masters in Wealth Management paper

Joining Fee: £25 or free if applying via prefilled application form   **Annual Subscription (pro rata):** £125

Using your new CISI qualification* to become an Associate (ACSI) member of the Chartered Institute for Securities & Investment could well be the next important career move you make this year, and help you maintain your competence.

Join our global network of over 40,000 financial services professionals and start enjoying both the professional and personal benefits that CISI membership offers. Once you become a member you can use the prestigious ACSI designation after your name and even work towards becoming personally chartered.

* ie, Investment Operations Certificate (IOC), IFQ, ICWIM, Capital Markets

Benefits in Summary...
- Use of the CISI CPD Scheme
- Unlimited free CPD seminars, webcasts, podcasts and online training tools
- Highly recognised designatory letters
- Unlimited free attendance at CISI Professional Forums
- CISI publications including *The Review* and *Change – The Regulatory Update*
- 20% discount on all CISI conferences and training courses
- Invitation to the CISI Annual Lecture
- Select benefits – our exclusive personal benefits portfolio

The ACSI designation will provide you with access to a range of member benefits, including Professional Refresher where there are currently over 100 modules available on subjects including Anti-Money Laundering, Information Security & Data Protection, Integrity & Ethics, and the UK Bribery Act. CISI TV is also available to members, allowing you to catch up on the latest CISI events, whilst earning valuable CPD.

Plus many other networking opportunities which could be invaluable for your career.

Revision Express

You've bought the workbook... now test your knowledge before your exam.

Revision Express is an engaging online study tool to be used in conjunction with most CISI workbooks.

Key Features of Revision Express:
- Examination-focused – the content of Revision Express covers the key points of the syllabus
- Questions throughout to reaffirm understanding of the subject
- Special end-of-module practice exam to reflect as closely as possible the standard you will experience in your exam (please note, however, they are not the CISI exam questions themselves)
- Extensive glossary of terms
- Useful associated website links
- Allows you to study whenever you like, and on any device

IMPORTANT: The questions contained in Revision Express products are designed as aids to revision, and should not be seen in any way as mock exams.

Price per Revision Express module: £35
Price when purchased with the corresponding CISI workbook: £105 (normal price: £116)

To purchase Revision Express:

call our Customer Support Centre on:
+44 20 7645 0777

or visit the CISI's online bookshop at:
cisi.org/bookshop

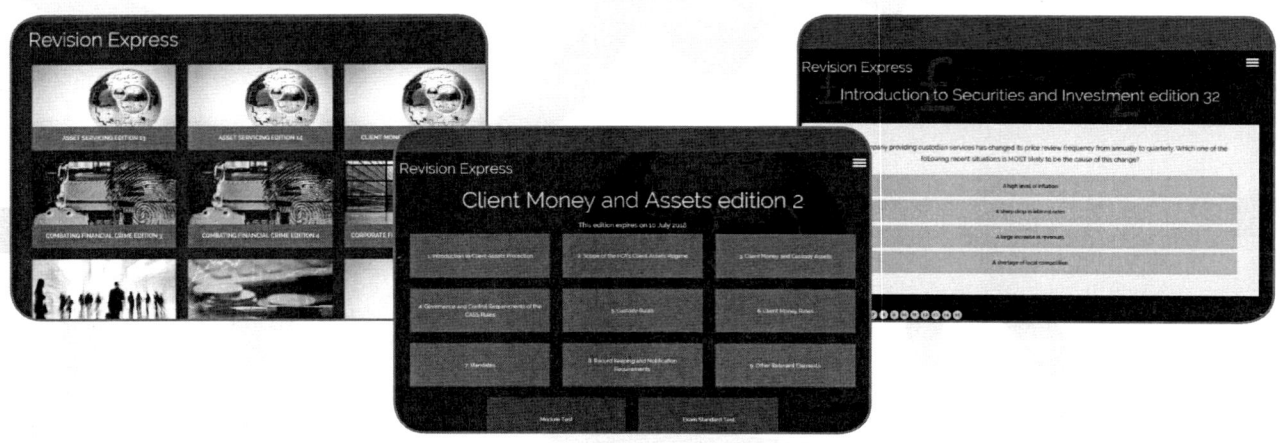

For more information on our elearning products, contact our Customer Support Centre on +44 20 7645 0777, or visit our website at cisi.org/elearning